In Defense
of the
Innocent

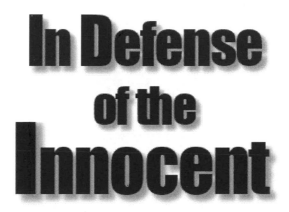

HOW TO RESPOND AND RECOVER
WHEN FALSELY ACCUSED OF SEXUAL ASSAULT
OR OTHER SERIOUS MISCONDUCT IN
THE NEW #METOO WORLD WHERE MEN ARE
GUILTY UNTIL PROVEN INNOCENT

E. F. Ferraro, SPHR

D0556711

In Defense of the Innocent
How to Respond and Recover When Falsely Accused of Sexual
Assault, or Other Serious Misconduct in Our New #MeToo World
Where Men are Guilty Until Proven Innocent

Publisher:
AuthorVista, LLC™
Denver, CO
info@AuthorVista.com

© 2020 Eugene F. Ferraro

Library of Congress Control Number: 2020907628
ISBN-13: 978-0937309032 (Paperback)

Names: Ferraro, Eugene, author.
Title: In defense of the innocent : how to respond and recover when falsely
    accused of sexual assault, and other serious misconduct in our new #MeToo
    world where men are guilty until proven innocent / Eugene F. Ferraro.
Description: First edition. | Pine, CO : AuthorVista, 2020. | Includes
    bibliographical references and index.
Identifiers: ISBN 978-0-937309-03-2 (paperback)
Subjects: LCSH: Men. | Work environment. | Sex crimes. | Actions and
    defenses. | Criminal law. | Social movements. | Investigations. |
    Truthfulness and falsehood. | BISAC: SOCIAL SCIENCE / Sexual Abuse
    & Harassment. | BUSINESS & ECONOMICS / Workplace Culture. |
    LAW / Civil Law. | LAW / Criminal Law / General.
Classification: LCC HQ1090.3 F47 2020 (print) | LCC HQ1090.3 (ebook) |
    DDC 305.31--dc23.

First Edition

Technical advice: Rae-Ellen Hamilton, GPHR, SHRM-SCP
Copy editing: Michelle Christensen
Content design and layout: AuthorVista, LLC
Cover design: AuthorVista, LLC

DISCLAIMER

THIS BOOK AND ITS CONTENTS IS PROVIDED FOR IINFORMATIONAL PURPOSES ONLY. NEITHER THE AUTHOR, NOR THE PUBLISHER ARE QUALIFIED OR LICENSED TO PROVIDE LEGAL ADVICE OR SERVICES. AS SUCH, TOGETHER AND INDIVIDUALLY THEY DISCLAIM ANY NOTION OR APPEARANCE THEREOF. EVERY EFFORT HAS BEEN MADE TO ENSURE THAT THE INFORMATION CONTAINED IN THIS BOOK WAS FACTUALLY CORRECT AND/OR CITED PROPERLY AT PRESS TIME. HOWEVER, NEITHER THE AUTHOR NOR PUBLISHER ASSUME ANY LIABILITY FOR ANY LOSS, DAMAGE, HARM OR DISRUPTION CAUSED BY ANY SUGGESTION, IDEA, ADVICE, STRATEGY, INACCURACY, ERROR OR OMISSION CONTAINED HEREIN, WHETHER SUCH INACCURACIES, ERRORS OR OMISSIONS ARE THE RESULT OF NEGLIGENCE, ACCIDENT, OR ANY OTHER CAUSE. **IF YOU ARE IN NEED OF LEGAL ADVICE OR ASSISTANCE PUT THIS BOOK ASIDE AND IMMEDIATELY SEEK OUT AND QUICKLY RETAIN A COMPETENT AND QUALIFIED ATTORNEY ADMITTED OR AUTHORIZED TO PRACTICE LAW IN YOUR JURISDICTION AND/OR STATE.**

"How is it that men can crush women time and time again and go unpunished?"

—*Wilkie Collins, Author*
The Women in White
Published **1859**

CONTENTS

FOREWORD

As an attorney and advocate for the falsely accused for nearly three decades, I have an abundant appreciation for the rule of law and that which we consider fair and proper justice. Integral to that obligation is that which we call *due process*. Due Process is both fluid and elusive, depending at all times upon the time, place, who, and what is at stake. We rarely recognize it, until it is taken from us. It is when fairness and equality are denied, that we begin to understand the meaning and importance of it. A fundamental component of due process is *the right to be presumed innocent when accused of an actionable offense.*

Lawyers who find it their passion to protect the innocent face the ongoing challenge of advocating on behalf of those who appear to be on the wrong side of an emotionally or politically polarizing issue. We reassure ourselves that everyone has the right to be defended against all allegations, and those allegations must be proven by credible evidence, in a fair forum, by objective triers-of-fact, through a reasonable and equitable process. Simple it is not. Defending those accused of sexual assault or harassment is a daunting task for which the population at large has little patience or sympathy.

Among the most insidious attacks on due process comes by way of that which we now refer to as the #MeToo movement. Generally, a force for good, giving a voice to the victims of sexual assault, it has been used unmercifully on university, college campuses, and in our workplaces across the country to demonize men accused of sexual assault and harassment. Often these allegations are made months, even years after the purported event, there is nothing that appears to be actual evidence, no eyewitness account, just allegations and speculation, followed by a vague and opaque procedure with byzantine protocols, all of which often ends before a tribunal that more often than not, seeks to maintain a pre-established cultural and

i

political agenda, *as well as its organization's reputation*. Thus, what little justice it serves is often self-serving.

Once the process has been completed, there is no independent avenue for appeal and sanctions run afoul of any sense of proportionality. There are none of the failsafe checkpoints that our forefathers ensured to protect against such abuses. The results are disastrous and life altering; attempted suicides, career paths and educations ripped away, replaced with an indelible, lifelong scarlet letter. Call it *Kafkaesque*, a star chamber, a labyrinth of lies and allusions from which there is no escape. In essence, what is created is a system built on bias and the quest for punishment, absent of any due process protections or presumptions of innocence. Left behind is an utter absence of impartiality and fairness, and ruined lives.

Until now, there has been little in the way of a guide for defending the accused in these cases, whether in our schools or workplaces, at either the administrative level or in the courts. It is critical that someone give a voice to the suffering and provide insight together with the strategy and tactics to combat this attack on fundamental reason and fairness. In the pages that follow, Mr. Ferraro does just that. Carefully and incrementally, he provides both the knowledge and tools necessary for the accused and his lawyer to ensure due process, and bring forth a proper defense. But perhaps most importantly, Mr. Ferraro has provided us all, the opportunity to help themselves and retain hope.

Andrew T. Miltenberg, Esq.
New York, New York
June 2020

PREFACE

This book is an effort to share my knowledge and experience defending those falsely accused of sexual assault and other crimes against women. My goal in writing this work is simple: I wish to provide assistance and hope to the falsely accused and his defenders. In following pages I will first provide a history of the #MeToo movement. I will challenge irrational thinking and contorted values. I will expose those responsible for the harm and injustice they have unleashed on our sons, brothers, fathers, husbands, and friends. I will defy mainstream thought and commentary, and critically assess the damage and harm the #MeToo movement has inflicted on our nation and our culture. I will do so by diving deeper and more critically into the concept of justice and the rule of law than others have attempted. Though hiding in plain sight, I will also expose some of the elites who hate and distrust men, and reveal their methods and ambitions.

But I am more than a writer—I am a practitioner. While I will briefly examine the truly malfeasant, I will quickly turn your attention to the secret methods of those who typically investigate allegations of sexual assault and other serious misconduct, and expose their deficiencies. I will then reveal in detail, how one can and should respond when falsely accused. I will also show those who represent him how to successfully protect and defend his rights, seek and obtain restitution, and restore his reputation and dignity.

In this book, you will find that I have arduously resisted ordinary conventions to offer new solutions to the most difficult challenges facing those falsely accused, as well his defenders. I will reveal new ideas, and offer sophisticated approaches and strategies to successfully confront and resist false allegations against the innocent. Nowhere, will you find better or deeper insight. I am confident you will find my approach as refreshing and inspiring as it is enlightening. Thank you for allowing me to join your journey to justice.

INTRODUCTION

Not all men are sexual predators, and indeed, some women are the tragic victims of violent sexual assault. However, a significant portion of our society has been convinced by a global social justice movement, which holds that most men are in fact dangerous predators. Co-opted by mindless enablers in the media, uninteresting, yet vocal celebrities, and a significant number of pandering lawmakers, many have been persuaded to believe men are dangerous marauders ceaselessly searching for prey. They believe that when accused of sexual assault or other serious misconduct, men deserve to be publicly exposed, professionally ruined, and when possible, criminally prosecuted. Their message is simple: men are evolutionarily inferior and inherently boorish pigs. As such, men must be relentlessly pursued and exposed whenever, and however possible.

For the intelligentsia that provide the rules for that which has become the #MeToo movement, guilt need not be proven in order to justify punishment. For their enlightened disciples, the mere allegation of impropriety is proof enough. We have been instructed that women are to be believed even in the absence of evidence. And why not? Their enablers have convinced the willing that the rule of law and our constitutional principle of being innocent until proven guilty is not necessary, nor must it ever be contemplated. They know best, and their message is clear: however and wherever found, the enemy must be destroyed. And to no end, they remind us of the need to do so because men are savage animals, and every woman is nothing less than a perfect angel.

But importantly, this book is not seeking sanctuaries for the guilty, or rationalizing boorish and offensive behavior. Nor is this book intended to change minds or persuade. Instead its purpose is to inform. Specifically, it is intended to inform men and the many women who know them, love them, and/or believe that men are citizens whose rights deserve protection under the law. This book is to help protect and preserve the reputations of the innocent. My intent is to help end some of the insanity that surrounds and propels the #MeToo movement and diminish its proponents' ability to destroy innocent people, their future, and our culture. As the chapter titles suggest, with the aid of an extensive appendices and a liberal use of endnotes, I will explore how this destructive force came about, how our system of justice has been shamelessly manipulated and co-opted, and how we, as rational and responsible citizens, can and should respond. Specifically, I will examine the evolution and current state of the law, its implementation, and most informatively, how the falsely accused should react and defend themselves. I will reveal how schools, institutions of higher-learning, and employers typically conduct internal investigations, what one can expect when falsely accused and that which he can do to prove his innocence and preserve his reputation when necessary.

I will also provide insights as to how to survive the inanity of hyper-sensitive, risk-adverse employers and institutions and their sometimes, flat-footed fact-finders who often neither know the law, nor the concept of fairness and impartiality. Using my years of expertise investigating allegations of harassment and discrimination and defending those investigations, as either the investigator who performed that investigation or as an expert witness who evaluated the investigations of others, I will reveal how decision-makers and triers-of-fact *should* determine guilt and deliver justice when appropriate. But possibly the most valuable thing I will provide the accused is hope. For without hope, even the strongest cannot survive.

Not all men are predators, nor are all women, breathless angels. This book will reveal why our enlightened elites wherever they may be found and the mindless obedient who pray at their altar are so often wrong and how we and their victims can *and* should respond.

CHAPTER ONE

IT WASN'T ALWAYS LIKE THIS

I recently had the pleasure of providing two days of instructor led training on the topic of conducting complex internal investigations. My client and host was a well-known global technology company and my students were a collection of male and female employees, most of whom were 40 and under. The audience was a mixture of experienced investigators and novices. They were engaged and very interested in improving their skills.

On the final day as I was packing my things a young female attendee approached me and asked if I was receptive to some feedback. I, of course said I was, stopped what I was doing and gave her my full attention. She began by asking if I had ever considered sensitivity training. "No, not actually. What have you in mind?" I asked. She proceeded to tell me that I had offended her, (and several others whom she did not identify), when earlier during the training, I had indicated that years earlier I had been surprised to learn that several members of my company's team of forensic psychologists, (coincidentally all but one were women at the time), had become very good investigative interviewers. The offended student then asked, "Why would you be surprised women could be good investigative interviewers?" In spite of my extensive experience responding to tough questions as both a fact and expert witness, I was caught off guard. Before I could respond, she suggested I seek counseling and sensitivity training, and that maybe residing inside me was an unacknowledged hatred of women. She informed me that if I dealt with my issue properly, maybe my future students would get more benefit from my experience and training. A single thought, which I left unspoken, filled my head—*Are you freaking kidding me?*

Completely missed on this fine and apparently very sincere woman, was that my comment had nothing to do with the gender of the psychologists. My point was that to my surprise, *clinicians,* possessing no investigative experience, in fact make very good investigative interviewers. Having mentioned they were almost all women, was simply a testimony to the success of my organization's affirmative action program and its vibrant diversity. But consider that for a moment. Somehow for reasons which still escape me, I apparently felt compelled to announce my support of women employed in positions of importance. Had I unconsciously sensed the need to defend myself in front of an audience of which I knew not a single individual? The mere thought of this absurdity sickens me. But that's how far we have allowed ourselves to be led. Today, even the innocent can and *should* feel guilty—regardless of their intensions or actions.

Sadly, being offended has become a competitive sport. A destructive sport where the most offended always gets a prize. It is a sport where the offended can even be offended by the truth. Remarkably, we're scolded that accusers are even entitled to their own truth and should never be disbelieved. The offended and eager-to-be-offended score points each time they find a new reason or excuse to be hurt. It is sick and culturally destructive.

It wasn't always like this. Admittedly, once upon a time some men were *dirty old men.* Some were boorish, crude and frequently behaved in very ungentlemanly ways. Some were, in fact, *male chauvinist pigs*. Unfortunately, some men still are. The women dominated by them were denied the right to vote, employment opportunities, excluded from clubs, public service, leadership roles, and treated as chattel. For centuries it seemed men could get away with anything. Even Shakespeare's Petruchio in *Taming of the Shrew* informed us, "Women are made to bear."[1]

But today is today and not all men are predators and they don't deserve to be treated like it. Nor should anyone tolerate their mistreatment or allow their destruction to be a form of restitution. The late Alex G. Karras reminds us, *"It takes more courage to think for ourselves than to allow others to dominate us. It takes courage to abide by thought-out principles rather than blind reflex. True character resides in the soul and spirit, not in the immature, unthinking mind."* [2]

Yet our institutions appear unable to help themselves. Everywhere it seems our leaders are seeking headlines, denouncing the *guilty* and pronouncing their commitment to change our *culture*. Facebook Inc. Chief Operating Officer, Sheryl Sandberg recently publicly reminded us that women still remain unrepresented within our nation's best known and important corporations. According to Ms. Sandberg, (one of the wealthiest self-made female billionaires in America today), progress has "dragged to a halt…we are at a critical moment where we need to invest in leadership."[3] Women are entering the U.S. workforce in the highest numbers in decades, but gender parity isn't improving, Ms. Sandberg told a panting audience in San Francisco in October 2018. According to a survey conducted by LeanIn.org, of which Ms. Sandberg is the founder and McKinsey & Co., only one in five senior business leaders are a women, and one in twenty-five are women of color.

Companies like Facebook have declared "Enough is enough." They and their leaders like Ms. Sandberg are "aggressively grappling with how sexual harassment impedes women's ability to scale the corporate ladder." We're told that, "In U.S. corporations, 35% of women and 55% of senior women surveyed said they experienced harassment—from sexist jokes to inappropriate touching—at some point in their careers."

But the consequences of the #MeToo movement trouble Ms. Sandberg as well. She reports that most male managers now feel "skittish" about having a meeting alone with a female co-worker. Men are also more hesitant about business travel or having dinner alone with their female colleagues. The stupefied and apparently very dim, former CEO of the Pacific Gas and Electric Company, Geisha Williams later countered by asking, "Why should you be worried about going out to with a woman or woman mentee for dinner or lunch?"[4] Ms. Sandberg responded with a thoughtful solution, "Treat all colleagues equally. If managers are uncomfortable having dinners alone with women, they should stop having dinners alone with men as well."

Let's unpack this overflowing thimble of wisdom: More women are entering the workplace than ever before.[5] More than half of the successful women surveyed said they experienced harassment—at some point in their careers. Men are now guilty until proven innocent, with women entitled to their "own truth"—and Ms. Williams is surprised men are now worried about dining alone with their female colleagues. Is anyone surprised that Ms. Williams is so shockingly surprised...and out of touch?

Knowing that an accuser need merely make an accusation to destroy a man's career, Ms. Sandberg suggests the perfect foolproof solution for men fearing women, is to "stop having dinners alone with men." Enlightening. Explained another way, these extremely well paid, self-identified, social scientists instruct us that to create a healthier and more civil workplace, we should spend less time with one another, and whenever possible, travel and dine alone. In other words, *shut up and keep your hands and eyes off us you hedonist pigs!* This thinking is so fundamentally flawed, I feel guilty wasting the ink *and your time* to relate it. But this is where we are. Up is down and down is up. Don't believe me? Get involved and join the "conversation" at LeanIn.org to find out more. If you do, you will be dining alone in no time.

Ground Zero

The #MeToo movement, (sometimes simply referred to as the *MeToo movement*), with its many local and international alternatives, is widely acknowledged to be ground zero of the grassroots response against sexual harassment and sexual assault that shook the globe. See Appendix A for a complete list of terms and definitions. #MeToo spread virally in October 2017 as a hashtag used on social media in an attempt to demonstrate the widespread prevalence of sexual assault and harassment, (especially in the workplace), and the solidarity of those who opposed it and supported its victims. The movement bloomed soon after sexual misconduct allegations against Harvey Weinstein, a successful American film producer, became public.

Ms. Tarana Burke, an American social activist and community organizer, is credited for having first used the phrase "MeToo" as early as 2006 on the then-trendy, social media platform, Myspace. The phrase was later popularized by Ms. Alyssa Milano, an actress using Twitter in 2017. Ms. Milano encouraged victims of sexual harassment to Tweet about it in order to "give people a sense of the magnitude of the problem." Her campaign enjoyed quick publicity and success after supportive posts by high-profile Hollywood celebrities, including Gwyneth Paltrow, Ashley Judd, Jennifer Lawrence, and Uma Thurman were then retweeted and retweeted.

Milano had Tweeted her first "#MeToo" around noon on

October 15, 2017, and by the end of the day it had been used more than 200,000 times. By the next day it had been retweeted more than 500,000 times. On Facebook, the hashtag was used by more than 4.7 million people in 12 million posts during the first 24 hours. Facebook later reported that 45 percent of users in the United States had a *friend* who had posted using the term.[6]

Everyone mobilized. Less than a month later, Congress Woman Jackie Speier proposed the Member and Employee Training and Oversight on Congress Act, (shortened to read, the ME TOO Congress Act). The full language of the bipartisan bill was revealed by the House on January 18, 2018 as an amendment to the Congressional Accountability Act of 1995. The purpose of the bill was to change how the legislative branch of the U.S. federal government treats sexual harassment complaints. Under the old system, complaints regarding the legislative branch were channeled through the Office of Compliance, which required complete confidentially throughout the process and took months of counseling and mediation before a complaint could actually be filed. Any settlement payments were paid using federal taxes, and it was reported that within a decade, $15 million of tax money had been spent settling harassment and discrimination complaints. The bill would ensure future complaints could only take up to 180 days to be filed. The bill would also allow the staffers to transfer to a different department or otherwise work away from the presence of the alleged harasser without losing their jobs if they requested it. The bill would require Representatives and Senators to pay their own harassment settlements. The Office of Compliance would no longer be allowed to keep settlements secret, and would be required to publicly publish the settlement amounts and the associated employing offices. For the first time, the same protections would also apply to unpaid workers, including pages, fellows, and interns.[7] To the dismay of many, the bill has yet to become law.

As for Weinstein, following the sexual abuse allegations against him, he was dismissed from his company and expelled from the Academy of Motion Picture Arts and Sciences within weeks of Milano's first Tweet. By October 31, over 80 women had made allegations against him. His "dirty little secret" had been exposed. The allegations against Weinstein sparked hundreds of sexual abuse allegations and the termination of powerful men around the globe. In memoriam, the phenomena has been called the Weinstein Effect.

On May 25, 2018, Weinstein was arrested in New York, charged with rape and other criminal offenses, and released on bail. On February 24, 2020, Weinstein was found guilty of a criminal sex act in the first degree and rape in the third degree, and acquitted on three further charges. As of the date of publication of this book, he has not yet been sentenced. For someone who apparently thought a job interview includes stuffing his penis in the mouth of a female applicant, a stiff stint (no pun intended), in a creepy prison surrounded by angry and sexually frustrated men would seem rather lenient.

The Weinstein Effect

The Weinstein Effect not only affected Hollywood, it shook corporate America. There cannot be a for-profit organization of more than 20 employees that hasn't taken notice. Large and small, organizations of all types and sizes decided to no longer do business as usual. HR professionals of all stripes suddenly acknowledged that the #MeToo movement cuts across all industries and all sectors of our nation's economy. Embarrassingly, global, high-profile companies have landed at the center of some of the most public and costly sexual harassment cases. Google, Facebook, Apple, and Uber have each found themselves painted as poster-children for all that is wrong in today's workplace.

"Today's story in the *New York Times* was difficult to read." said Google CEO, Sundar Pichai in an email sent to every Google employee recently. "We are dead serious about making sure we provide a safe and inclusive workplace. We want to assure you that we review every single complaint about sexual harassment or inappropriate conduct, we investigate and we take action." he wrote. According to Pichai, 48 employees were fired *without* an exit package for sexual harassment in the two years prior to his message, and 13 of those terminations were individuals in senior management positions. Just imagine the indignity and hardship of being terminated and receiving an exit package of as much as $90 million in the case of an alleged misbehaving Google executive.[8] That will teach him! Pichai also did not disclose what, if anything the victims were paid.[9]

To get an idea of how serious Google and Mr. Pichai think the problem is, let's take a quick look at the math. Google, today has approximately 85,050 employees—I know that because I Googled it. If indeed, 48 employees were fired for sexual harassment in two years prior to Pichai's announcement, one could conclude that on average, Google terminated roughly 24 people a year for the offense. If true, Google annually terminates about .028 percent of its workforce for policy violations involving sexual harassment, AND of them, about .009 percent of them were senior management. To enjoy such little piggish, workplace behavior, Google must hire nothing but saints. But then again, Pichai's candid disclosure fails to reveal how many people Google paid to go away. Had it been less than the 48 he fired I have no doubt he would have told us. So how many did Google actually pay off? Based on my litigation experience, sadly, almost all are paid off, with the highest earners receiving the most. Google understands that in the long run it is cheaper, quieter, and cleaner to simply make the guilty go away with a fat wallet.

The truth be told, sexual misconduct at Google goes right to the top. Pichai's email was precipitated by Alphabet Inc., Google's parent company, admitting it had fired its, Chief Legal Officer, David Drummond for having a sexual relationship (and a child in 2007) with one of his subordinates. *The Times* had reported that Drummond had not disclosed the relationship as required by organizational policy, of which Drummond had some responsibility in enforcing. Of course Drummond's lover was transferred out of his chain of command and later voluntarily resigned. I could drone on, but I will spare you the agony.[10]

What the #MeToo movement has spawned of value is a greater awareness of sexual harassment and discrimination in the workplace. It has also highlighted an apparent gender gap. The new champions of justice, albeit outside our real justice system, call themselves *management experts*. They assert that sexual harassment and the gender gap are inextricably linked. The experts tell us that harassment is a direct side effect of a workplace that slights women on everything from compensation and promotions to creating the perception that "men run the show," and women cannot speak up. I don't see the connection frankly, but then again I am just a man. But as a practicing management consultant, I can assure you the management experts and HR consultants love opportunities like this. Here is what some of them do:

Step 1: Reframe an existing and well recognized issue;

Step 2: Write an article or paper about it and liberally speculate as to its cause and effect;

Step 3: Tell those who will listen that which they already know;

Step 4: Using slick marketing and packaging to sell a solution for which there is no need or rationale; and

Step 5: Behave like a guru while carefully networking into an industry of their choice and with a little luck become a regular on one of the three-letter, nonstop news networks until the next new social or industry crisis comes their way.

On and on, the management experts and HR consultants tell us, organizations need better policies, honest dialog, clearly defined boundaries, the promotion and advancement of more women, more civility, more seminars and time-wasting summits, more compassion, deeper understanding, safe-spaces, and the requirement of dining and traveling alone.

What we don't need are millionaire scolds like Ms. Sandberg and Geisha Williams or some talking-head vacationing on Martha's Vineyard telling us what to think and how to view the world around us. We need men *and* women to stand up, respect one another, and genuinely acknowledge men and women are different. At the same time, we should recognize that just because we are different, doesn't mean we cannot work together, trust one another, respect each other, and treat one another like adults.

The lessons are manifold. Workplace behavior and culture matter. A corrosive culture in which women are mistreated, excluded and considered chattel, is not a formula for success. The sooner our society wakes up to it, the sooner we and our nation will be better off.

Academia Prepares for War

Academia has long been a champion of women's rights.[11] Its left leaning academicians and cowering administrators, (Harvard's hapless Larry Summers comes to mind), have rarely missed an opportunity to share with us their thoughts about the powerlessness of women and their oppression. Such insights are particularly enlightening when the likes of Elizabeth Warren, whose annual compensation as a Harvard Law School professor approached, $330,000 in 2015. Today, Senator Warren rarely misses an opportunity to remind us how oppressed she and others of her gender continue to be.[12] But Northeastern University professor, Suzanna Danuta Walters took the message to new heights in an op-ed piece published in June 2018.[13]

Ms. Danuta Walters identifies herself as a "professor of sociology and director of the Women's, Gender, and Sexuality Studies Program" at Northeastern. Her June 10, 2018, piece published in the *Washington Post* is headlined, "Why Can't We Hate Men?" The headline and her question are both rhetorical. She can nothing, but hate men—*all men*. Her reasoning goes like this: Although it's true that not every male on earth is a bad person, feminists should never qualify an argument with the statement that *not all men are bad*. She tells the reader everyone knows most men are actually really terrible. Between their tools of war ("red pill men's groups and rape camps"), and the institutional power they have claimed for themselves and refuse to share, men do not deserve to exist.

She tells her female readers they should, "Lean out so we can actually just stand up without being beaten down. Pledge to vote for feminist women only. Don't run for office. Don't be in charge of anything. Step away from the power. We got this. And please know that your crocodile tears won't be wiped away by us anymore. We have every right to hate you. You have done us wrong. #BecausePatriarchy. It is long past time to play hard for Team Feminism. And win." Go Girl!

A careful reader might wonder how the professor's demand that men step aside and *let women win*—a demand premised on the supposition that men are stronger and more determined—is supposed to further the cause of modern feminism. In what historical conflict was it ever revealed that when the strong and powerful allowed themselves to be pushed aside and the weak to become their rulers, peace, happiness and prosperity miraculously ensued? As any kindergartener knows, *sharing is caring*. But who the hell does

Professor Walters think she is? Real leaders are not crybabies, they do not lead from behind, and they do not demand they be given control of others. But then again, our universities have become places we send our youth to be indoctrinated. They have become places where women's gender, and sexuality studies have replaced the study of American History and that ancient misogynist fool known as William Shakespeare.

So deeply has this rot infected the American academy, consider this job posting for an Assistant Nordic Skiing Coach at Williams College:

"Our expectation is that the successful candidate will excel at working in a community that is broadly diverse with regard to race, ethnicity, socioeconomic status, gender, nationality, sexual orientation, and religion. We are especially interested in individuals who have experience with diverse populations who can contribute to the diversity and excellence of athletic opportunities at Williams. Candidates from under-represented groups are strongly encouraged to apply. In your cover letter, please highlight your experience with and commitment to supporting diverse and inclusive communities.

Responsibilities include providing assistance to the Head Coach in all aspects of the Nordic Ski program, including, but not limited to student-athlete development, coaching, training plans, travel, waxing, equipment management, driving team vans, video analysis, recruiting, team website updates and other duties as assigned."[14]

On the webpage where this job posting appeared, Williams informs would-be applicants, that it "is a coeducational liberal arts institution located in the Berkshire Hills of western Massachusetts with easy access to the culturally rich cities of Albany, Boston, and

New York City. The College is committed to building and supporting a diverse population of approximately 2,000 students, and to fostering an inclusive faculty, staff, and curriculum. Williams has built its reputation on outstanding teaching and scholarship and on the academic excellence of its students."

Very noble. While reasonable people support inclusion and diversity, in the job posting above Williams uses 84 words to express its all-out commitment to the cause with the expectation that the *successful applicant* will excel in a *"community with regard to race, ethnicity, socioeconomic status, gender, nationality, sexual orientation, and religion."* Yet, the college expends a mere 44 words describing the actual responsibilities of the individual seeking the job. If Williams College is so inclusive and open minded why doesn't it consider an applicant's gang-affiliation, criminal record, drug addiction, and handgun skills? Failing to do so potentially gives one gang member an unfair advantage over another. Doesn't everyone belong to the *community*?

And by the way folks, isn't naming a sport as something *Nordic* a little nationalistic and white? Think about it—it wasn't that long ago that the Nazis occupied Norway.[15] Having done so, how is it possible that they did not influence the culture of those they oppressed…at gun point? How did the Nazis not influence something as culturally important as skiing in a nearly all white and affluent nation? Heck, if President Trump has been able to bring out his followers' inner-Nazi in the mere first three years of his presidency, just think of the impact the real Nazi's must have had on the Norwegians during their six-year occupation, not to mention their impact on the stoops who attended the 1939 Olympic Games, in Berlin no less!

My point is not to trash good intentions, but to trash political correctness and the inanity it fosters. It is corrosive and destructive. It also distracts us from achieving obtainable solutions to real problems. My advice to Williams College and its brain trust—get over it, it's just a sport…and when you have the time, try teaching, you may find it rewarding. Who knows, maybe a few students will actually appreciate it and God forbid, learn something useful.

No, You Cannot Have a Lawyer!

Sadly, identity politics has entrenched its miserable self in both our schools and institutions of higher learning. It seems the further away we allow our kids to get out of our sight, the greater the influence our educators and their culture police have over their minds. The influence is particularly intense wherever humanities are studied. It seems some of our most expensive and prestigious colleges and universities think the greater the concentration on gender, race, victimology, and diversity studies, the greater the chance of success in life.

Coddling the minds of students and providing them trigger warnings, safe-spaces, and speech codes softens the mind. It invites female, black, Hispanic, trans, gay and other minority students to see themselves as victims of oppression and discrimination. The environment and mindset it produces encourages student to believe he or she is the target of unrelenting bigotry and danger. Our campus raging and all powerful "rape culture" is their proof.[16]

The sexual revolution of the 60's and 70's was meant to liberate. First it gave us premarital sex without guilt. That freedom eventually devolved into hookups and the debasement of femininity and eventually birthed the #MeToo movement. With it we now have campus administrations marshaling kangaroo courts where the accused student is not allowed to examine evidence, question the accuser, have representation, and most outrageously—is presumed guilty until proven innocent. If that stack of cards is not enough, our elites in the media then pile on. For the innocent, the means by which to confront this insanity and prevail with dignity is one of the chief purposes of this book. I intend to reveal exactly how these faux trials work and how the accused can turn the process on his oppressors and the institutions they claim to protect.

The Kavanaugh Effect

What a fiasco. For more than a month, the Bret Kavanaugh Supreme Court nomination hearings breathlessly dominated our 24-hour news cycle for all September 2018. Painfully, we endured report after report, commentary after commentary, and countless talking heads telling us who to believe and what to expect next. It was an embarrassment only a free democracy could endure.[17] As I partook in the consumption of the spectacle, I couldn't help but be reminded of Milton Friedman's timeless observation that to understand the motivation of an individual or organization, you need only to "follow the self-interest." Both Republicans and Democrats were all in. Panting, our public servants shamelessly vied for the spotlight, each hoping to share with us their Spartacus moment. It was as shameful as it was embarrassing.

The United States Senate Committee on the Judiciary, informally the Senate Judiciary Committee (or as wizards in Washington call it, SJC), is a standing committee of 21 U.S. Senators whose role is to oversee the Department of Justice (DOJ). Its purpose includes the consideration of executive nominations, and the review pending legislation. Of its many important duties, among its most important is approval of presidential nominations to the U.S. Supreme Court. There can be no argument that the appointment of a Supreme Court Justice is an event of major significance in American politics. Each appointment is of consequence because of the enormous judicial power the Supreme Court exercises as the highest appellate court in the federal judiciary.

To receive appointment to the Court, a candidate must first be nominated by the President and then confirmed by the Senate. Although not mentioned in the Constitution, an important role is played midway in the process, (after the President selects, but before the Senate considers), by the SJC. Specifically, the SJC, rather than the Senate as a whole, assumes the principal responsibility for investigating the background and qualifications of each Supreme Court nominee, and typically the committee conducts an intensive, if not comprehensive, investigation of each nominee. Since the late 1960s, the Judiciary Committee's consideration of a Supreme Court nominee almost always has consisted of three distinct stages—(1) a pre-hearing investigative stage, followed by (2) public hearings, and concluding with (3) a committee decision on what recommendation to make to the full Senate. During the pre-hearing investigative stage, the nominee responds to a detailed Judiciary Committee questionnaire, providing biographical, professional, and financial disclosure information to the committee.[18]

In addition to the committee's own investigation of the nominee, the FBI also investigates the nominee and provides the committee with confidential reports related to its investigation. During this time, the American Bar Association also evaluates the professional qualifications of the nominee, rating the nominee as "well qualified," "qualified," or "not qualified." Additionally, prior to hearings starting, the nominee pays courtesy calls on individual Senators in their offices, including Senators who do not serve on the Judiciary Committee. Once the Judiciary Committee completes its investigation of the nominee, he or she testifies in hearings before the committee. On average, for Supreme Court nominees who have received hearings from 1975 to the present, the nominee's first hearing occurred 40 days after his or her nomination was formally submitted to the Senate by the President.

Questioning of a nominee by Senators has involved, as a matter of course, the nominee's legal qualifications, biographical background, and any earlier actions as public figures. Other questions have focused on social and political issues, the Constitution, particular court rulings, current constitutional controversies, and judicial philosophy. For the most recent nominees to the Court, hearings have lasted for four or five days (although the Senate may decide to hold more hearings if a nomination is perceived as controversial—as was the case with Robert Bork's nomination in 1987, who had 11 days of hearings). Usually within a week upon completion of the hearings, the Judiciary Committee meets in open session to determine what recommendation to "report" to the full Senate. The SJC's usual practice has been to report even those Supreme Court nominations opposed by a committee majority, allowing the full Senate to make the final decision on whether the nomination should be approved. Consequently, the committee may report the nomination favorably, report it unfavorably, or report it without making any recommendation at all. Of the 15 most recent Supreme Court nominations reported by the Judiciary Committee, 13 were reported favorably, 1 was reported unfavorably, and 1 was reported without recommendation. When requested, additional Congressional Research Service (CRS) reports are used to provide additional information and analysis related to other stages of the confirmation process for nominations to the Supreme Court.[19] Ugh.

Nominee Kavanaugh ran the gauntlet and collided with reality at the hearings. Clearly, the Right hoped to approve him and the Left sought to destroy him. The spectacle began with the SJC scheduling three or four days of public hearings, commencing September 4, 2018. What followed was both instructive and ridiculous. The hearings were at the onset delayed with objections from the Democratic members, concerning the absence of records during Judge Kavanaugh's time in the George W. Bush administration, prior to his service as a federal circuit court judge. The Democrats also complained they hadn't the time to analyze the 42,000 pages of documents that they had received at the 11th hour, the night before Day One of the hearing.

Adding complexity to an already chaotic process, the press published a letter, which it claimed had been leaked to it. Reportedly in July, Representative Dianne Feinstein (D-CA) received the following letter, from an alleged constituent, later identified as Dr. Christine Blasey Ford. For reasons, Representative Feinstein later had difficultly explaining to SJC Chair, Charles E. Grassley, she never disclosed the letter to anyone other than some of her staff. Only after it was "leaked" did members of the SJC become aware of it.[20]

The letter reads:

July 30 2018   CONFIDENTIAL

Dear Senator Feinstein;

I am writing with information relevant in evaluating the current nominee to the Supreme Court. As a constituent, I expect that you will maintain this as confidential until we have further opportunity to speak.

Brett Kavanaugh physically and sexually assaulted me during high school in the early 1980's. He conducted these acts with the assistance of **REDACTED**. Both were one to two years older than me and students at a local private school.

The assault occurred in a suburban Maryland area home at a gathering that included me and four others. Kavanaugh physically pushed me into a bedroom as I was headed for a bathroom up a short stair well from the living room. They locked the door and played loud music precluding any successful attempt to yell for help.

Kavanaugh was on top of me while laughing with **REDACTED**, who periodically jumped onto Kavanaugh. They both laughed as Kavanaugh tried to disrobe me in their highly inebriated state. With Kavanaugh's hand over my mouth I feared he may inadvertently kill me.

From across the room a very drunken **REDACTED** said mixed words to Kavanaugh ranging from "go for it" to "stop." At one point when **REDACTED** jumped onto the bed the weight on me was substantial. The pile toppled, and the two scrapped with each other.

After a few attempts to get away, I was able to take this opportune moment to get up and run across to a hallway bathroom. I locked the bathroom door behind me. Both loudly stumbled down the stair well at which point other persons at the house were talking with them. I exited the bathroom, ran outside of the house and went home.

I have not knowingly seen Kavanaugh since the assault. I did see **REDACTED** once at the **REDACTED** where he was extremely uncomfortable seeing me.

I have received medical treatment regarding the assault. On July 6 I notified my local government representative to ask them how to proceed with sharing this information. It is upsetting to discuss sexual assault and its repercussions, yet I felt guilty and compelled as a citizen about the idea of not saying anything.

I am available to speak further should you wish to discuss. I am currently **REDACTED** and will be in **REDACTED**.

In confidence, **REDACTED**.[21]

After agonizing delays, motions, grandstanding, and copious quantities of speculation among those in the media, and much adult foolishness, on September 27, the SJC resumed fulfilling its responsibilities. Intended was an additional day of public hearings to discuss allegations revealed in the letter, known then to have been written by Ford. The only witnesses scheduled were Kavanaugh and Christine Blasey Ford, his accuser. The Republican committee members chose Rachel Mitchell, a career prosecutor from Maricopa County, Arizona to question Ford on their behalf. It was painful to watch. By midday, the Republican committee members put an end to their experiment and politely dismissed Ms. Mitchell and resumed their proper role.

Ford, a professor of psychology at Palo Alto University and a research psychologist at the Stanford University School of Medicine was questioned first. She proved to be almost everything a victim could be. She was pained, timid, sufficiently embarrassed, and sympathetic. And in spite of her impressive education and background she portrayed herself as meek and vulnerable. It was almost impossible to not believe her or *feel her pain*. During her testimony she repeated and expanded upon her earlier written allegations, claiming that Kavanaugh and his companion, Mark Judge, both "visibly drunk", had locked her in a bedroom, where Kavanaugh groped her and tried to take off her clothes while Judge watched. She said she "believed he was going to rape me" and feared for her life when he held his hand over her mouth. Allegedly, when Judge attempted to assist Kavanaugh, the trio rolled off the bed and she escaped.

The media and her supporters on the left believed her to be the quintessential victim. "She must be believed!" the feeble public was told. However, she proved not to be the witness her champions had hoped. She could neither recall exactly when or where the alleged attack had occurred; how she got to the "party" and got home that awful night; why she, a 15 year-old at the time was at a "party" attended by men in college; why she drank beer (one allegedly) while at the party; or why she hadn't reported the attack to her parents or the authorities. There were other loose ends as well. In fairness, human recollection of horrific events is rarely perfect and it is not uncommon that victims of sexual assault provide testimony that is seemingly irrational and weak.

Judge Kavanaugh testified next and sufficiently portrayed himself human, an imperfect young man who drank beer in college, thought passing gas in front of others was funny, and looked forward to enjoying "beach week" with his buddies. He passionately defended himself, his past, his record, his love of family and faith, and his integrity. But after two more, albeit seemingly less-than credible allegations of sexual misconduct by two adult women, and another FBI background investigation of him, his seat on the Supreme Court as an Associate Justice was ultimately confirmed by the U.S. Senate. With little fanfare he took his oath of office on October 6, 2018, with his entire family present.

For those hungry for more salacious details of this historical event go to Appendix B and read Chairman Grassley's referral of the Ms. Julie Swetnick and Michael Avenatti, (Ms. Swetnick's lawyer) allegations regarding Kavanaugh to the U.S. Department of Justice. It contains many inconvenient details some lawmakers would rather you not know and the very biased media *accidently* overlooked.

This sliver of history is filled with useful insights and tragic lessons. Not only were many of the lessons procedural and tactical in form, everyone present learned something. Unsurprisingly, some of the participants attempted to use the events surrounding Judge Kavanaugh and his confirmation proceedings to make headlines and affirm their credentials as protectors of women. Not all women, however. Only women who thought like they did, voted like they did, and hated masculinity and all that they thought it represented, as they did. The wreckage left casualties everywhere.

The first casualty, was that which constitutes credible evidence. Next was the notion of credibility and the reliability of witness testimony, (of which Ford failed to produce a single witness). Then was the concept of fairness, and last and very possibly the most important, was the tragic dismissal of our once cherished belief that one is innocent until proven guilty. These, by any measure, are remarkable outcomes and defining alterations to our once common sense of that which is justice and principled fairness.

The consequences of this debacle will impact every man accused of sexual assault or misconduct outside of our criminal justice system. It is now only within our criminal justice system that a man's constitutional rights and legal protections still exist. In our schools, colleges, and workplaces EVERY man is now subject to the rule that they are guilty until proven innocent and that only the accuser is EVER to be believed. All that is needed to justify punishment is an accusation. It is unfair and frightening. These are rules by which witches were once identified and punished. These are the new rules by which men, young, and old will be judged and their punishment decided.

Lying is learned, while the reputation for honesty is earned.

---

[1] Shakespeare, William, *The Taming of the Shrew*, Act II, Scene I, circa 1590. It should be noted that in the end, the arrogant Petruchio was no match for Katherine, the razor-sharp tongued shrew he came to adore.

[2] Alexander George Karras was an American football player, professional wrestler, sportscaster, and actor. He was a four-time Pro Bowl player with the Detroit Lions of the National Football League, where he played from 1958 to 1970. Paraphrased for readability.

[3] In June 2012, Sheryl Sandberg became the first woman to serve on Facebook's Board of Directors. Before she joined Facebook as its COO, Sandberg was Vice President of Global Online Sales and Operations at Google, and was involved in launching Google's philanthropic arm, Google.org. Before Google, Sandberg served as Chief of Staff for United States Secretary of the Treasury, Lawrence Summers. As Facebook's COO Sandberg's total 2017 compensation was $25,196,221. Of this total, $795,769 was received as a salary, $640,378 was received as a bonus, $21,072,431 was awarded as stock and $2,687,643 came from other types of compensation. Information obtained from Facebook proxy statements filed for the 2017 fiscal year (Source: Salary.com).

---

[4] As Chief Executive Officer and President at PG&E CORP, Geisha J. Williams made $7,600,410 in total compensation in 2017. Of this total, $991,667 was received as a salary, $6,500,168 was awarded as stock and $108,575 came from other types of compensation. This information was found in PG&E proxy statements filed for the 2017 fiscal year (Source: Salary.com). Following her termination as CEO after the lethal California wild-fires in 2017 and 2018, she received a $2.5 million cash severance package

[5] Wall Street Journal, Harriet Torry, October 22, 2018, p A2.

[6] https://en.wikipedia.org/wiki/Me_Too_movement. Sourced, October 29, 2018 by the author.

[7] Ibid.

[8] According to the *New York Times* article it was Mr. Andy Rubin, the creator of the Android operating system, who was fired. Allegedly, Google paid him a $90 million exit package, paid in installments of about $2 million a month for four years. The last payment was scheduled for November 2018. https://www.nytimes.com/2018/10/25/technology/google-sexual-harassment-andy-rubin.html

[9] It was subsequently reported in the New York Times that Google's largest single payout was in the vicinity of $90 million. On November 1, 2018, in response to the disclosure several thousand Google employees staged an internationally coordinated walkout in protest to the alleged payout and for the usual basket of deplorable behaviors everyone knows Google management is famous. Pichai's response was classic for such controversies. He told the protesters and the panting media that he supported the walkouts and appreciated his employees courage to express their dissatisfaction with management. History will decide what the shareholders think.

[10] Drummond's relationship with Google is a bit more complicated. After his separation from the tech giant, Drummond moved over to Alphabet Inc., Google's parent. There he became Alphabet's Senior Vice President of Corporate Development and Chief Legal Officer. According to a story written by Caroline Spiezio, a writer for Law.com, Drummond made more than $47 million in 2018 at his new job at Alphabet (see https://www.law.com/corpcounsel/2019/05/01/despite-sexual-misconduct-report-alphabets-chief-legal-officer-earned-47m-in-2018/?kw=Despite%20Sexual%20Misconduct%20Report%2C%20Alphabet%27s%20Chief%20Legal%20Officer%20Earned%20%2447M%20in%202018&utm_source=email&utm_medium=enl&utm_campaign=breakingnews&utm_content=20190502&utm_term=cc&slreturn=20190402084222).

[11] ac·a·de·mi·a *noun* the environment or community concerned with the pursuit of research, education, and scholarship.

[12] http://www.hcs.harvard.edu/~pslm/livingwage/originalpage/salaries.html

[13] https://www.washingtonpost.com/opinions/why-cant-we-hate-men/2018/06/08/f1a3a8e0-6451-11e8-a69c-b944de66d9e7_story.html?noredirect=on&utm_term=.b5ad3fc50628

[14] https://fasterskier.com/fsarticle/williams-college-seeks-assistant-coach-4 (captured November 2018)

[15] German forces invaded the neutral Norway on April 9, 1940. The country remained occupied and under Nazi rule until the capitulation of Nazi Germany on May 9, 1945. During their occupation, the Nazis arrested, detained, and/or departed 775 Jews. 742 were sent to concentration camps.
https://en.wikipedia.org/wiki/German_occupation_of_Norway

[16] For a short and very readable exposé on this topic see Heather Mac Donald's, *Why Are College Students So Afraid of Me?*, *Wall Street Journal*, Wednesday, November 27. 2019, p A15.

[17] With no disrespect to Associate Justice Bret Michael Kavanaugh, for the purpose of readability I will refer to him simply as Kavanaugh.

[18] In Kavanaugh's case, he responded to 1,287 written questions, which amounted to more than 260 pages—the most comprehensive ever posed to a nominee. In fact, the number of questions posed to Kavanaugh was more than the combined number of written questions submitted to every prior Supreme Court nominee in the entire history of the United States.
https://www.judiciary.senate.gov/press/rep/releases/
scotus_committee-democrats-continue-delay-tactics-with-volume-of-written-
questions-for-kavanaugh

[19] https://fas.org/sgp/crs/misc/R44236.pdf. The document is well worth the read for those interested in a criminal justice perspective and the machinations of the process.

[20] Thought Senator Feinstein denies it, it is widely believed that either she and/or her staffers withheld disclosure of the letter and the tactically leaked it when Kavanaugh and his defenders hadn't the time to investigate its authenticity or the allegations it contained.

[21] This letter is fascinating at several levels. As an investigator and the founder of one of the world's largest whistleblower hotline providers (more on that topic in Chapter Four, *The Anatomy Of A Proper Internal Investigation*), I have had the opportunity to examine and analyze many letters and/or reports that allege misconduct. In doing so, among other things one of the first challenges is to determine if the communication is authentic and if the individual claiming authorship is in fact the author. In this instance, there has been no challenge to its authenticity. However, authenticity is not the same as *authorship*. Two aspects of this document suggest to me that Ms. Ford had a lawyer(s) assist her in writing this letter. First is the claim, "(He)…*physically and sexually assaulted* me during high school…" Most anyone, including a psychologist, who has been *attacked*, does not initially describe the attack as a *physical* or *sexual assault*, unless coached to do so. Next, after identifying the assailant as "Bret Kavanaugh", she thereafter identifies him as "Kavanaugh." Though it appears obvious she and *Kavanaugh* were not friends, her use of only his last name is suspicious. Most victims when knowing the attacker's first name, typically refer to him by it. Typically, lawyers in their pleadings and papers refer to the assailant by his last name after first identifying by his full name. Professional investigators similarly use only last names after an individual have been fully identified.

CHAPTER TWO

THE SCARCITY OF RIGHTS AND PROTECTIONS AFFORDED THE ACCUSED

T o many, the instrument we call law is a peculiar thing. Take for example the legal issues and national discussion regarding the employee walkouts mentioned in the prior chapter. Well organized and orderly, thousands of Google employees walked off the job on November 1, 2018, to protest a perceived culture that allegedly fosters sexual harassment and rewards bad behavior. Protest organizers demanded an assortment of changes at Google relative to organizational practices and policies. Among them were, equal pay, a clear process for reporting sexual misconduct, an end to forced arbitration, a publicly disclosed sexual harassment transparency report, and for the organization's chief diversity officer to answer directly to the CEO.

The public response was mixed. Though the protestors were described as heroic by many in the media, the business community was generally left scratching its collective head. To anyone informed, at first blush, the act of walking off the job appeared to be what the law calls *job abandonment.* Job abandonment is generally considered an *actionable offense.* That is, if determined guilty of the offense, the offending employee can face disciplinary action up to and including termination. The punishment is often final and swift. It is easy to appreciate why, for some walkouts can have serious consequences. Unhappy TSA workers cannot simply get up and walk off their posts at airport security checkpoints, nor can a critical care nurse walk out, leaving his or her most feeble patients unattended and without care. While getting up and walking away from one's workstation or work area may not put the safety or lives of others at risk, the practice is in fact intended to be disruptive and though we rarely hear the word anymore, it can be equally *disrespectful* to those that it affects.

However, under the National Labor Relations Act (NLRA), employees in the United States have the right to protest peacefully without retaliation if their walkout is sparked by workplace-related issues or conditions. The NLRA and caselaw pertaining to "protected activities" prohibit employers from retaliating. Thus, in most cases it would be unlawful for an employer to discipline an employee or subject him to an *adverse employment action* simply because of his participation in a walkout.

On the other hand, organizations can discipline employees for tardiness and absences related to walkouts, if there were policies in place that were routinely followed. But even neutrally applied attendance *work rules* are complicated if walkout participants choose to use paid time off to protest. Organizations sometimes attempt to reduce confusion by informing employees of their rights when choosing whether to walk off the job. What most don't know is that this doctrine and the statutes and rules that permit walkouts were long in the making. Here's how we got here.

Magna Carta

Magna Carta Libertatum (Medieval Latin, meaning "the Great Charter of the Liberties"), is a charter of rights agreed to by King John of England at Runnymede on June 15, 1215.[22] First drafted by the Archbishop of Canterbury to make peace between the unpopular

King and a group of rebel barons, it promised among other things, the protection of church rights, protection for the barons from illegal imprisonment, access to swift justice, and limitations on compulsory payments to the Crown. The charter eventually became part of English political life and was typically renewed by each monarch taking the throne. Its significance over time diminished as the fledgling English Parliament passed new laws and gained power. From it came the concept and institutionalization of *common law*, or what was known at the time as the law of the common people.

Common law was intended to be applied uniformly and therefore be consistent among all jurisdictions and courts in England. It became the law which applied to common everyday situations and people. To ensure uniformity and fairness, among other inventions, torts evolved and their utility and application became codified. Per common law, a tort is a civil wrong that causes a claimant to suffer loss or harm. When triggered, should the claimant prevail, he may be awarded damages. Over time, the courts became a convenient and usually expeditious means of resolving tort claims arising from common disputes.[23]

The Path to a New Nation and a Bill of Rights

Pre-revolutionary colonists in the New World however, enjoyed few of the protections and rights afforded the citizens of England. Among the colonists, many gripes were the burdens of military occupation, taxation without parliamentary representation, and a myriad of seemingly arbitrary and unfair trade tariffs. Ultimately, the colonies formed an alliance and revolted. Familiar with the value of written protestations and declarations, the colonial leaders crafted a careful and inspiring declaration proclaiming their independence from England in 1776. The *Declaration of Independence* was fully ratified a year later.

Violent rebellion in the Colonies ensured and lasted until 1783. But it wasn't until 1790 that the last of the newly created states, Rhode Island, ratified a constitution. Almost two years later on December 15, 1791 the states ratified the *Bill of Rights*. Having recognized the need to establish and codify the rights of the citizens in the new nation they had created, it has been argued that the founders listed them so that each right is iterative and relies on the foundation of the rights that precede it. Collectively they constitute the first amendments to the Constitution. In summary, The Bill of Rights provides the following:

I. *Freedom of religion, speech, press, assembly, and the petition of the government for redress of grievances.*

II. *Right to keep and bear arms.*

III. *No forced quartering of soldiers in time of peace.*

IV. *Protection against unreasonable search and seizure.*

V. *No unlawful imprisonment; double jeopardy, self-incrimination; or taking of private property without just compensation, and trial by jury in criminal matters.*

VI. *Speedy and public trial, opportunity to confront witnesses and know the charges that one faces.*

VII. *The guarantee of trial by jury in federal court for civil matters.*

VIII. *No excessive bail, no cruel or unusual punishment.*

IX. *Ensures that the individual rights that are not enumerated in the Constitution are secure—that is, that these rights should not be automatically infringed upon because they are omitted from the Constitution.*

X. *Limits the power of federal government by reserving for the states all powers that are not explicitly granted to the federal government by the Constitution.*

A learned reader or constitutional lawyer might find the above summary wanting. However important such precision might seem, for our purposes it is principally within the Fifth and Sixth Amendments we find the rights which are under attack by those in the #MeToo movement. To appreciate that, let's first look at the Fifth Amendment a little closer.

The Fifth Amendment

The Fifth Amendment of the U.S. Constitution provides:

"No person shall be held to answer for a capital, or otherwise infamous crime, unless on a presentment or indictment of a grand jury, except in cases arising in the land or naval forces, or in the militia, when in actual service in time of war or public danger; nor shall any person be subject for the same offense to be twice put in jeopardy of life or limb; nor shall be compelled in any criminal case to be a witness against himself, nor be deprived of life, liberty, or property, without due process of law; nor shall private property be taken for public use, without just compensation."

Critically, as we will see shortly, the clauses incorporated within the Fifth Amendment outline basic constitutional limits on the *government,* not the people. Today these limits are incorporated in police procedures and further defined by statute. Not surprisingly, the framers derived the *Grand Juries Clause* and the *Due Process Clause* from the Magna Carta, the principle reference of their time.

Scholars consider the Fifth Amendment as capable of breaking down into the following five distinct constitutional rights:

1. The right to indictment by the grand jury before any criminal charges for felonious crimes;
2. A prohibition on double jeopardy;
3. A right against forced self-incrimination;
4. A guarantee that all criminal defendants have a fair trial, and;

5. A guarantee that government cannot seize private property without providing fair compensation.

While the Fifth Amendment originally only applied to federal courts, the U.S. Supreme Court has partially incorporated the Fifth Amendment to include the states through the Due Process Clause of the Fourteenth Amendment. The right to indictment by the Grand Jury has not been incorporated, while the right against double jeopardy, the right against self-incrimination, and the protection against arbitrary taking of a private property without due compensation have all been incorporated, (additionally assigned) to the states. Let's dig deeper.

Grand Juries

The concept and the use of grand juries are a holdover from the early British common law. Deeply-rooted in the Anglo-American tradition, the grand jury was originally intended to protect the accused from overly-zealous prosecutions by the English monarchy. In the early phases of the development of the U.S. Constitution, the founders decided to retain the grand jury system as a protection against over-zealous prosecution by the central government. Although the Supreme Court in Hurtado v. California in 1884 has refused to incorporate the grand jury system to all of the states, most states have independently decided to retain a similar form of grand jury, and currently, all but two states, (Connecticut and Pennsylvania), employ grand juries.

The Double Jeopardy Clause aims to protect against the harassment of an individual through successive prosecutions of the same alleged act, to ensure the significance of an acquittal, and to prevent the state from putting the defendant through the emotional, psychological, physical, and financial troubles that would accompany multiple trials for the same alleged offense. Courts have interpreted the Double Jeopardy Clause as accomplishing these goals by providing the following three distinct rights: a guarantee that a defendant will not face a second prosecution after an acquittal, a guarantee that a defendant will not face a second prosecution after a conviction, and a guarantee that a defendant will not receive multiple punishments for the same offense. Courts, however, have not interpreted the Double Jeopardy Clause as either prohibiting the state from seeking review of a sentence or restricting a sentence's length on rehearing after a defendant's successful appeal.

Jeopardy refers to the danger of conviction. Thus interestingly, jeopardy does not attach unless a risk of the determination of guilt exists. If some event or circumstance prompts the trial court to declare a mistrial, jeopardy has not attached if the mistrial only results in minimal delay and the government does not receive added opportunity to strengthen its case.

Self-Incrimination

The Fifth Amendment also protects criminal defendants from having to testify if they may incriminate themselves through their testimony. A witness may "plead the Fifth" and not answer if the witness believes answering the question may be self-incriminatory.

In the landmark Miranda v. Arizona ruling, the United States Supreme Court extended the Fifth Amendment protections to encompass any situation outside of the courtroom that involves the curtailment of personal freedom. 384 U.S. 436 (1966). Therefore, any time that law enforcement takes a suspect *into custody*, law enforcement must make the suspect aware of all rights. Known as Miranda rights, these rights include the right to remain silent, the right to have an attorney present during questioning, and the right to have a government-appointed attorney if the suspect cannot afford one.

31

Courts have since then slightly narrowed the Miranda rights, holding that police interrogations or questioning that occur prior to taking the suspect into custody does not fall within the Miranda requirements, and the police are not required to give the Miranda warnings to the suspects prior to taking them into custody, and their silence in some instances can be deemed to be implicit admission of guilt.

If law enforcement fails to honor these safeguards, courts will often suppress any statements by the suspect as violating the Fifth Amendment protection against self-incrimination, provided that the suspect has not actually waived the rights. An actual waiver occurs when a suspect has made the waiver knowingly, intelligently, and voluntarily. To determine if a knowing, intelligent, and voluntary waiver has occurred, a court will examine the totality of the circumstances, which considers all pertinent circumstances and events. If a suspect makes a spontaneous statement while in custody prior to being made aware of the Miranda rights, law enforcement can use the statement against the suspect, provided that police interrogation did not prompt the statement.

Self-incrimination can also be the product of carelessness and ignorance. In my home state of Colorado for instance, it is not uncommon for investigators to ask the alleged victim to call the accused and listen in on the call during the investigation of an allegation of date rape. The caller may be coached to ask the accused to apologize for his transgression or otherwise incriminate himself in some fashion. If the call produces useful evidence, the recording can then be used to make an arrest or seek a grand jury indictment. These methods are particularly effective in cases involving students. Not only do the parties often know one another, they may have dated or previously slept together. In such circumstances, a mere apology or innocent thank you for a nice evening can ruin an innocent man's life. In Chapter 5, *How to Respond and Defend Oneself When Falsely Accused* we will revisit the challenge in more detail.

In the meantime, it is useful to point out that the Fifth Amendment does not extend to an individual's voluntarily prepared business papers because the element of compulsion is lacking. Similarly, the right does not extend to potentially incriminating evidence derived from obligatory reports or tax returns.

Due Process Clause

The guarantee of due process requires the government to respect all rights, guarantees, and protections afforded by the U.S. Constitution and all applicable statutes before *the government* can deprive any person of life, liberty, or property. Due process essentially guarantees that a party will receive a fundamentally fair, orderly, and just judicial proceeding. While the Fifth Amendment only applies to the *federal government*, the identical text in the Fourteenth Amendment explicitly applies this due process requirement to the states as well.

Courts have come to recognize that two aspects of due process exist: procedural due process and substantive due process. Procedural due process aims to ensure fundamental fairness by guaranteeing a party the right to be heard, ensuring that the parties receive proper notification throughout the litigation, and ensures that the adjudicating court has the appropriate jurisdiction to render a judgment. Meanwhile, substantive due process has developed during the 20th century as protecting those substantive rights so fundamental as to be "implicit in the concept of ordered liberty."[24]

The Sixth Amendment

The Sixth Amendment reads:

"In all criminal prosecutions, the accused shall enjoy the right to a speedy

and public trial, by an impartial jury of the State and district wherein the crime shall have been committed, which district shall have been previously ascertained by law, and to be informed of the nature and cause of the accusation; to be confronted with the witnesses against him; to have compulsory process for obtaining witnesses in his favor, and to have the Assistance of Counsel for his defense."[25]

While the Sixth Amendment sets forth rights related to criminal prosecutions and guarantees afforded to the accused, it is instructive for it establishes guidance relative to the treatment of those accused of misconduct beyond the jurisdiction of the federal government. Like the other amendments, the Sixth Amendment not only restricts the authority of the federal government but, as we will see shortly, it establishes reasonable expectations of *anyone* accused of an offense, regardless of the jurisdiction in which the alleged offense occurred, or by whom the accusation was made. What's more, the amendment's *Confrontation Clause*, relates to the common law rule preventing the admission of hearsay, that is to say, testimony by one witness as to the statements and observations of another person to prove that the statement or observation was accurate. The rationale was that the defendant had no opportunity to challenge the credibility of and cross-examine the person making the original statements. Certain exceptions to the hearsay rule have been permitted; for instance, admissions by the defendant are admissible, as are dying declarations.

The Fourteenth Amendment

The Fourteenth Amendment to the United States Constitution was adopted on July 9, 1868, as one of the Reconstruction Amendments. Arguably one of the most consequential amendments to this day, the amendment addresses citizenship rights and equal protection of the laws and was proposed in response to issues related to former slaves following the American Civil War. The amendment was bitterly contested, particularly by the states of the defeated

Confederacy, which were forced to ratify it in order to regain representation in Congress. The amendment, particularly its first section, is one of the most litigated elements of the Constitution, forming the basis for landmark decisions such as Brown v. Board of Education (1954) regarding racial segregation, Roe v. Wade (1973) regarding abortion, Bush v. Gore (2000) regarding the 2000 presidential election, and Obergefell v. Hodges (2015) regarding same-sex marriage. Importantly, the amendment limits the actions of all state and local officials, including those acting on behalf of such an official.

The amendment's first section includes several clauses: the Citizenship Clause, Privileges or Immunities Clause, Due Process Clause, and Equal Protection Clause. The Citizenship Clause provides a broad definition of citizenship, nullifying the Supreme Court's regrettable decision in Dred Scott v. Sandford (1857), which had held that Americans descended from African slaves could not be citizens of the United States. Since the Slaughter-House Cases (1873), the Privileges or Immunities Clause has been interpreted to do very little.

Similar to the Fifth Amendment, the Fourteenth Amendment addresses Due Process. However, in this amendment, its *Due Process Clause* prohibits state and local government officials from depriving persons of life, liberty, or property without legislative authorization. This clause has also been used by the federal judiciary to make most of the Bill of Rights applicable to the states, as well as to recognize substantive and procedural requirements that state laws must satisfy. The Equal Protection Clause requires each state to provide equal protection under the law to *all people*, including all non-citizens, within its jurisdiction. This clause has been the basis for many decisions rejecting irrational or unnecessary discrimination against people belonging to various groups.[26]

So What and Who Cares?

It would not be surprising if you have not yet said to yourself, *so what, who cares and what if anything does all this have to do with me and/or the purpose of this book?* The answer is that it may have everything to do with you, and if not, it has to do with everything about the topic of this book and its purpose. If and when accused of non-criminal sexual misconduct, whether at work or in school, the rights of the accused are very limited. It is common for the accused, and sometimes those who defend them, to believe the accused enjoys an abundance of constitutional and statutory protections just waiting to be exercised. Nothing is further from the truth. All the rights and protections discussed thus far in this chapter, are available only to those accused of an offense *by the government.* The Constitution, the Bill of Rights and almost all of the amendments to the Constitution protect us against the government, not each other. In fact, that was precisely the founders intension. The Constitution and its amendments constitute a pact between a free people and a limited government to which the people voluntarily surrendered limited powers to their elected government. The Constitution places restrictions on the government, thus protecting the people *from the government* and the intrusions it might impose on the people. To protect citizens from each other we have created *laws.*

Thus, it appears that when accused of sexual assault or other serious misconduct by anything (or anyone), other than the government (or its agent), the accused has nearly no constitutional protections. And of those that exist, are either voluntarily provided by the organization to which the accuser belongs or its affiliates, or those provided by regulatory agencies and institutional policies, and/or past practices should any exist. From a constitutional standpoint, almost entirely under these circumstances, the accused is on his own!

However, many organizations and those responsible for

investigating and adjudicating allegations of sexual harassment or misconduct don't know the extent to which the rights of the accused are limited. As such, an astute and informed individual can demand and often obtain benefits and protections of which are not otherwise available. This shift of power can make the difference between one receiving punishment or a humble apology. Regardless, information is power. He who has the most of it has a decided advantage.

There is possibly more good news for the falsely accused. It has been argued that institutions that receive federal government aid and/or financial support (via grants for example), may in fact be *agents* of the government. If held to be true, due process protections afforded by the Bill of Rights may be available to those who the *government's agents* might investigate. The term describing this concept and resultant condition is called *agency*, but the determination of agency requires more than just receiving money from the government. The institution or its employee(s) must aid or actually conduct the investigation in question. If agency can be established and the institution fails to honor or recognize the accused's Constitutional rights, the accused may have the opportunity to make a constitutional claim against the institution and its agents (those who performed the investigation). What's more, any evidence procured while violating the rights of the accused may be inadmissible and may not be used against him.

We will come back to this topic in the next chapter. In the meantime, let's examine some of the rights the accused actually has.

The Civil Rights Act of 1964

The Civil Rights Act of 1964 is a landmark civil rights and US labor law that prohibits discrimination based on race, color, religion, sex, or national origin.[27] It prohibits unequal application of voter registration requirements, racial segregation in schools, employment, and public accommodations. Over time the power and influence of this landmark legislation has vastly changed our culture and the nature and texture of our relationship with one another. Since its passing, Congress and the courts have used the act to assert increasing legislative authority over several different parts of the United States Constitution. Principally enhancements were the power to regulate interstate commerce under Article One (section 8), its duty to guarantee all citizens equal protection of the laws under the Fourteenth Amendment, and its duty to protect voting rights under the Fifteenth Amendment.

During debate, and prior to its passing, the prohibition on sex discrimination was added to the bill by Representative Howard W. Smith. Smith, a powerful Virginia Democrat who chaired the House Rules Committee, strongly opposed the legislation. Smith's amendment was passed by a teller vote of 168 to 133. Historians debate Smith's motivation, whether it was a cynical attempt to defeat the bill by someone opposed to civil rights both for blacks and women, or an attempt to support their rights by broadening the bill to include women.[28] Though not entirely bi-partisan, the final bill passed with the assistance of votes of Republicans and Northern Democrats.

As amended, the law today contains nine distinct *Titles*, each enumerating legal and regulatory authorities over different institutions and aspects of American life. For our purposes, only two are relevant, Title VII and Title IX.

Title VII

Title VII prohibits discrimination by *covered employers* on the basis of race, color, religion, sex or national origin...having "fifteen (15) or more employees for each working day in each of twenty or more calendar weeks in the current or preceding calendar year."[29] Title VII also prohibits discrimination against an individual because of his or her association with another individual of a particular race, color, religion, sex, or national origin, such as by an interracial marriage. Over time, Title VII has also been supplemented with legislation prohibiting pregnancy, age, and disability discrimination (see Pregnancy Discrimination Act of 1978, Age Discrimination in Employment Act and the Americans with Disabilities Act of 1990). [30]

Later, Justice William Rehnquist mused in Meritor Savings Bank v. Vinson, "The prohibition against discrimination based on sex was added to Title VII at the last minute on the floor of the House of Representatives...and we are left with little legislative history to guide us in interpreting the act's prohibition against discrimination based on sex."[31] For some time, everyone including the Supreme Court seemed a bit confused.

Flowing from Title VII, we find the most basic protections against discrimination based on gender. Its protections extend into both the public and private sectors and applies to employers with 15 or more employees, and ALL state and local public sector employers. As it applies to the topic of this book, sexual harassment claims under Title VII come in two varieties: quid pro quo claims and hostile work environment claims. A quid pro claim is cognizable when an employee's "submission to the unwelcome advances [of a supervisor] was an express or implied condition for receiving job benefits or her refusal to submit resulted in a tangible job detriment."[32] A hostile work environment occurs "[w]hen the workplace is permeated with 'discriminatory intimidation, ridicule, and insult'...that is 'sufficiently severe or pervasive to alter the conditions of the victim's employment and create an abuse working environment.'"[33]

While it is possible to delve deeper into the nature of these claims and the mountain of case law surrounding them and their application, it is not necessary for our purposes. These claims cannot be brought against an employee. They can only be brought against an employer! However, when behaviors giving rise to these claims are made in a whistleblower complaint or outright alleged by an employee against another worker, the employer has the duty to respond. Generally, it is the complainant that first brings forth the allegations and it is the employer that then decides how to respond. Should the employer determine the allegation(s) credible and sufficiently serious, it may choose to investigate. In that case, the accused is questioned and a determination of guilt and punishment are eventually decided. The employer's failure to respond in a timely and appropriate fashion can give rise to a civil action brought by the alleged victim. In that case, the accused becomes a witness, and the employer is the defendant. Rarely, is justice so tidy and life so interesting.

In many cases the underlying allegations against the accused include unwanted and/or inappropriate touching. Unwanted or inappropriate touching can be both a tort claim and crime. As a crime, the offense is called battery. Thus, in the worst of circumstances, the accused can ultimately find himself: 1) fired; 2) sued; and 3) charged with a crime. To justify such, the employer and/or law enforcement must exercise their duty to investigate. Regardless, the message is clear: keep your hands and sexual impulses to yourself and no fishing off the company pier…regardless of how inviting the water may appear.

Title IX

Passed as part of the Education Amendments of 1972, Title IX is another federal civil rights law which addresses institutional discrimination. However, contrary to the belief of many, Title IX is not an original component of The Civil Rights Act of 1964 and has no historical or legislative relationship with Title VII as discussed above.

Initially encouraged by the tenacious and outspoken activist Bernice Resnick Sandler and the fledging Women's Equity Action League in 1969, Congress was pressured to act on a growing body of evidence of sexual discrimination in admissions, hiring, pay and sports on American campuses. The bill that became Title IX, was co-authored and introduced by Senator Birch Bayh in the U.S. Senate, and Congresswoman Patsy Mink in the House. It was later renamed the Patsy T. Mink Equal Opportunity in Education Act following Mink's death in 2002. The original bill was signed into law by President Richard Nixon in 1972.[34] In summary, the law provides:

"No person in the United States shall, on the basis of sex, be excluded from participation in, be denied the benefits of, or be subjected to discrimination under any education program or activity receiving Federal financial assistance."

Using its power of the purse, the law permitted Congress to expand its antidiscrimination agenda and change college athletics and campus life in America forever. Dutifully, in the 1990s, the U.S. Supreme Court issued three decisions clarifying that Title IX requires schools to respond appropriately to reports of sexual harassment and sexual violence against female students. Civil rights activists and organizations such as the American Civil Liberties Union (ACLU) laid in waiting. Mind you, the intentions of Congress, higher-ed, Russlynn and the likes of the ACLU were fundamentally well intended, few could resist the opportunity to put a thumb on the scales of justice. So as to preclude any confusion, according to an April 2011 letter issued by the Department of Education's Office for Civil Rights, "The sexual harassment of students, including sexual violence, interferes with students' right to receive an education free from discrimination and, in the case of sexual violence, is a crime." See Appendix C for the salient portions of the 19 page letter authored by Russlynn Ali, United States Department of Education, Office of Civil Rights, Assistant Secretary for Civil Rights.

The letter, dubbed the *Dear Colleague Letter*, states that it is the responsibility of institutions of higher education "to take immediate and effective steps to end sexual harassment and sexual violence." The letter illustrates multiple examples of Title IX requirements as they relate to sexual violence, and makes clear that, should an institution fail to fulfill its responsibilities under Title IX, the Department of Education can impose a fine and potentially deny further institutional access to federal funds. To suggest that the letter was meant to trigger hysteria, is an understatement. From page two, the reader is offered:

> "The statistics on sexual violence are both deeply troubling and a call to action for the nation. A report prepared for the National Institute of Justice found that about 1 in 5 women are victims of completed or attempted sexual assault while in college. The report also found that approximately 6.1 percent of males were victims of completed or attempted sexual assault during college. According to data collected under the Jeanne Clery Disclosure of Campus Security and Campus Crime Statistics Act (Clery Act), 20 U.S.C. § 1092(f), in 2009, college campuses reported nearly 3,300 forcible sex offenses as defined by the Clery Act. This problem is not limited to college. During the 2007-2008 school year, there were 800 reported incidents of rape and attempted rape and 3,800 reported incidents of other sexual batteries at public high schools. Additionally, the likelihood that a woman with intellectual disabilities will be sexually assaulted is estimated to be significantly higher than the general population. The Department is deeply concerned about this problem and is committed to ensuring that all students feel safe in their school, so that they have the opportunity to benefit fully from the school's programs and activities."

Assistant Secretary Ali's "statistics" deserve scrutiny. With "about 1 in 5 women" becoming "victims of completed or attempted sexual assault while in college" it would appear no one on campus is safe. Moreover, a closer look at the Clery statistics don't support the hysteria. Regardless, were such studies accurate, our college campuses would look more like crisis relief centers instead of institutions of higher learning. Between the women being treated for assault and other injuries and the men spending their days before administrative tribunals and being carted off to jail, no one would have the time or inclination to study. Yet today, more women seem to want to attend college than men. Go figure.

According to the U.S. Department of Education, women comprise about 56 percent of the students on campuses nationwide.[35] Of the roughly 16.9 million undergrads in 2017, there were some 2.2 million fewer men than women.[36] So of the 9.7 million women on campus today, almost 2 million of the them have been "victims of completed or attempted sexual assault" while at college. If true, given the breadth of the epidemic shouldn't parents be considered negligent for sending their daughters to college? What kind of parent would send their 18 year old *anyplace* knowing that she would have a 1 in 5 chance of becoming a victim of sexual assault upon arriving at her destination?

But no crises should ever be wasted. Somebody has to be held responsible, the scolds demand. Ah yes, of course, the champions of the social justice movement know exactly who. It is the men who are responsible, they tell us and it is they who should pay the price. Remember, only men are guilty until proven innocent and all women are entitled to their own truth and should always be believed. What's more, why insult the parents of the alleged victims who are picking up the tab. Isn't it easier to sweep up a few dopey frat boys and subject them to a kangaroo court where they are denied the opportunity to question their accuser or be permitted professional representation? Of course it is. It also makes for good headlines.

In October 2012, an Amherst College student (class of 2014),

Angie Epifano, wrote an explicit, personal account of her alleged sexual assault and the ensuing "appalling treatment" she received when coming forward to seek support from the college's administration. In her narrative, Ms. Epifano alleged that she was raped by a fellow Amherst student and described how her life was affected by the experience; she stated that the perpetrator harassed her at the only dining hall, that her academic performance was negatively affected, and that, when she sought support, the administration coerced her into taking the blame for her experience and ultimately institutionalized her and pressured her to drop out.

Subsequently, in an essay Ms. Epifano offered, "The fact that such a prestigious institution could have such a noxious interior fills me with intense remorse mixed with sour distaste. I am sickened by the Administration's attempts to cover up survivors' stories, cook their books to discount rapes, pretend that withdrawals never occur, quell attempts at change, and sweep sexual assaults under a rug. When politicians cover up affairs or scandals the masses often rise up in angry protestations and call for a more transparent government. What is the difference between a government and the Amherst College campus? Why can't we know what is really happening on campus? Why should we be quiet about sexual assault?"

When the Amherst case reached national attention, Annie E. Clark and Andrea Pino, two women who were allegedly sexually assaulted at the University of North Carolina at Chapel Hill connected with Amherst student, Dana Bolger, and Alexander Brodsky to address the parallel concerns of hostility at their institution, filing Title IX and Clery Act complaints against the university on January 2013, both leading to investigations by the U.S. Department of Education.

Following the national prominence of the UNC Chapel Hill case, organizers Pino and Clark went on to coordinate with students at other schools. In 2013, complaints citing violations of Title IX were filed by Occidental College, on April 18, Swarthmore College and the University of Southern California, on May 22. These complaints, the resulting campaigns against sexual violence on college campuses, and the organizing of Bolger, Brodsky, Clark, Pino, and other activists led to the formation of an informal national network of activists. Bolger and Brodsky also started *KnowYourIX.org*, an organization of student activists focused on legal education and federal and state policy change.

Additionally to its use for the handling of formal complaints submitted to the Department of Education, Title IX has been utilized in civil litigation. In 2006, a federal court found that there was sufficient evidence that the University of Colorado acted with "deliberate indifference" toward students Lisa Simpson and Anne Gilmore, who were sexually assaulted by student football players. The university settled the case, promising to change its policies and pay $2.5 million in damages.

In 2008, Arizona State University was the subject of a lawsuit that alleged violations of rights guaranteed by Title IX. Resultantly, the university expelled a football player for multiple instances of severe sexual harassment, but readmitted him; he went on to rape a fellow student in her dorm room. Despite its claim that it bore no responsibility, the school settled the lawsuit, agreeing to revise and improve its official response to sexual misconduct and to pay the plaintiff $850,000 in damages and fees.[37]

Fortunately, the Trump administration has made some changes to the guidelines put forth in the *Dear Colleague Letter* and were subsequently implemented during the Obama administration and directly overseen and promoted by then Vice President, Joe Biden, (himself later accused of sexual assault by a former aide). These changes shift the determination of sexual assault from "preponderance of the evidence" to a "clear and convincing" evidence standard. Though the *clear and convincing evidence standard* is a substantially lower threshold than the *standard of beyond reasonable doubt* used in criminal cases it is far better suited for alleged campus sex crimes.

On September 22, 2017, US Secretary of Education Secretary Betsy Devos rescinded the Obama-era guidelines that had prodded colleges and universities to more aggressively investigate allegations of sexual assaults on campus and punish those responsible.

Sanity Might Be On Its Way

Secretary DeVos's new Title IX Rule finally arrived on May 6, 2020. In the spirit of her original proposal, the new rules appear to provide definitive guidance and clarity for schools and their administrators. According to a November 16, 2018, DOE press release, Secretary DeVos stated she intended to provide, "due process rights for all." In part her 2018 announcement read:

> "WASHINGTON — Continuing its efforts to ensure equal access to education free from discrimination, today the U.S. Department of Education released its proposal on improving schools' responses to sexual harassment and assault. The proposed regulation under Title IX, the federal civil rights law that prohibits discrimination on the basis of sex in education programs or activities that receive federal funding, was developed after more than a year of research, deliberation, and gathering input from students, advocates, school administrators, Title IX coordinators, and other stakeholders.

> Throughout this process, my focus was, is, and always will be on ensuring that every student can learn in a safe and nurturing environment,' said U.S. Secretary of Education

Betsy DeVos. 'That starts with having clear policies and fair processes that every student can rely on. Every survivor of sexual violence must be taken seriously, and every student accused of sexual misconduct must know that guilt is not predetermined. We can, and must, condemn sexual violence and punish those who perpetrate it, while ensuring a fair grievance process. Those are not mutually exclusive ideas. They are the very essence of how Americans understand justice to function."[38]

From the casual reader, one might have expected a big yawn.[39] Yet critics wasted no time disparaging DeVos while claiming the new rules were unfair to women and they'd embolden a fresh stock of sexual predators on America's campuses. More sober minds quickly pointed out that with our schools shut down, the timeline for implementation does not give administrators enough time to seek input from their various stakeholders and make sure that any modification to existing policies are fairly evaluated and considered.

However, the proposal and resultant new rules represent an immense shift to how DOE wishes to see Title IX enforced. Briefly, the new guidance, which takes effect August 14, 2020, will allow Title IX officials to apply either the "preponderance of the evidence" or "clear and convincing" standard in deciding guilt, with the latter setting the higher burden of proof. However, the stand selected for students must be *the same standard that is applied to the institution's own employees*. Genius really. DeVos had original proposed to raise the standard of proof to the much higher, clear and convincing standard. However, the press, scholars, faculty, tenured educators, visiting professors, and administrators howled. DeVos backed off and in the final rule, instead tied the standard of proof to that which applied to the institution's own employees—a standard which those same scholars, faculty, tenured educators, visiting professors and administrators had long established for themselves!

The new guidance also requires colleges to provide a live hearing and allows student advisers (inclusive of their lawyers), to cross-examine the parties and witnesses involved. According to a summary of its major provisions (See Appendix D), statements made by parties that are not cross-examined cannot be relied on to determine guilt. Critics have already claimed cross-examination of the accused will re-traumatize victims and prevent victims from coming forward.

The new regulations also define the scope of an institution's responsibility to respond to sexual misconduct complaints, stating colleges must act upon complaints of misconduct whether occurring on or off-campus, to include fraternity or sorority housing, in "a building owned or controlled by a student organization that is officially recognized by a postsecondary institution," and "locations, events, or circumstances" where the institutions have "substantial control" over students and activities where the alleged event occurred. The initial draft of the rules had precluded schools from investigating off-campus incidents. But schools will be allowed to only investigate episodes which occur within their programs and activities, exempting student housing and residents not affiliated with a university.

To find a school legally culpable for mishandling accusations, it would have to be proved "deliberately indifferent" in carrying out mandates to provide support to victims and investigate complaints fairly. The 2,000-page document emphasizes "equitable" treatment and the presumption of innocence. Variously, the new rules also require or provide:

1. Covered entities to promulgate and maintain clear policies and fair processes so as to sustain a "fair grievance process."

2. Define the complainant, "as an individual who is *alleged* to be the victim of conduct that could constitute sexual harassment."

3. All Title IX Coordinators, investigators, decision-makers, people who facilitate any informal resolution process) to be free from conflicts of interest or bias for or against complainants or respondents.

4. Describe the range, or list the possible remedies a school may provide a complainant and disciplinary sanctions a school might impose on a respondent, following determinations of responsibility.

5. State whether the school has chosen to use the preponderance of the evidence standard, or the clear and convincing evidence standard for all formal complaints of sexual harassment (including where employees and faculty are respondents).

6. Describe the school's appeal procedures, and the range of supportive measures available to complainants and respondents.

7. Training of Title IX personnel must include training on the definition of sexual harassment in the Final Rule, the scope of the school's education program or activity, how to conduct an investigation and grievance process including hearings, appeals, and informal resolution processes, as applicable, and how to serve impartially, including by avoiding prejudgment of the facts at issue, conflicts of interest, and bias.

8. A school must ensure that decision-makers receive training on any technology to be used at a live hearing.

9. A school's decision-makers and investigators must receive training on issues of relevance, including how to apply the rape shield protections provided only for complainants.

10. Include a presumption that the respondent is not responsible for the alleged conduct until a determination regarding responsibility is made at the conclusion of the grievance

process.

11. Recipients must post materials used to train Title IX personnel on their websites, if any, or make materials available for members of the public to inspect.

12. Include reasonably prompt time frames for conclusion of the grievance process, including appeals and informal resolutions, with allowance for short-term, good cause delays or extensions of the time frames.

13. At the request of either party, the recipient must provide for the entire live hearing (including cross-examination) to occur with the parties located in separate rooms with technology enabling the parties to see and hear each other.

14. Only relevant cross-examination and other questions may be asked of a party or witness. Before a complainant, respondent, or witness answers a cross-examination or other question, the decision-maker must first determine whether the question is relevant and explain to the party's advisor asking cross-examination questions any decision to exclude a question as not relevant.

15. If a party does not have an adviser present at the live hearing, the school must provide, without fee or charge to that party, an advisor of the school's choice who may be, but is not required to be, an attorney to conduct cross-examination on behalf of that party.

16. If a party or witness does not submit to cross-examination at the live hearing, the decision-maker(s) must not rely on any statement of that party or witness in reaching a determination regarding responsibility; provided, however, that the decision-maker(s) cannot draw an inference about the determination regarding responsibility based solely on a party's or witness's absence from the live hearing or refusal to answer cross-examination or other questions.

17. Live hearings may be conducted with all parties physically present in the same geographic location or, at the school's discretion, any or all parties, witnesses, and other participants may appear at the live hearing virtually.

18. Schools must create an audio or audiovisual recording, or transcript, of any live hearing; and more generally;

19. Adopt and formalize basic "due process protections" to include:

    a. Live proceedings open to both the accuser and her accused;
    b. A presumption of innocence for the accused;
    c. Written notice and specification of the allegations;
    d. The opportunity to examine all evidence and cross-examine witnesses;
    e. Cease the use of the "single investigator" or "investigator only" model, thus bifurcating the roles of fact-finders and decision-makers; and
    f. A fair and functional appeal process for all parties.

One needn't be a lawyer or a seasoned harassment or discrimination investigator to view these directives and not realize how unfair and arbitrary the "process" had been. Even the most naïve would have to wonder how the accused might have mounted a defense if he wasn't fully aware of the allegation(s) and the evidence against him? Even the Salem witch trials allowed the accused to prove their innocence by being dunked until death by drowning. But when one starts with the presumption all men are predators and all women are perfect victims, actually proving guilt is merely an inconvenience. The Obama-era appointees and their DOE acolytes had no intention of being inconvenienced by actually proving guilt. Instead, they and Title IX's poster child and mouthpiece Vice President Joe Biden, sought the fastest and most convenient path to punishment.

The resultant damage was immense. Not only were the *investigators* not properly screened, selected, or trained, few had any experience in such matters. Those responsible for creating this form of justice and they who defended it should ask for forgiveness. Those who embraced it and participated in it should be ashamed of themselves. Rarely, in modern times have we seen such high-mindedness and injustice. Thank you Secretary Betsy DeVos.[4041]

> *Faced with what is right, to leave it undone*
> *shows a lack of courage.*
>
> —*Confucius*

---

[22] It is believed six of the seventeen original copies of the Magna Carta known to exist are in private hands. Microsoft founder, Bill Gates is the owner of one of them. He purchased it in 1994 for what is believed to be $12.3 million at auction. To the best of anyone's knowledge, it is still in his possession.

[23] The common law—so named because it was "common" to all the king's courts across England—originated in the practices of the courts of the English kings in the centuries following the Norman Conquest in 1066. The British Empire spread the English legal system to its colonies, many of which retain the common law system today. These *common law systems* are legal systems that give great weight to judicial precedent, and to the style of reasoning inherited from the English. Thus today, common law (also known as judicial precedent or judge-made law) is the body of law derived from judicial decisions of courts and similar tribunals. The defining characteristic of *common law* is that it arises as precedent. In cases where the parties disagree on what the law is, a common law court looks to past precedential decisions of relevant courts, and synthesizes the principles of those past cases as applicable to the current facts. If a similar dispute has been resolved in the past, the court is usually bound to follow the reasoning used in the prior decision (a principle known as *stare decisis*). If, however, the court finds that the current dispute is fundamentally distinct from all previous cases (called a "matter of first impression"), and legislative statutes are either silent or ambiguous on the question, judges have the authority and duty to resolve the issue (one party or the other has to win, and on disagreements of law, judges make that decision). The court states an opinion that gives reasons for the decision, and those reasons agglomerate with past decisions as precedent to bind future judges and litigants. Common law, as the body of law made by judges, stands in contrast to and on equal footing with statutes which are adopted through the legislative process, and regulations which are promulgated by the executive branch. Stare decisis, the principle that cases should be decided according to consistent principled rules so that similar facts will yield similar results, lies at the heart of all common law systems. The common law of today is contrasted by that which is called, *civil law*. In civil law systems, individual decisions have only advisory, not binding effect. In civil law systems, case law only acquires weight when a long series of cases use consistent reasoning, called *jurisprudence constante*. Civil law lawyers consult case law to obtain their best prediction of how a court will rule, but comparatively, civil law judges are less bound to follow it. Today, Great Britain has a civil law system. For more details see: https://en.wikipedia.org/wiki/Common_law

[24] Courtesy Legal Information Institute. See https://www.law.cornell.edu/wex/fifth amendment

[25] The word defense as spelled in the original document ss *defence*.

[26] https://en.wikipedia.org/wiki/Fourteenth_Amendment_to_the_United_States_Constitution

[27] Public Law 88–352, 78 Statute 241, enacted July 2, 1964.

[28] https://en.wikipedia.org/wiki/Civil_Rights_Act_of_1964#Title_VII

[29] As written in the Definitions section under 42 U.S.C. §2000e(b)

[30] Age Discrimination in Employment Act of 1967.

[31] 477 U.S. 57, 63–64.

[32] Ogden v. Wax Works, Inc. 214 F.3d 999, 1006 (8th Cir. 2000); also see Burlington Indus. V. Ellerth, 524 U.S. 742, 751 (1998).

[33] Harris v. Forklift Sys. , Inc., 510 U.S. 17, 21 (1993).

---

[34] Public Law No. 92-318, 86 Stat. 235 (June 23, 1972), codified at 20 U.S.C. §§ 1681–1688.

[35] https://nces.ed.gov/programs/digest/d16/tables/dt16_303.70.asp.

[36] https://nces.ed.gov/programs/coe/indicator_cha.asp

[37] More details can be found at https://en.wikipedia.org/wiki/Title_IX (retrieved November 18, 2018).

[38] https://www.ed.gov/news/press-releases/secretary-devos-proposed-title-ix-rule-provides-clarity-schools-support-survivors-and-due-process-rights-all

[39] So important did I think these changes were necessary, I submitted a comment via the Regulations.gov website (comment ID: ED-2018-OCR-0064-0001).

[40] Just as this book is going to press, more than a dozen state attorneys general have filed a lawsuit against U.S. Secretary of Education Betsy DeVos and the U.S. Department of Education in an attempt to block the department's final Title IX regulations. According to the lawsuit, if the regulations take effect, they will "reverse decades of effort to end the corrosive effects of sexual harassment on equal access to education" and will require institutions to "completely overhaul" their current systems for addressing sexual misconduct in less than three months—all while dealing with the coronavirus pandemic. The complaint asserts that the new rule conflicts with federal and state statutes and Supreme Court precedent and that it creates a set of "one-size-fits-all formal procedures" that do not allow for institutions to fairly judge a complaint. The attorneys general also state the rule will chill the reporting of sexual harassment due to extensive and unnecessary new procedural requirements. The lawsuit has been filed on behalf of attorneys general from California, Colorado, Delaware, the District of Columbia, Illinois, Massachusetts, Michigan, Minnesota, New Jersey, New Mexico, North Carolina, Oregon, Pennsylvania, Rhode Island, Vermont, Virginia, Washington and Wisconsin.

[41] I do not know Secretary DeVos nor have I ever met her. My expression of appreciation to her is at several levels. First and foremost, is appreciation for accepting the difficult and a rarely appreciated position of U.S. Secretary of Education. At another level, I have immense appreciation and respect for her keeping her word by overhauling Title IX's rules and making both the American workplace and our schools better prepared to protect those who have been falsely accused of sexual assault or other serious misconduct.

CHAPTER THREE

TRIAL BY ORDEAL

W atching the Kavanaugh Senate confirmation hearings was painful. On full display was the pomposity and arrogance of lawmaking elites caring little about anyone or anything other than themselves and their imaginary importance. But as an investigator who had spent his career conducting the very type of investigation many were demanding, I was both puzzled and deeply troubled. What puzzled me most was the apparent absence of process. How was it possible Chairman Grassley and his committee, (or those who had served before them), had not put into place a process for handling last minute allegations regarding a nominee's suitability or qualifications. Apparently, also absent was a process for performing a formal investigation of allegations of serious sexual misconduct or criminality. I was left thinking to myself, what exactly are we paying these people for? Had no one in the Senate remembered the Clarence Thomas or Robert Bork hearings? Had no one thought ahead and prepared?

Sadly, everyone knows sexual assault, harassment and discrimination occurs in the workplace, our schools, and places of higher learning. Since the launch of the #MeToo movement, a little over a year prior to the confirmation hearings, the Equal Employment

Opportunity Commission reported it had experienced a sizable increase in the number of sexual harassment charges it received. Some agencies serving as a state counterpart to the federal EEOC had seen even greater increases. At the same time, the EEOC's filing of sexual harassment lawsuits against employers more than doubled, while the monetary damages paid by those targeted increased from $47 million to $70 million. To appreciate the scale of this trend, consider that these numbers do not include the costs of sexual harassment cases brought by private plaintiff attorneys or other forms of harassment investigated or litigated by the EEOC or private parties.

Damage awards and litigation costs are not the only financial consequences of organizational failures to stop and prevent sexual harassment. Employees and students who are harassed, as well as those who are around them, suffer adverse physical and mental health consequences, sometimes resulting in absenteeism and higher healthcare costs. Research shows that harassment reduces the productivity of both harassed individuals and those closest to them when the harassment occurs. In the case of harassed employees, they may leave if they are able, and employees who witness unchecked harassment and its consequences on their coworkers may also leave. Because it is believed that almost 70 percent of harassment incidents are *never reported* to the employer, talented and highly-skilled employees may leave without employers knowing why they left or that their organization has suffered because of an unrecognized hostile work environment.

Reputational harm resulting from outspoken victims and media exposure can add to the devastation. Organizations in which it is known that harassment occurs and has been known to have apparently tolerated it, are less likely to attract talented employees and may lose customers and clients. If workplace harassment becomes public, the harm to the organization's reputation may be expensive and long lasting. The list of examples is long and includes many well-knowns such as Miramax, Wynn Resorts, CBS, Fox News, Google and Uber.[42] Notwithstanding the cost and emotional devastation suffered by the victims and those falsely accused, our nation and culture has been severely damaged as well.

Had no one on the Senate Judiciary Committee known any of this? Had no one read a newspaper or watched the news?

Borking Comes of Age

The Brett Kavanaugh nomination to replace Associate Justice, Anthony Kennedy on the U.S. Supreme Court in September 2018 was a watershed event that brought out the worst in nearly everyone associated with it. The entire affair was distasteful and horribly disappointing. And while some have claimed victory and others defeat, there were no real winners, and like it or not, every American is now a loser.

Judge Kavanaugh was not the first to have his fate decided by trial by ordeal. Before him was Clarence Thomas and then Robert Bork. So memorable was the mistreatment of former Solicitor General of the United States, Bork in 1987, the words *Bork, Borked,* and *Borking* shamefully entered the American English lexicon. So common are these words today, I needn't even define them for you. But consider the spectacle: Judge Kavanaugh's nomination for the U.S. Supreme Court, the embodiment of our modern rule of law, was decided by the medieval practice of trial by ordeal. Though he needn't survive physical torture, armed combat against a better armed and more powerful opponent, exposure in fire or immersion in boiling water, he was forced to confront an ordeal that had been outlawed by the Lateran Council in 1215.[43] It was clear, Kavanaugh's opponents intended to claim his withdrawal from consideration proof of his guilt. At the same time, they surely would claim the same, had he not. The strategy and theater used to execute it was as embarrassing as it was disgraceful. Even those such as myself, who simply watched, felt dirty after it was over.

What had begun as tragedy, would soon end in farce. A respectable and seemingly, very credible professor by the name of Christine Ford accused Kavanaugh of sexual assault when she was 15 and he a mere 17. The accusation, though known to at least Senate Judiciary Committee member, Dianne Feinstein, for six weeks was not revealed until the eleventh hour. Knowing the accusation could neither be proved nor disproved, the opposition knew it had political value. Like many of the other #MeToo episodes before it, the grandstanding was not really about the pursuit of justice, it was about taking someone down. The higher the profile of the target, and in some cases his organization, the more valuable the allegations and the greater the opportunity to destroy the *powerful*. Discovered was a weapon against which there is no defense. In the Dark Ages, the tactic became known as *trial by ordeal*.

However this time, it was an ordeal that was to consume not only Kavanaugh but others as well. First was Ms. Ford, whose privacy was violated by Senator Feinstein. Ms. Ford had entrusted the senator to not reveal her allegation or identity. Soiled were also her family, friends, and colleagues. Disgraced, if not embarrassed were her alleged witnesses and former friends, as well as her professional colleagues and students. Used as bludgeons and weapons to exact maximum shame, were Judge Kavanaugh's wife, children and parents. It was embarrassing to even watch.

Character assassination is nothing new in politics. As in the case of Judge Kavanaugh, he was powerful, polished, and respectable. His alleged victim was presented as powerless, sympathetic, and suitably traumatized. It was the perfect political conflict. It had everything: the powerful and the powerless; an assailant and victim; disgust and sympathy; and a terrifying graphic sexual assault. To complicate matters, and to their own disgrace, Ms. Ford's attorneys and her psychologist assisted her with "resurrecting" her memory of the event.

But Kavanaugh's ordeal was not just about unprovable and uncorroborated allegations, it was about the denial of due process. It birthed a new standard of proof that effectively eliminated any burden of proof. Remarkably, his distracters in chorus, declared him guilty until proven innocent. This new standard required one only to believe Ms. Ford, and poof…Kavanaugh was at once, guilty as charged! And like the practices that now have become "industry standards" he was further denied the opportunity to examine his accuser, challenge her credibility, engage in any legal discovery, or mount a defense. The conduct of those who mounted this assault against him was as appalling as it was dishonest. The entire affair was an offense on the rule of law and our expectation of common decency.

Henceforth, many of those accused of sexual assault, and other serious misconduct will be deemed guilty until proven innocent. No male regardless of age, color, faith, political persuasion, or reputation will be immune to this savagery. Sadly, the men attending our universities and colleges will be no less immune, nor will any male in the modern workplace or public view. Compounding the risk, is the limitation of rights afforded the accused who are outside our criminal justice system. So as to refresh your recollection, I previously offered:

"It is common for the accused and sometimes those who defend them, to believe the accused enjoys an abundance of constitutional and statutory protections just waiting to be exercised. Nothing is further from the truth. All the rights and protections discussed [previously], are available only to those accused of an offense *by the government*. The Constitution, the Bill of Rights, and almost all of the amendments to the Constitution protect us against the government, not each other. In fact, that was precisely our founders intension…The Constitution places restrictions on the government, thus protecting the people from the government and the intrusions it might impose on the people. *To protect citizens from each other we have created laws* (emphasis added)."

Resultantly, when accused of sexual assault or other serious misconduct by anyone or anything other than the government, (or a government financed or funded institution), the accused has nearly no constitutional rights (return to Chapter 2 for a refresher regarding those rights). But in the search for social justice, no opportunity to settle a score or find justice where none is due, can any allegation of sexual misconduct be wasted. To our detriment, any allegation can and must be weaponized!

Weaponizing Allegations of Sexual Misconduct

Often, the purpose of this movement is not justice at all. Its purpose is the pursuit of power and the extraction of money from wherever it may be found. The ability to punish those who are dislikeable and have deep pockets are the best targets. Allegations of sexual assault are particularly suited for this purpose for two very good reasons: a) in most jurisdictions there are no statute of limitations, and those that exist can sometimes be circumvented; and b) most sexual assaults involve only two people—the victim and the assailant, thus there are no pesky witnesses available to screw up the accuser's (and his or her handlers) version of the event. As a thought experiment try to come up with another offense for which the following elements exist:

1. No statute of limitation;
2. No obligation to explain why one did not disclose the alleged offense in a timely fashion nor explain the untimeliness of eventually doing so;
3. No requirement of a witness or even the thinnest amount of

corroboration;

4. No requirement of physical or forensic evidence;

5. Little or no recollection of when or where the alleged offense occurred;

6. No explanation as to how the victim arrived at or was transported to the crime scene or how or when she left it; and

7. The ability to use a licensed clinician or some form of therapy to "resurrect" the victim's recollection.

Sorry, time's up. Answer: there is no such crime. One needn't be a lawyer to appreciate the injustice in this. The last time we had what might have been considered a civilized society that tolerated such was over 1000 years ago. Our Founding Fathers thought otherwise as well, ergo our Constitution and the Bill of Rights. But hysteria, social panic, and political ambition has a way of enabling the willing to act and think, irrationally. When hysteria, panic and ambition converge, social movements are birthed. And while the movements' followers are soft-minded at best, they are loyal, and they are led by the ambitious. Power and money are often their leaders only ambition. Sadly, today, we live in such a place and time. Get ready, it appears things will get worse before they get better.

The Lasting Impact of the #MeToo Movement

As you are reading this book, the #MeToo movement is in fact transforming our nation and its understanding of justice. The supporters of the movement are unleashing a sweeping and destructive torrent of gender and race quota demands on our economy and national identity. They and their leaders believe that all disparities in our culture, schools, and workplaces are the product of unbridled harassment, discrimination, and bias. The resulting distortions of policy and law-making they foster will largely remain out of sight, except for those they directly affect. Few will notice the carnage they will bring, learn of the employment candidates who were passed over, or the college applicants overlooked in the name of gender parity and equality. Few have captured the import of this phenomena and its consequences better than Heather Mac Donald. She recently offered the following in the Hillsdale College publication, *Imprimis*:[44]

"Pressures for so-called diversity, defined reductively by gonads and melanin, are of course nothing new. Since the 1990s, every mainstream institution has lived in terror of three lethal words: "all white male," an epithet capable of producing paroxysms of self-abasement…But however pervasive the diversity imperative was before, the #Me Too movement is going to make the previous three decades look like a golden age of meritocracy. No mainstream institution will hire, promote, or compensate without an exquisite calculation of gender and race ratios. Males in general, and white males in particular, will have to clear a very high bar in order to justify further deferring that halcyon moment of gender equity…

Corporate boardrooms, executive suites, and management structures are going to be scoured for gender and race imbalances. Diversity trainers are already sensing a windfall from #MeToo. Gender, diversity, and inclusion were the dominant themes at this January's [2018] World Economic Forum in Davos, Switzerland. The conference was chaired exclusively by women. Windows were emblazoned with slogans like "Diversity is good for business" and "Gender equality is a social and economic issue." CEOs shared their techniques for achieving gender equity. It's actually quite simple: pay managers based on their record of hiring and promoting females and minorities, as Hilton CEO Christopher Nassetta explained. Never mind the fact that by introducing irrelevant criteria such as race and gender into an evaluation process, you will inevitably end up with [fewer] qualified employees [and eventually a smaller bottom-line]…

Academia, the source of identity politics, will double down on its diversity quota-izing in the wake of #Me Too. A panel at the annual American Economic Association meeting in January charged that gender discrimination was pervasive in economics—an argument that fit into the "larger national examination of bias and abuse toward women in the work force," *The New York Times*. In March, the Chronicle of Higher Education and Priya Satia, former diversity chair of Stanford University's Department of History, went into diversity meltdown over a history conference that Hoover Institution Fellow Niall Ferguson had organized. Though Ferguson had invited females to speak, none had accepted. Not good enough, according to Professor Satia. Ferguson should have suspended the conference entirely unless he could persuade females and minorities to participate. Although Satia did not identify any scholarly gaps that resulted from the actual lineup, Stanford University was so shaken by the controversy that it issued a statement on behalf of the president and provost assuring the public that it had made its concerns about the lack of diversity known to the conference organizers…

The #MeToo movement has uncovered real abuses of power. But the solution to those abuses is not to replace valid measures of achievement with irrelevancies like gender and race. Ironically, the best solution to sexual predation is not more feminism, but less. By denying the differences between men and women, and by ridiculing the manly virtues of gentlemanliness and chivalry and the female virtues of modesty and prudence, feminism dissolved the civilizational restraints on the male libido. The boorish behavior that pervades society today would have been [less likely] in the past, when a traditional understanding of sexual propriety prevailed. Now, however, with the idea of "ladies and gentlemen" discredited and out of favor, boorishness is increasingly the rule.

Contrary to the feminist narrative, Western culture is in fact the least patriarchal culture in human history; rather than being forced to veil, females in our society can parade themselves in as scantily clad a manner as they choose. As we have seen, every mainstream institution is trying to hire and promote as many females as possible. As the #MeToo movement swells the demand for ever more draconian diversity mandates, a finding in a Pew Research Center poll on workplace equity is worth noting: *the perception of bias is directly proportional to the number of years the perceiver has spent in an American university.* The persistent claim of gender bias, in other words, is ideological, not empirical. But after #MeToo, it will have an even more disruptive effect."

Mac Donald is not shy. She clearly argues that the #MeToo movement is not only unfair, it is destructive. And if Pew's poll result is accurate, no male anywhere is safe from being falsely accused and unjustifiably punished.

There is no escaping it, *men are fair game and should be punished.* Men deserve better. And, it should be clear by now, I believe men deserve fair treatment, a level playing field, and the opportunity to defend themselves—and receive only the punishment they deserve. The remainder of the book is about just that. But to survive the journey, the accused must know the maniacal maw he is entering. He must play the game better and smarter than those who choose to pursue him. It is a jungle. For the accused, he must acquire the knowledge and skills necessary to evade his hunters and turn their weaknesses and inadequacies against them.

There Remains Hope

In a perfect world, following what might appear to be a credible accusation of an actionable offense, should be an investigation. By understanding the principles and methods of a proper investigation, the falsely accused and his defenders can begin the process of mounting a successful defense. And should the accused not evade punishment, understanding how an investigation should be performed will provide him and his defenders the ability to bring a credible legal offensive (in the form of a civil action) against those who were responsible for harming him and his reputation.

In the next chapter I will reveal how an investigation of alleged misconduct *should be properly conducted*. I will also detail for you the manner in which decision-makers and triers-of-fact *should determine guilt*, and when appropriate, deliver justice. But possibly the most valuable thing I will provide the accused from this point forward, is hope. For without hope, even the strongest cannot survive.

Those with wisdom proportion their beliefs with the quality and strength of the evidence in their possession.

---

[42] For a near complete list of #MeToo casualties visit https://www.vox.com/ a/sexual-harassment-assault-allegations-list/. Offered is a fascinating list of the "252 celebrities, politicians, CEOs, and others who have been accused of sexual misconduct since April 2017." Though I did not go through the entire list, those that I did examine were fairly and seemingly accurately reported upon. The list identifies only a few women. Of them, former Fox News commentator Kimberly Guilfoyle's "profile" is rather embarrassing (for her) and disappointing. I will let those interested to see for themselves: https://www.vox.com/a/ sexual-harassment-assault-allegations-list/kimberly-guilfoyle

[43] Trial by ordeal was an ancient judicial practice by which the guilt or innocence of the accused was determined by subjecting them to a painful, or at least an unpleasant, usually dangerous experience. The test was one of life or death, and the proof of innocence was most often death. In some cases, the accused was considered innocent if they escaped injury or if their injuries healed, from such ordeals as being buried alive or burned at the stake. Religious cooperation in trials by fire and water was forbidden by Pope Innocent III at the Fourth Lateran Council of 1215 and replaced by compurgation (see https://en.wikipedia.org/wiki /Compurgation). Trials by ordeal became rarer over the Late Middle Ages, but the practice was not fully discontinued in much of the world until the 16th century. Certain trials by ordeal would continue to be used in the New World well into the 17th century during the witch trials in what became the Colonies. https://en.wikipedia.org/wiki/Trial_by_ordeal

[44] Mac Donald, Heather, *The Negative Impact of the #MeToo Movement*, Imprimis, Volume 47, Number 4, Hillsdale College, Spring Arbor, MI, 2018; with permission. Heather Mac Donald is the Thomas W. Smith Fellow at the Manhattan Institute and a contributing editor of *City Journal*. She earned a B.A. from Yale University, an M.A. in English from Cambridge University, and a J.D. from Stanford Law School. She writes for several newspapers and periodicals, including *The Wall Street Journal, The New York Times, The New Criterion*, and Public Interest, and is the author of four books, including *The War on Cops: How The New Attack on Law and Order Makes Everyone Less Safe* and *The Diversity* Delusion: How Race and Gender Pandering Corrupt the University and Undermine Our Culture (2018).

CHAPTER FOUR

THE ANATOMY OF A
PROPER INTERNAL INVESTIGATION

E
Tymologically, to investigate something is to look for
traces, or vestiges of them. The word can be traced to the
Latin word investīgāre, meaning "search into", a compound
verb based on vestīgāre, meaning track or trace, which was a
derivative of vestīgium meaning footprint. Ergo, the silly and terribly
over-used human footprint, (or shoe print) as a component of the
business logos of many private investigators. However today, the
noun version of the word, *investigation,* is used for many purposes and
means different things to different organizations. For general
purposes, most consider an investigation to be *the examination, study,
searching, tracking, and gathering of factual information so as to enable the
formulation of answers to a question or solve a problem.* Acceptable, but a
little unwieldly. Better yet, might be my definition:

> *An investigation is the logical and careful collection of information
> through inquiry and examination for the purpose of developing
> evidence so as to solve a problem or disagreement.*[45]

Therefore, is seems apparent that regardless of the circumstances,
the *investigation* of alleged assault, harassment, and discrimination (in
all of their variants), is often appropriate, if not necessary. And as

67

mentioned earlier, an employer or an institution of any type, may in fact be statutorily obligated to undertake an investigation under a variety of circumstances. What's more, it is well established that sometimes people actually do bad things and hurt others. Sadly, not all men are angels. Thus, the need for a thorough investigation is not only uncommon but regrettably, sometimes necessary.

Investigations of alleged serious misconduct are complex undertakings. They are time consuming and fraught with enormous potential for unwanted publicity and liability. However, when done properly, they combine an intricate mixture of planning, experience, and skill and can produce startling results. Those who attempt such investigations without a clear understanding of the fundamentals and inadequate training are recklessly naive. An improperly conducted private sector investigation can be ruinous and destroy the careers and reputations of everyone who touches it, including that of the investigator(s) and the accuser.[46]

Reflect for just a moment and try to identify someone who hasn't heard about the Joe Paterno and Jerry Sandusky scandal and the subsequent investigation performed by ex-FBI Director, Louis Freeh on behalf of Penn State. An investigation for which the university paid Freeh and his organization, Freeh, Sporkin & Sullivan approximately $8.1 million. After considerable (and justifiable) criticism, Freeh later recharacterized the effort as a *review*.[47] Of course I could go on, but you get the point. The investigation of allegations of serious misconduct and criminal behavior are often complicated and expensive. If the former director of the FBI, a law enforcement officer of the then most respectable kind and himself a lawyer with nearly unlimited resources couldn't get it right, what chance has the average private investigator, HR manager, or campus Title IX investigator? Sadly, their failures are typically not the lack of tools or the absence of good intentions, it is the absence of process and the use of a qualified team.

But before we dig in, let's start with the means by which such matters are typically reported and how the recipients of these reports should respond. And if you are a lawyer intending to defend the accused and recover his or her reputation, I suggest you break-out your yellow pad and start taking notes. As this chapter and those that follow unfold, you are likely to identify opportunities in formulating claims, and preparing motions and deposition questions you have not yet imagined. You might even find some quality grist for an opening statement or better yet, the persuasive elements of what may be a successful settlement demand.

The Means by Which Alleged Misconduct is Typically Communicated

On Tuesday, October 5, 1999 I had an epiphany. At the time, I was the CEO of the Denver based company, Business Controls, Inc., an organization that I had founded in 1994. BCI was a professional services company that, among other things, specialized in employment related matters. Our forte was the investigation of workplace and school-place misconduct in all of its various forms. Most often our clients engaged us to investigate known or suspected theft, dishonesty, fraud, sexual assault, harassment, discrimination, and threats of violence.

While discussing business development at our weekly staff meeting, it occurred to me that most of the opportunities we received were the result of a client receiving a "tip." Typically, someone associated with the client organization, an employee, student, customer, or vendor for example, had provided information alleging others had engaged in some form of misconduct involving the organization or institution. While audits, management review, and direct observation all play a role in detecting misconduct, overwhelmingly it is by means of *whistleblowing* that management is first alerted of a possible problem.[48] Thus, I thought, if we could somehow make the work of reporting suspected or known wrong-doing easier for would-be *tipsters*, our clients would receive more tips and we would resultantly be the beneficiary of more opportunities to provide our services. To generate more tips, my idea was to allow the whistleblower to provide their tip via the telephone, but also by way of the internet! As obvious as this is for us today, in 1999 my idea to use the internet in such a fashion was sufficiently original, that I subsequently filed a number of patent applications and was eventually awarded three U.S. patents for the idea.[49] Remember, Google had launched a mere year before, while Facebook, Twitter, Instagram, LinkedIn, and YouTube did not yet exist. Not only were my ideas patentable, once incorporated as fundamental components of the services we offered, they soon became the cornerstone on which our business was re-invented.[50]

The idea of allowing whistleblowers to disclose their concerns or report misconduct quickly and anonymously (if they chose), blossomed and became our newest service offerings. These offerings were branded and customized for each vertical they served. We resultantly offered customized reporting portals and identified them by their URL. Among them, the most successful were MySafeWorkplace.com, MySafeCampus.com, MySafeSchool.com and MySafeHospital.com. In 2004 our service offerings became more sophisticated and we began to move these "solutions" onto a single platform I named, Convercent, Inc. That business and its various service offerings (including our investigative and consulting services) quickly dominated the market and we become the industry leader. Had our eventual competitors not rolled-up their businesses into a single entity which they eventually named, Navex Global, Convercent would have remained the largest player in that space. Yet today, Convercent remains the second largest whistleblower/hotline provider in the world and arguably the best. Today it serves millions of users in more than 147 countries and in 70 languages, 24-7 every day. If interested, you can find out more at Convercent.com. And though I remain its largest individual shareholder, and indeed its true founder, I am no longer involved with the company or its management, nor am I mentioned on its website.

Of course, there are other means by which an organization learns of internal problems. The Association of Certified Fraud Examiners, bi-annually publishes its *Report to the Nations: Global Study on Occupational Fraud and Abuse* that examines those means. For the lack of a better or more comprehensive resource, the 2018 *Report* reveals that 40 percent, (down 2 percent from 2016) of all financial frauds are disclosed first by a tip. Other means of discovery include internal and external audit, management review, document examination, surveillance/monitoring, and by accident. Navex Global's 2018 annual *Corporate Compliance Benchmark Report* reveals that of the organizations responding to the survey, 71 percent provided their employees access to an anonymous reporting "channel", which, most of the respondents identified as a "hotline." And like the 2018 *Report*, the Navex 2018 *Benchmark Report* revealed that overwhelmingly, it was by way of tips that organizations first learned of internal problems.

Other than governmental regulatory authorities, I have found only the international employment law firm, Littler Mendelson, P.C. in its *Annual Employer Survey, 2019* to have reliably broken out survey data specific to the frequency of workplace discrimination and harassment claims based on credible methods.[51] The survey included employers in private industry but also those in the field of public and private education. The survey revealed that of the respondents, 61 percent had received harassment claims and 49 percent had received retaliation claims against their organization filed by those who had originally filed a discrimination or harassment claim. As detailed as the report is, Littler's *Employer Survey* did not reveal the means by which the reports that generated the claims were reported.

Hotline Best Practices

Returning our attention to whistleblower management, best-practices suggest the organization intending to use this technology create a means by which:

1. The whistleblower can report without revealing his/her identity if they desire to do so, (surprisingly, the overwhelming majority of whistleblowers self-identity and many ask that the accused be told it was he or she who blew the whistle!);
2. The whistleblower can report whenever or however they wish (i.e.: either via the telephone, text messaging, email or the Web)...24-7-365 in the language of their choice;
3. The whistleblower can upload or transmit electronic evidence if they so wish;
4. The complaint or allegation can be categorized by its nature or the issue underlining it;
5. The complaint or allegation can be expeditiously distributed to the proper people in the organization (and in some cases, outsiders); and
6. The recipient can further communicate and follow up with the whistleblower or reporting party whether directly, or such that anonymity is maintained as long as the "reporter" wishes.

Once received and preliminarily assessed, there must be procedures and protocols in place delineating how the report should be handled. Most sophisticated hotline service providers have these issues all worked out. They provide their customers expansive options and choices as to the functionality of their "*helpline*" and how they wish to manage it. And while modern service providers like Convercent and Navex Global still offer users the option of making reports telephonically, more than 95 percent of all reports are made electronically. In the Far East (and categorically, China) everyone seems to mistrust telephonic communications, yet curiously, few fear using the web. Resultantly, it has been my experience, almost 100 percent of all helpline reports originating in Asia are made electronically.

Before moving on let me address the topic of offering monetary rewards to tipsters. Oldest of the commercially available helpline providers is probably WeTip. Founded in Ontario, California in 1972, a year later it was endorsed by then California Governor Ronald Reagan and became a statewide crime reporting hotline known as 800-78-CRIME. In 2007, WeTip began accepting anonymous tips via the Internet and in 2015 it received its 1 millionth "crime" report. WeTip's success, in part, is believed to be its practice of offering the reporting party (the *reporter*) a reward. According to WeTip's website, in 2013 it celebrated the landmark of precipitating 15,000 criminal arrests and the payment of $1,000,000 in rewards. Good for the communities in which the criminals were arrested and those who justly received a reward. However, it is widely accepted that the offering of rewards tends to drive down the reporting of crime!

As is evidenced by the testimony of IRS informants and qui tam relators, many (if not most) withheld information of ongoing or suspected crimes. Their intent was to receive the largest reward possible. Unlike IRS tipsters, in a qui tam action, a private party called a *relator* brings a civil action on the government's behalf. However, the government, not the relator, is considered the real plaintiff. If successful, a relator in a *False Claims Act qui tam action* may receive up to 30 percent of the government's recovery! Simply put, the larger the loss the government suffers (and the corresponding recovery), the larger the reward. Consider Bradley Birkenfeld's 2012, remarkable $104 million reward from the IRS[52]. According to sources, of the roughly 100 rewards awarded each year under the False Claims Act, roughly 50 will be for $2 million or less. Resultantly, the legal advisors and consultants who service this market, generally tell their clients to not report *too quickly*. So while monetary rewards may incentivize some types of whistleblowers, it is a practice generally not recommended for businesses or places of learning (whether public or private)…unless of course the objective is to receive fewer, but more expensive tips.

Hotline/Helpline Secrets

The purveyors of commercial and private helpline services, and the administrators of the web portals through which the reporting party uses to make an electronic report, rarely reveal the sophisticated technology behind them. Here are some of the features the reporting party is not told:

1. Almost all reports are retained indefinitely and rarely is the reporting party able to delete a submitted report;[53]

2. Activity logs maintained by the helpline provider record:

    a. The date and time the report was submitted;

    b. The IP address of the sender;

    c. Any modification or attempts to modify the original report;

    d. The IP address, date, time, and identity of anyone who examines or prints the report after its submission, including that of the reporting party;

    e. All electronic communications between those authorized to access a specific report (or a thread containing multiple reports), including the date and time they communicated;

    f. Reports deleted by authorized parties (i.e. administrators, investigators, and HR personnel) are often archived such that they can be "recovered" and used later if ever needed or subpoenaed; and that

g. System administrators can secretly provide law enforcement and others, including attorneys access to a specific report(s) and associated records when requested.

Other Means of Reporting

As mentioned earlier, anecdotally I observed that most employer investigations of misconduct were precipitated by the actions of a tipster. Second to helpline tipsters were *drop-ins*, individuals who "stopped by the office" and openly reported their concerns to a supervisor or a member of HR. Most drop-ins were employees or students, and most of them alleged they were the victim or a first-hand witness to the offense. Interestingly, second to employees and students coming forward in this manner were a mix of family members, (including parents) and vendors.

Other means of reporting include:

1. Anonymous written/or electronic messages, or the leaving of recorded telephone messages;

2. Going to the press;

3. Notifying law enforcement in any manner;

4. Having friends, family, or others report on behalf of the tipster;

5. By witnesses or friends who possess first or second hand knowledge;

6. Accidental disclosure by any means; and

7. Simple carelessness or unintentional disclosure.

Carelessness and unintentional disclosures in some cases might be too generous. Reporting parties have been known to accidently lose or misplace notes, journals, diaries, images, videos, phones, computers and other evidence. Others have shared such with people whom they thought could be trusted, or in fact knew they could not be trusted to keep the information to themselves.

Yet some reporters are just unthinking. In one of my cases, a woman who strongly insisted on anonymity and refused to engage in any face-to-face communication with me, revealed that she was particularly offended by the behavior of a certain supervisor whom she readily identified. However, during her "sharing" she told me she did not want him confronted or punished, but merely wanted him to stop his harassment of her (a very common request, actually). But in describing the specifics of his offensive conduct, she carelessly stated she was the only woman who worked for him at the time of the alleged offense. At the end of the exchange, she gave me her phone number and said I could contact her after her request for my intervention was fulfilled. Go figure.

Establishing Expectations

The simple receipt of tips and complaints however, does not solve problems or necessarily answer difficult questions. Every report or complaint should be evaluated, and when appropriate, acted upon. An organization that is serious about managing the behavior of its members, (and those interacting with it) and better serving their community, must properly respond when behavioral and performance expectations are not met.

In order to do so properly, among other things, the organization must create policies and procedures (what may be called protocols) relative to the distribution and handling of the reports it receives. From an architectural standpoint, the downstream out-flow of expectations begins at the top of the organization and typically begins with a Mission Statement. From there the distribution of expectations unfold iteratively, such that each level of activity is dictated (or inspired), by the holdings and expectations preceding it. By memorializing this process in writing, the organization is able to manage both expectations and measure results, thus enabling process improvement and increasing organizational performance. The tools organizing the elements that establish an organization's behavioral and performance expectations might look something like this:

Figure 4.1

Each level is dependent upon the aggregate of those above it. Resultantly, failures or shortcomings at any level, will impact the organization's behavior and performance and ultimately, its actual structural practices. When out-facing, the organizations *practices* are that which we as outsiders see and experience. In aggregate, they are commonly identified as the most significant component of the organization's image. Sadly, in the case of Penn State mentioned above, this image was further formed by the press it relentlessly received. And though it is said in Hollywood, *any ink is good ink*, such was not the case when that ink turned its attention on Joe Paterno and his pal, Jerry Sandusky.

However, when it comes to internal investigations, we typically find investigations mentioned only at the policy level. As such, internal investigators are commonly left creating their own procedures and practices. The resultant processes they create are rarely written, poorly communicated, and inconsistently followed. Because so few know anything about performing fair and proper investigations, many organizations outsource them to law enforcement or those with former law enforcement experience. And often when the conduct of internal investigations are not outsourced, and kept in-house, the organization hires former law enforcement officers to manage all things having to do with physical security, that is guards, gates, cameras, fences, and locks, *and* internal investigations. This mindset is so prevalent, that in the loss prevention/asset protection profession, retired FBI agents have organized themselves and created a confidential network that regularly publishes a directory allowing its "members" to remain in contact with one another. The *Secure FBI Directory*, which replaced the FBI's old and outdated *Trapline*, among other things, assists former agents find FBI friendly employment. After decades of friendly referrals, some very large organizations have no one but former FBI agents running their internal security and investigative operations.

Other organizations assign the task of internal investigations to HR and some hire lawyers to perform their investigations, as Penn State did. However, most thinking people know that when directed to report to HR, the dean's office, or the campus Title IX officer, it is not for the purpose of receiving recognition or an award. And as I tell those I train, never, ever talk to an attorney acting in the capacity of an investigator.[54] Rarely does anything good ever come from such meetings.

So, who then should the organization turn to perform its internal investigations? The answer should be found in the organization's *investigation policy*. But rarely do organizations ever have an investigation policy, and those that do more rarely offer procedures supporting the policy. Regardless, whomever is designated the task should be sufficiently skilled and qualified. He or she should possess the requisite, education, training, and experience to properly perform the job. They in fact may be former law enforcement or a member of HR, but above all, they must be qualified and properly trained. Once identified, we call these individuals *fact-finders*. And in the perfect world, fact-finders report to *decision-makers*. Fact-finders are responsible for finding facts, whereas decision-makers are responsible for making decisions. However, it is very common that decision-makers play the role of fact-finders. Imagine our system of criminal justice where in addition to fact-finding, law enforcement played the role of judge, jury, and executioner. Who would ever cooperate or talk to a police officer?

In practice, when formulated properly and all of the necessary procedures and practices are bundled and in place, and the requisite responsibilities properly assigned, what is created is a *system* driven by *process*. Aptly, I call that process, *The Process of Investigation*.[55] That process is diagramed in Appendix E, page 295. It is structured so as to minimize the effects of incompetence, poor decision-making, and disorder. Instead, it assures the *subject* that the process of which he has entered is structured, fair and impartial. Furthermore, it assures that the fact-finders and decision-makers are competent and not flying by the seat of their collective pants. Every organization that performs internal investigations should have such a process. Because having investigative processes has been formally recognized as an established industry best practice, those that haven't an investigative process, often find their conduct characterized as either *nonconformant* or more generally, lacking sufficient rigor. As such, when their fact-finding methods and practices are demonstrated to be lacking, their investigative deficiencies can expose them and their organization to bad publicity and possibly, civil liability.

To better understand these terms and concepts, allow me to digress and briefly introduce the fascinating, (or is the word arcane?) and highly structured world of national standards and the terminology and value that accompanies them.

The Role and Importance of Standards and the Best Practices They Offer

A standard is a written document created by consensus that provides rules, guidelines, or characteristics for products, services and activities or their output. Standards play an important role in everyday life. A standard may establish the size, shape, or capacity of a product, *process* or system. Standards can specify guidance regarding the performance of products or personnel. They also can define terms so that there is no misunderstanding among those using the terms while attempting to implement a particular standard. While a standard is a technical expression of how to make a product, activity, or process safe, efficient, and effective, a standard alone cannot guarantee performance or outcomes. It is up to the organization that adopts a standard to ensure its guidance is properly implemented and its benefits are maximized. Unknown to many fact-finders, and those who employ them, standards are particularly suitable for designing and managing investigations of all types. To better appreciate this assertion let's look a little more closely at the terminology associated with the use and application of standards.

Depending upon the technical specifications of the standard, one's *conformity* with a standard is determined by means of formal audit or structured examination and evaluation. Thus, *conformity assessments* increase public and/or consumer confidence by providing assurances that products, processes, or services are evaluated against the requirements or specifications of the relevant published standard. ANSI, American National Standards Institute, coordinates the U.S. voluntary consensus standards system, by providing a neutral forum for the development of standards. Additionally, it serves as the watchdog for standards development and conformity assessment programs and their functioning. On the other hand, *conformance* is a state of general conformity and may be determined by simple observation. Thus in the world of standards, conformance is to *conform*, but such is not considered conformity.

Alternatively, according to Merriam-Webster, a *best practice* is a "procedure that has been shown by research and experience to produce optimal results and that is established or proposed as a [practice] suitable for widespread adoption." For our purposes consider a best practice as a procedure, routine or process that when properly employed, produces results that are superior in their effectiveness and usefulness. Best practices are generally acknowledged by those in the industry to which they apply as valid and useful when published and/or referenced in trade journals, industry magazines, and blogs, or other industry publications recognized by that industry and those in it. Thus, it is nearly impossible for any successful business or institution to not rely on the use of best practices and the processes that support them in some material and useful manner.

However, unlike best practices, standards are created in a highly structured environment and rely upon the consensus of carefully selected, qualified practitioners and experts. Standards are intentionally crafted so as to be neither unreasonable nor overly burdensome. Thus, conforming to the standards and best practices referenced in the documents we shall discuss shortly are well within the reach of most organizations. Collectively, these standards and best practices constitute a very practical and economical approach to the type and form of the processes and procedures around which an organization should form its investigation practices. Among all of the ANSI standards, the ANSI/ASIS INV.1-2015 Investigations Standard is the most applicable to the topic of this book.[56] This

Standard specifically provides guidance for individuals and organizations conducting internal investigations.[57] The Standard uses a systems approach for developing an investigation program consistent with the business management principles related to the Plan-Do-Check-Act (PDCA) Model. PDCA is a circular process designed to provide improved performance. Often confused with Deming's Cycle or Plan–Do–Study–Act (the PDSA cycle), PDCA is strictly a method of process improvement and enhanced system development.[58]

Graphically, it is typically expressed like this:

Figure 4.2

The ANSI/ASIS INV.1-2015 Investigations Standard

In 2015, ASIS International, the largest international membership organization for security management and investigation professionals, published the first national standard addressing the administration and conduct of investigations in the private sector. That standard is now formally identified as ANSI/ASIS INV.1-2015 Investigations Standard.[59] Not only was I a member of the ASIS INV Standard Development Committee, which was responsible for the development and construct of this important document, for 10 years

I was a member of the ASIS Standards and Commission that oversaw and managed its successful development. An effort, I might add, took the development committee's roughly 200 volunteer members, more than seven years to complete. The ANSI/ASIS INV.1-2015 Investigations Standard ("The Standard") is a certified American National Standards Institute standard. It is available to anyone and though it is an American National Standard, it is used by organizations throughout the world. It is invaluable in many ways as we will shortly examine.[60] But for the moment, the Standard provides not only guidance relative to the use of PDCA, it provides a standardized and legally defensible architecture for the planning and performance of internal investigations in the private *and* public sector, generally. Remarkably, many fact-finders and decision-makers fail to use it. Some have not even heard of it. As a result of their failure to consider its use, no less conform to it, the credibility of the investigations they perform or relies upon when properly challenged, are often less than defensible (if you are a lawyer, highlight this sentence). Fortunately for the accused and astute, this failure can be the first of many potential legal challenges thrown at his or her accusers' investigators.

Reflect on the importance of that for a moment.[61] If the fact-finder intending to investigate allegations of serious misconduct (whether in the workplace, higher-ed, or a K-12 school), fails to consider the professional best-practices and processes as provided in the Standard, the resultant investigation and its findings can, and should, be challenged as potentially defective and unreliable. Regardless of his or her job title, experience, alleged skills, or self-importance, the investigation the fact-finder performs should be questioned and its results potentially considered unreliable as evidence. Thus, *short of a voluntary admission provided by the accused, any discipline or corrective action considered or implemented may be successfully challenged if the Standard was not used to guide the underlying investigation!* As both a seasoned professional fact-finder and an expert witness, it pains me to think of how many skilled and well-meaning attorneys overlook this opportunity when defending or advocating on behalf of an innocent client.

To reiterate, for other than law enforcement purposes, the Standard provides consensus approved insight and guidance for generally accepted practices and processes one should contemplate and consider when undertaking an internal investigation. Offered as guidance, the Standard does not contain requirements, nor is it intended for third-party certification. However, if implemented properly, the framework it offers will provide fact-finders and decision-makers a high degree of assurance that the resultant investigation was fair, impartial and defensible.

Other Applicable Standards

Risk assessment is the identification, analysis, and evaluation of uncertainties as they pertain to an organization's objectives and operations. A risk assessment analyzes whether the uncertainties identified during the assessment are within acceptable boundaries and compatible with an organization's capacity to manage that risk. Of the many published ANSI standards, ANSI/ASIS/RIMS RA.1-2015, entitled *Risk Assessment* provides organizations, and the consultants and security professionals that serve them, (people such as me), guidance relative to evaluating, developing, and sustaining an effective risk assessment program and managing an overall risk assessment program.

Another relevant standard, ANSI/ASIS PAP.1-2012, entitled *Physical Asset Protection*, provides an approach to systematically identify, apply, and manage security program activities in order to safeguard an organization's assets, *people*, property, information, and intangibles that are based or stored in its facilities.

I should note that loss prevention, asset protection, and security management are terms of art widely used by those in the security profession and in the standards that guide them. When used collectively, as in the preceding sentence, I am referring to the activities associated with safeguarding an organization's assets and those of its customers whom have entrusted the safekeeping of their assets or children. For the purpose of readability, I will refer to the collective: loss prevention, asset protection and security management as simply, a *security program*. A security program, however, is more than the use and deployment of guards, gates, cameras, fences and locks. It is an interconnected system of activities and tools, that when organized and deployed properly, protect assets and people while preventing losses. What's more, the implementation of investigative policies, procedures, and practices are an integral component of a successful security program. When advising my clients, I suggest they think of it holistically as a system that allows an organization to report, deter, detect, and respond to all that threatens them and for those whose safety they are responsible.

An Overview of the Process of Investigation

More than twenty-five years ago, I coined the term, *The Process of Investigation*. As mentioned earlier in this chapter, *The Process of Investigation* is the embodiment of the ANSI/ASIS INV.1-2015 Investigations Standard. The *Process* holds that in order for the results of an internal investigation to be useful, it must have meaningful and well defined objectives, be properly and lawfully executed, be fair and impartial, and the results accurately documented and communicated. In order for investigations driven by process to achieve maximum efficiency, they must unfold incrementally and progressively in distinct phases. Each progressive phase is engineered to build on the phase that precedes it. Collectively, professional investigators refer to these phases as the *Seven Phases of Investigation*. They include:

1. Assessment

2. Preparation and planning (goal and objective setting)

3. Information gathering and fact-finding

4. Verification and analysis

5. Decision-making

6. Disbursement of disciplinary and/or corrective action

7. Prevention and education

Informed employers and institutions know that an effective and proper investigation is the foundation on which all fair and defensible discipline or corrective action, (when appropriate) should rest. Unfortunately for the accused not all investigations are fair or driven by process. Regrettably, even experienced and talented fact-finders frequently rush to interview the accused. Short on facts and big on ego, they rush to confront the accused and attempt to convince him or her to make a *confession*.[62] Hotshots of this type are dangerous and frequently precipitate more problems than they solve. As a matter of best-practice, interviewing the suspected or known wrong-doer should take place *after* the fact-finding portion of the investigation is properly completed, not before. In a perfect world, the interview of the subject is merely a verification of that which was learned during the information gathering and fact-finding phase…thus we title that phase, *verification and analysis*.

But proper investigations are more than just processes. They typically involve the convergence of many disciplines and an assortment of uncommon skills. More often than not, the private sector fact-finder must often have a comprehensive understanding of criminal, civil, and employment law. They also require a considerable investment of time, money, and patience. Then finally, to ensure success, the process must be highly structured and near-flawlessly executed. As discussed in detail earlier in this chapter, fortunately for the falsely accused and his defenders, the elements and processes providing the architecture for the conduct of a proper and fair investigation are memorialized in the ANSI/ASIS INV.1-2015 Investigations Standard. Thus, when falsely accused, the target (and his defenders) have the opportunity to credibly challenge an improperly performed investigation with more than bravado and passion. They can confidently attack the efficacy and quality of the investigative effort and its findings with confidence.

Resultantly, investigations are fraught with liability for those who perform them improperly. Internal investigations of even the simplest variety are not for the faint-hearted. By their very nature they involve the investigation of people who have a relationship with the organization. Most often those individuals are either employees, contractors, customers, volunteers, or students. They are insiders. They are people with whom the organization employs, does business, teaches, or is in some fashion responsible for their behavior. As such, the subject of the investigation in some cases, in fact, has special rights, expectations, and very often, carry a sense of entitlement or inflated sense of their protections. These considerations significantly add to the complexity of the fact-finding process and the manner in which the accused may respond to the investigative effort and the decision-makers' corrective or disciplinary actions when applied.

For the unknowledgeable and unprepared organization there is a virtual legal minefield in front of it. An improperly conducted or otherwise defective investigation can be expensive and horribly embarrassing. That is, of course good news for the accused—whether innocent or not. On the other hand, the totality of these complexities gives the properly prepared and equipped organization a decisive competitive advantage. An entity that is able to efficiently bring an end to incidents of assault, harassment, and discrimination, without litigation or a public relations debacle has a significant competitive advantage over the organization that cannot. Let's look deeper.

The Subject versus Suspect

It has only been within the last forty years that those without law enforcement experience have been openly welcomed to conduct private sector investigations. Historically, most private sector investigators worked first in the public sector. Typically, those with former law enforcement or military investigative experience were the people selected to conduct private sector investigations. For a host of obvious reasons this choice made sense. These investigators were not only well trained; they were disciplined and knew how to obtain results. With them they brought not only the tools of the trade, but the vernacular its practitioners used. So while we have recently seen more private sector investigations conducted by those without law enforcement experience, much of the vernacular used by their predecessors remains in use today. As harmless as this may seem, it has consequences.

Of the claims made by those who have been the focus of a private sector investigation, one of the most common is that the investigation was unfair and that the investigator(s) that performed it were heavy-handed and behaved improperly—the investigators acted like cops. So when an investigator conducting an investigation uses the language of a cop, the accusation he acted like one seems more credible. In fact, isn't it often possible to identify one's profession by the way he communicates? If you disagree spend several hours with a lawyer or doctor sometime.

So when private sector investigators communicate like public sector investigators, we are conditioned to expect them to behave like it as well. This mistake by the person conducting an investigation may superficially make him or her appear more professional, but will likely invite challenges otherwise not encountered. Among them might be claims asserting constitutional rights violations, due process violations, the unlawful use of police-like coercion and intimidation as well as the entire banquet of companion torts associated with these—all because the well-meaning private sector investigator used the vernacular of another profession.

I tell my student investigators, the first word they should eliminate from their vocabulary is, *suspect*. The word is harsh and accusatory. If you use the word, replace it with *subject*. Throughout the remainder of this book you will see, I only use the word subject to describe the investigation's person of interest. So while I may suspect someone, I never call him or her the suspect. Investigators that use the word, do themselves and their *customer* a disservice.

Interview versus Interrogation

Few words used by fact-finders are more misleading and confusing than interview and interrogation. Without much thought, most people use the words interchangeably. Some private sector fact-finders think that by using the word interrogation, they and their methods sound more sophisticated. Confusing the matter further, organizations such as the highly regarded firm, John E. Reid and Associates, Inc., which teaches The Reid Technique® and The Reid Technique of Interviewing®, insists that all proper admission seeking processes involving questioning of a subject include both an interview and an *interrogation* component. Heaping more confusion onto the matter are reference resources like USLegal.com that offer the legal definition of interrogation as:

"Interrogation is, in criminal law, the process of questions asked by police to a person arrested or suspected to seek answers to a crime. Such person is entitled to be informed of his rights, including right to have counsel present, and the consequences of his answers. If the police fail or neglect to give these warnings, the questions and answers are not admissible in evidence at the trial or hearing of the arrested person."

Suffice it to say, there is little agreement as to what these words mean and how they should be used. What appears to be agreeable to most, however, is that an *interview* seems less structured, less formal and maybe even less accusatory than an *interrogation*. And it is precisely because of this presumption that I prefer to use the word interview, exclusively.

Investigative Interviews

Investigative interviews are interviews that are reserved for fact-finders who know, or have a strong reason to believe, the subject they intend to interview has committed the offense in question. These interviews are highly structured and carefully choreographed. Generally, they are not fact-finding in nature. Instead they rely on the facts generated during the fact-finding process that preceded it. They are also non-accusatory. Surprisingly, most often the primary purpose of an investigatory interview is to corroborate that which was discovered during the fact-finding process and obtain an *admission* from the subject. Admissions are simple statements of guilt. Admissions are unlike confessions in that they need not contain all of the elements of the crime.

Unless established by an organization's past practices or its written policies and protocols, in the private sector it is on properly obtained admissions that disciplinary and/or corrective action are most often based. Thus, properly conducted investigative interviews are the most powerful tool available to modern workplace fact-finders and those whom they provide their services. However, because of their usefulness, fact-finders tend to instinctively default to investigative interviewing, employing them before the investigation has progressed to the point of completion and interviews are actually appropriate.

Investigative interviews are valuable in other ways as well. When done correctly, they enable the fact-finder to:

1. Fulfill many of their real or expected due process obligations;

2. Obtain the subject's side of the story and motive, should one exist;

3. Uncover extenuating and/or mitigating circumstances;

4. Learn who else might be involved and why; and

5. Uncover the means by which a reoccurrence of the offense might be prevented.

Thus, investigative interviews are useful and powerful tools. However, to appreciate their enormous power and how to implement them properly, and might I add consistently, the proper place to begin is with examining the elements of a successful investigation.

The Elements of a Successful Investigation

I am frequently asked by my clients what is needed for an investigation to be successful. At the expense of sounding trite, the answer I offer is quite simple. In order to be successful, every private sector or institutional investigation requires the following elements:

1. Management (or organizational) commitment

2. Meaningful objectives

3. A well-conceived strategy

4. Properly pooled resources and expertise

5. Lawful and proper execution

Let's now examine each of these critical elements in detail.

Management Commitment

Because private sector and institutional investigations can be extremely complex and often involve potential litigation, a commitment by management is an essential component, if success is to be achieved. From the very beginning, management must be prepared to commit the requisite time, patience, and resources in order to achieve its objectives. It is misleading and dishonest for the individual responsible for driving the investigative process, a person from this point forward we shall refer to as the *project manager*, to allow anyone (typically his or her employer or client), to believe anything less. To obtain quick results with little effort, or with few resources is often impossible and even reckless. In accepting the assignment, the project manager must be prepared to accept responsibility and communicate honestly with his customer, whether internal or external to the organization. Only with the proper information and a thorough understanding of the issues and options can his *customer* make decisions that are sound and appropriate. Anything less will diminish the return on investment and invite potential litigation.

Time is a precious commodity. Each of us is allocated just so much of it. Therefore, how we use it, by-in-large, will determine that which we produce and how much. Because investigations are dynamic, the use of time and the allocation of it to any particular task is a critical aspect of project management. The project manager is responsible, among other things, for the formulation and confirmation of the project's objectives. In doing so, she will define milestones and deadlines. It is he or she who will ensure that the investigative team remains on course and the project is accomplished in a timely fashion. In many organizations the project manager is a member or HR or the administration.

A successful investigation also requires patience, a virtue few practitioners seem to have. The simple truth of the matter is that a proper investigation takes time. Investigations frequently unfold in fascinating and often unexpected ways. Although the experienced project manager can influence the pace in which his or her investigation unfolds, there are aspects of it that may be uncontrollable. Despite the anxiousness of the other parties involved, (the employer-client or the administration), the investigation must unfold at its own pace.

Additionally, there may be events, which impact the pace of the investigation, that are beyond the control of anyone. Things like illnesses, weather, holidays, schedules, and the unavailability of the parties are all things that sometimes no one can control. In order to endure such delays, the organization and the project lead, as well as the fact-finders, must have patience.

In addition to time and patience, a successful investigation requires the dedication of resources—in the form of money. Regardless of the simplicity or complexity of the undertaking, some investment of financial resources will be necessary. Like the free enterprise system, money is the essential fuel, that in many ways powers the investigation.

My clients sometimes debate this. With all sincerity, they will sometimes contend that they can conduct the investigation under consideration cheaper and faster than I. In rare instances this may be so. However, most often they have neither the skill nor the experience to conduct the investigation properly, no less materially achieve its specific objectives. The mere availability of manpower, technology, and other resources does not assure success. The fact that the entity already employs a security director, human resources manager or house counsel does not mean that they or the organization, is capable, qualified or even has the time to conduct a proper investigation. Even if capable and qualified, it may make more economic sense to outsource the effort. Consider the organization to which you belong for a moment; does it have the human resources, talent, and time necessary to undertake a complex internal investigation that may span weeks or possibly months? Probably not.

Meaningful Objectives

No investigation of any complexity will be successful without meaningful objectives. The investigation's objectives define the fact-finder's purpose, allow him or her to benchmark their progress, and provide the framework by which the project manager coordinates the effort to achieve its stated goals. I am astounded by how many of my colleagues fail to appreciate this critical fundamental and begin their investigations without articulating, or even contemplating their objectives. Those that do, often still miss the point. The investigative objectives must be carefully articulated *at the beginning of the process*, for they establish the investigation's starting point and where it intends to finish.

I embrace this concept to such a degree, that it is my practice to begin every investigation by negotiating the effort's objectives with my customer. By negotiating, I mean we together decide what it is we are going to pursue, what information we are seeking, and what tools or methods we are going to use to obtain that information. Together we talk through that which we are intending to do, how we intend to do it, and who is responsible for each step taken. The objectives make it clear that the investigation's purpose is proper and lawful. When properly articulated, they demonstrate that both the organization and the fact-finder have pure intentions and that the length they will go to achieve success has been carefully contemplated and is reasonable. Once the objectives are fully negotiated and agreed upon, I memorialize them in writing. Thus, the first objective might be to determine the *true nature and scope of an alleged problem(s) or the behavior(s) which underlies it*. Without identifying the alleged perpetrator(s), I needn't change the objectives as the investigation unfolds and potentially produces additional subjects and more actionable behaviors.

By articulating and documenting the project's objectives early, the sophisticated fact-finder is also laying a defensive foundation against the claim of bias and discrimination or some other form of investigative misconduct at the conclusion of the project. In the event of subsequent litigation and discovery, we should want the plaintiff that has claimed bias, discrimination, targeting, and/or other abuse to sustain an early setback when handed documents that demonstrate, from the start of the investigation, the fact-finder's intentions (and that of the decision-maker) were pure, honest, and reasonable. Practical experience has also shown that early setbacks for plaintiffs of this type tend to demoralize them. It tends to take some of the wind out of their sails. At the very least it demonstrates to them, and, most importantly, the trier-of-fact that the defendant is no amateur and an easy victory for the plaintiff is less likely. The most common objectives of the type of investigation we are discussing should articulate the desire to:

1. Seek out and identify the true nature and scope of the allegation or problem;

2. Identify who is involved and to what extent, and why;

3. Gather any and all information in such a fashion as to allow the proper distribution of disciplinary and/or corrective action, if appropriate;

4. Engineer the process in a fashion that is least disruptive to the organization and its operations; and

5. Achieve the best possible return on investment.

This is no small order. However, taking the time to articulate and record the objectives of the intended investigation in advance saves time and money. Moreover, as you have probably already recognized, the objectives stated above are nearly universal. They are so useful, I sometimes call them the *universal objectives*. From a practical standpoint, who could argue with them? Also note that these objectives, as I have penned them, do not speak in the language of law enforcement. Instead they demonstrate an appreciation of fairness, the organization's culture, and general practicality.

Most importantly, an investigation that hasn't defined objectives is nearly impossible to defend. As an expert witness, to affirm that assertion, I point out to the lawyer that hired me that she need only to read the *ANSI/ASIS INV.1-2015 Standard*, specifically pages 18 and 19 to learn why.

Well-Conceived Strategy

The next key to success is the development and deployment of a sound investigative strategy. There are many different types of issues that may call for an internal investigation; therefore, I will forgo describing strategies for each of them here. However, the topic of the book deserves some brief examination at least.

Effective investigative strategies involve more than mixing and matching investigative methods and collecting information. The successful project manager needs strategy. That strategy must be sufficiently structured, such that it provides efficiencies and the opportunity to measure results. However, the strategy must be sufficiently flexible so that it permits the changing of objectives and strategy as new relevant information is developed. The project manager and her investigators must have the ability to modify their strategy as new information is obtained.

In the furtherance of developing one's strategy, one should consider the following;

1. Credibility of the allegation(s);

2. Identity of those known to be involved;

3. Jurisdictional implications and boundaries;

4. Existing policies and guidelines;

5. Prevailing precedents;

6. Past practices; and

7. External notification and communication up and down the organization's chain of command.

Collectively, I refer to this list as one's *pre-investigation investigation.* And like the investigation's objectives discussed earlier, documentation regarding the above is highly recommended. Doing so will go a long way in establishing the sophistication and the credibility of the project lead and his or her team members.

Properly Pooled Resources

Nothing can derail a well-planned investigation more effectively than an organization's failure to support it with the proper resources. The failure to dedicate adequate talent results in a lengthier investigation which will assuredly fail to achieve the desired objectives.

Investigations, or the sort we are discussing are complex and as I said earlier in this chapter, successful investigations require the investment of time, patience, and resources. If the organization in question isn't prepared to make the requisite investment in each, its investigation will be difficult and likely fail to produce the desired results. It is worth noting that in matters involving complex issues it is often necessary to bring to bear resources that have special expertise. Failing to use the right resource often produces disappointing, if not useless, results.

Lawful and Proper Execution

Fact-finders, and those who conduct internal investigations for their employers, have enormous responsibility. The outcomes of their effort often impact the organizations they serve, and most certainly those whom they investigate. The *Process of Investigation* hasn't a rule book, though consistent with the guidance of the ANSI/ASIS INV.1-2015 Investigations Standard it is not governed by any oversight body, and it is not necessarily bound by civil code or criminal law. It and the people who conduct such investigations are governed largely by organizational policies, past practices, and ethics. Usually not until someone complains or sues, and the fur begins to fly, does anyone ever really scrutinize the typical private sector investigation or the people who performed it.

Consider for a moment the investigations, if any, you are familiar with. How many of them were ever really scrutinized and picked apart? Who critiqued those involved or the decisions they made? Certainly, there must be exceptions, but by and large very few internal investigations are looked at carefully. Unless someone challenges the outcome, is dissatisfied with the punishment, or the effort was so glaringly defective, no one cares and no one looks. The case is closed and never looked at again. Regardless of the venue or the likelihood of critical examination, every investigation should be conducted ethically and lawfully. To do otherwise is a disservice to the subject, the organization for which the investigation was performed, and society at large.

The Eight Methods of Investigation

Fundamentally, there are eight basic methods of investigative fact-finding:

1. Physical surveillance

2. Electronic surveillance

3. Research and internal audit

4. Forcnsic analysis

5. Undercover

6. Interviews

7. Grand jury

8. Search warrants and subpoenas

That's it. There are no others. Every other form of investigation one can identify is a subcategory of one of these. You might have observed, the use of a grand jury and search warrants and subpoenas are almost exclusively available to only those who conduct criminal investigations and have jurisdictional authority to do so. For our purposes the investigations we're discussing have but only the first six methods of investigation available for use.

Every investigation of the type we are discussing uses one or more of these six methods. The challenge for the designated fact-finders is to select the method(s) most suitable for his or her particular circumstances and deploy them properly and in the correct sequence. In many instances, the fact-finder will find that he must combine the methods in some fashion or mix and match them. Only with knowledge and experience can he know which methods to use and when. It is this unique ability to combine these methods properly and efficiently that separates exceptional investigators from merely, good investigators. Let's look at each of them briefly.

Physical Surveillance

In the context of our purposes, physical surveillance is nothing more than watching people, places, things, and activities. Physical surveillance has only two requirements; there must be something to watch, and someone to watch it. As such, physical surveillance is relatively inexpensive and fairly easy to use. Those who have conducted surveillance know that as simple as it may seem, to be done properly, it requires significant skill and patience. Not everyone is capable of surveillance or doing it well. In some instances it requires sitting patiently in close quarters, such as an automobile or van. In other instances it requires following the subject as they drive or move about. This form of physical surveillance is called moving surveillance and requires even greater skill.

Physical surveillance, however, has its limitations. Because it is not interactive, that is the observer has no interaction or communication with whom or that which he is observing. The evidence physical surveillance produces is typically only *corroborative*. That is, it only supports or corroborates other evidence.

Electronic Surveillance

Electronic surveillance is similar to physical surveillance in that it, too, is nothing more than watching and monitoring people, places, things, and activities. However, unlike physical surveillance electronic surveillance materially employs the use of electronic technology in order to improve the results. It, too, is relatively inexpensive and easy to use. Electronic surveillance can also be used in places and circumstances, simple physical surveillance cannot. Because electronic surveillance uses technology such as video, covert cameras and personal computer monitoring software, and surreptitious voice recording, etc. it can be used when and where physical surveillance is not possible. For example, if the subject of interest was deep inside a building, working primarily inside the school's science lab, all the physical surveillance conducted in the building's parking lot would never capture anything of value.

However, the use of electronic surveillance can be challenging. Because electronic surveillance is possible in so many circumstances, users must be careful not to deploy it where its use might violate the rights of others. Among them is the right of privacy. The courts have widely held that even in the workplace, employees enjoy a limited right to privacy and the expectation thereof. The limitations of which vary from jurisdiction to jurisdiction. Regardless, an individual's right to a reasonable expectation of privacy is nearly universal, and to violate it may be both criminally and civilly actionable.

In this method category also falls surreptitious voice recording. The information technology revolution has irreversibly changed the way we communicate and do business. Never before have employers had so many ways to monitor their employees and their behavior. Not only can employers and administrators monitor their employee's communications, they can now know their exact whereabouts. The technology available offers a host of amazing investigative options for the fact-finder. While the opportunities are plentiful, so are the risks. For the inexperienced and untrained fact-finder, voice communication interception and monitoring provides for a legal minefield that only a masochist would attempt to enter. The Omnibus Crime Control and Safe Streets Act of 1968 (Title III) prohibits private individuals, organizations, and employers from intentionally intercepting or recording wire or oral communications. Amended as the Electronic Communications Privacy Act of 1986, 18 U.S.C. §§2510-2520 (commonly referred to as the *wiretap statute*, states:

"[A]ny person who willfully uses, endeavors to use, or procures another person to use any electronic, mechanical, or other device to intercept an oral communication when…such use or endeavors to use…take place on the premises of any business or other commercial establishment the operations of which affect the interstate or foreign commerce…shall be punished."

There are several exemptions:

(1)   Where there is consent of one party to the communication;

(2)   Where an employer uses a telephone extension to monitor an employee in the ordinary course of business, which can include:

(a)   providing training on interaction with the public;

(b)   determining whether an employee is discussing business matters with a competitor;

(c)   determining whether an employee is making personal telephone calls;

(d)   a phone company monitoring calls for mechanical or service purposes.

The amended Act of 1986 also prohibits the interception of wire communications, including e-mail. Section 2515 reads:

"Whenever any wire or oral communication has been intercepted, no part of the contents or such communications and no evidence derived therefrom may be received in evidence in any trial, hearing, or other proceeding in or before any court, grand jury, department, officer, agency, regulatory body, legislative committee, thereof if the disclosure of that information would be in violation of this chapter."

Clearly, lawmakers intended to extend employee privacy rights to include the protection of electronic mail and messaging. Only in the arena of workplace drug testing has the clash of employer interests and individual rights been more vivid.

In 2001, the United Nations Committee on Crime and Criminal Justice tagged employees as the greatest security threat to employers. Many employers agree. A survey released by the American Management Association the same year revealed that 78% of U.S. firms monitor employee communications in some fashion. The survey also found that two-thirds of the new survey respondents cited legal liability as the most important reason for their monitoring. My personal experience is that most employers monitor because they suspect employee misconduct or are simply curious. Statutorily, these reasons are insufficient. Citing the exemptions above, an employer's options are extremely narrow. However, creative employers have not surrendered.

One very practical workaround is the implementation of a *monitoring policy*. By establishing a policy that notices employees (and others) of the organization's intent to monitor, and insisting employees consent to it as a condition of employment, exemption (1) above is satisfied. Employers with such a policy should be able to monitor as they choose.

However, while a properly constructed monitoring policy may satisfy federal law, it may not satisfy state law. Many states require all parties to a communication provide individual consent before they can be monitored. Employers and schools desiring to intercept and monitor employee workplace communications should first consult a competent employment law attorney. The intricate web of federal, state, and local statutes provides big opportunities for legal missteps.

So what kind of communications can be legally monitored? The answer is limited only by one's imagination. Most frequently, intercepted and monitored are voice and e-mail communications. In the case of voice communications, the principal tool is the telephone. While some organizations may occasionally listen in, others record all telephone activity. But legal problems persist. Even with the consent of their party, the organization may not have the consent of the other party. You may recall the problem Linda Tripp had recording her friend Monica Lewinski during the Clinton administration. While Washington D.C. adheres to the federal standard of requiring one-party consent, Maryland requires the consent of all-parties, (according to PImall.com, only twelve states currently require all party consent). Thus, because the women were not both in D.C. during the recorded conversation, Maryland claimed that Tripp violated state law by not obtaining Lewinski's permission to record their telephone conversations. Other states, such as Florida have asserted the same over calls coming into their states. Go to http://www.pimall.com /nais/n.tel.tape.law.html to determine if recording in your state of interest is permissible.

Intercepting and monitoring e-mail may also be regulated by state law. As such, the rummaging through e-mail could be risky. Still employers do it all the time. The effort is time consuming and often futile when one does not know what they are looking for. A better method is to ask the subject, or a cooperative witness to provide it. Many fact-finders overlook this simple but effective method of information gathering. In many instances, recruiting the assistance of a cooperative party is the most practical approach. If an investigation leads you to believe e-mail messages may be helpful, ask one of the parties involved to provide you the information you are seeking. Alternatively, if you find yourself in a situation where an interception or monitoring policy does not exist, ask the subject for permission to conduct a search. Unless the subject has something to hide, he or she will generally grant permission.

Tracking Devices

Global Positioning Satellite technology, or GPS is a remarkable technology. Using 32 satellites in geosynchronous orbit about 11,000 miles above the surface of the earth, GPS allows one to reliably identify his location anywhere on the planet within several meters. Using one's phone or a small handheld device will permit them to identify their location, land navigate, or find their way when lost. The technology is even more exciting when used for investigative purposes.

Contrary to that which is portrayed in some movies, GPS technology that allows one to track a target in real time is available to most anyone. In order to do so, a GPS device and transmitter must first be attached to something belonging to the subject, such as his vehicle. The receiver is then placed in the tracking vehicle. As it is produced by the transmitter, the tracking data is received by a hand-held device or a computer. Using preinstalled software, the system will display the position of both the tracking device and reception device overlaid on a map of the area(s). As theoretically simple as it sounds, these systems are technologically complex. Because they typically rely on low energy transmitters to conserve battery power and use line-of-sight communications, they are vulnerable to electronic interference and loss of reception.

Other systems are even more complicated and expensive. Similar to those used on some commercial vehicles, the GPS uploads data to a satellite. These systems as used in commerce, allow the precise tracking of the vehicle and two-way communication between the operator and his base. Speed, fuel state, and maintenance data is also uploaded and made available to the base station. These systems require a constant and reliable source of power and, unless specially configured, cannot operate on batteries. They also require large antennas to be placed atop the vehicle. In sum, this technology does not easily lend itself to the typical workplace investigation.

The more common and far less expensive, technology also requires a GPS device to be temporarily placed on the target vehicle without the subject's knowledge. However, instead of a transmitter, a recording device is attached to it. The whereabouts of the vehicle cannot be determined contemporaneously with its movement. Instead, the recorder is periodically recovered or replaced, and its data is downloaded for analysis. Again, using software provided by the manufacturer, the route, speed, destination, and other aspects of the vehicles prior travel is made available. These systems work well and have many applications.

Although state statutes, regulations, and current case law addressing vehicle tracking devices used for investigative purposes is evolving, that which has been decided suggests that placing a tracking device on a privately owned vehicle without the owner's knowledge is actionable if not criminally unlawful in some jurisdictions. The civil causes of action theoretically could include trespass, invasion of privacy, and even intentional infliction of emotional distress. What is clear is that electronically tracking a private citizen as he goes about his private affairs, whether in his vehicle or not, likely constitutes an invasion of privacy at some level. Interestingly, however, is that the conduct of physical surveillance does not. Barring another limitation, whether the observer was visible to the subject or not does not alter its permissibility. Apparently the fact that the observer is physically present is the differentiator.

Conversely, tracking devices placed on organizational vehicles driven by an employee or other authorized individual does not pose the same problem. Because the vehicle is owned (or controlled) by the organization, the driver hasn't the same expectation of privacy as when the vehicle is his. This significantly expands the usefulness of this tool. Nevertheless, the privacy implications need always to be considered prior to the initiation of any surveillance. Contractual restrictions or requirements pursuant to a collective bargaining agreement may exist as well.

Electronic surveillance used for investigative purposes offers no interaction or communication with those that it is observing or monitoring. As such, like physical surveillance, the evidence it produces is typically only corroborative.

Research and Audit

The third method of investigation is the combination of research and audit. This method involves the collection and examination of information from both public and private sources. Incorrectly many investigators use the terms research and audit interchangeably. For our purposes the activity called *research* defines work involving the collection and examination of public records or public sources. Such sources include the Department of Motor Vehicles, the county clerk's office where criminal and civil records are typically stored, and the county recorder's office where all manner of records involving real estate transactions are recorded and kept.

On the other hand, *audit* applies to those records and documents internal to the organization—specifically the examination of documents and information that would not normally be available to someone outside the organization. Such records include, attendance records, productivity records, financial records, transcripts, test scores, medical information, and even prior investigations. Today, the amount of information organizations generate is staggering. Modern enterprises are far beyond merely watching the numbers or monitoring a student's grades. Keeping records on customer wants, needs, buying patterns and consumption; vendor capacity, capability, delivery time and reliability; productivity, up-time, down-time, capacity, and even the amount of waste produced are common. Regardless of venue, no detail, event, outcome, or result is too small to document. In fact, modern management tools such as ISO business methods standards and Six-Sigma require everything to be measured. Assuredly, no organization of any size is short on data, nor any school short on information about its students and faculty.

Forensic Analysis

Forensic analysis is the fourth method of investigation. It includes all manners of investigation that employ science and/or the technologies that support that science. In this category are bodily fluid analysis, chemical and substance analysis, fingerprint examination and comparison, computer forensics, various deception detection methods, and forensic document examination, and of course digital forensics. For the purposes of our study, forensic analysis is the catch-all category where science, technology, and fact-finding meet.

Because of the significance electronic communications play in our lives today, it also plays a significant role in modern investigations. Technology not only makes it easy to communicate and entertain, it also makes some investigations much easier than others. Whether they be text messages, emails, web posts, or digital images and streaming, technologies such as Instagram, LinkedIn, Twitter, YouTube, or Facebook, often produce troves of potential evidence capable of either proving an allegation or undeniably refuting it. As such, these tools and technologies play an ever increasing role in modern fact-finding.

Another interesting application of forensics is in the field of psychology. Many consider forensic psychology the intersection where psychology and criminal investigation meet. Forensic psychology, for our purposes involves the application of psychological theory, knowledge, skills and competencies to the pursuit of civil and criminal justice. Similar to the other forensic methods mentioned above, it too is a tool. When properly used, it potentially allows a peek into the mind of the subject and permits the fact-finder a fundamental understanding of why the subject of one's investigation behaved in the manner he did—or may behave in the future. It has applications in a wide array of environments both clinical and investigative. Within our investigative realm, a working knowledge of the subject's mindset is sometimes essential in order to manage and possibly predict his future behaviors. In matters involving threats or acts of violence, it is frequently imperative to understand the motivation of the aggressor and their capacity to do harm. Armed with a psychological appreciation for the way environmental stressors and other emotional influences impact behavior, the fact-finder and his team can better engineer an intervention strategy.

The professionals that provide this type of assistance are specialists. It is a mistake to presume that any attending physician, family psychologist, campus counselor, or career advisor can provide the forensic assistance necessary for most investigations.

While forensic psychology does not play a role in every investigation, the fact-finder ought to be familiar with this tool and be able to properly deploy it when appropriate.

If you would like to learn more about forensics and forensic analysis, or any of the methods of investigations mentioned in the book, obtain a copy of my book entitled, *Investigations in the Workplace, Second Edition* (2012). Whether you are simply curious or defending the falsely accused, you will find it both fascinating and edifying.

Undercover

Undercover investigation is one of the most powerful and challenging methods of investigation. By definition, it is nothing more than the surreptitious placement of a properly trained and skilled investigator into an unsuspecting environment for the purpose of gathering information. Undercover is one of only two forms of investigation that are interactive. That is, it permits the investigator to interact and communicate with those he or she is investigating. However, undercover is immensely complex and is fraught with significant challenges. When conducted improperly it can create unfathomable liabilities for both the employer-client and the fact-finder.

Undercover investigations are also time consuming and expensive. The typical investigation might take three to six months and cost as much as $100,000 to complete properly. Because of the cost and liability associated with undercover, I tell my clients it should only be used as the option of last resort. After all other alternatives and solutions have been thoroughly contemplated, only then should undercover be considered. That said, I have personally supervised or managed over a thousand undercover investigations in my career. For a short period of time, my team ran 30 or more undercover cases simultaneously at one time…in seven different states. I have successfully placed undercover investigators in nearly every environment imaginable. Over the years, my undercover investigators have harvested trees, planted lettuce, built airplanes, sorted recyclables, emptied bedpans, refined oil, directed traffic, made bath tissue, tended bar, drove trucks, sorted mail, enrolled as students, bought illegal drugs and firearms, and posed as *gangstas* and one-percenters.[63]

But undercover is not for the faint-hearted. It requires a motivated, disciplined investigator and close supervision. It generally cannot be done in-house. Those who wish to use this method of investigation should always use a vendor—and good vendors are hard to find.[64] For more information about undercover investigations and their management, seek out a copy of my book entitled, *Undercover Investigations in the Workplace*, (1999). Though dated, it is a fascinating read filled with case studies, actual events, and sound advice regarding undercover investigations and the challenges that accompany them. In the meantime, let's move on to that which is unquestionably most powerful tool in the fact-finder's tool chest, interviewing.

Interviewing

The sixth and final method of investigation is the systematic collection of information via interviewing. Though some fact-finders prefer the term interrogation, *interviewing* seems less harsh and more palatable. However, Merriam-Webster® defines these terms similarly, distinguishing interrogation as a process in which one "questions formally and systematically." But in actuality, the word interrogation is rarely used to describe a formal and systematic interview. Instead, the word conjures up images of an offensive and coercive interview, during which the subject is harshly questioned in a windowless room, with hands and feet bound while seated under a bright light. It's stigmatized, carrying with it the inference or suggestion of coercion, intimidation, and thuggery. Some even consider an interrogation to be unlawful. As such, I use the word very cautiously. I don't like the inferences that are associated with it and don't care to offer qualifiers or explain myself every time I use the word. Hence, for the purposes of our study of the subject I will restrict my use of it.

Interviews conducted during an investigation fall into two categories. The less formal of the two are *administrative interviews*. These include interviews of witnesses, by-standers, process owners, stakeholders, administrators, and others not culpable, or unlikely culpable, of the offense or matter under investigation. *Investigative interviews* on the other hand, are reserved for those who we have very convincing reasons to believe committed the offense or had direct involvement in it. Both forms of interviews are highly structured, but neither is confrontational or accusatory. Largely what distinguishes the two categories is the intended outcome. During administrative interviews we are simply looking for information. We are attempting to learn, gain insight and collect information. During investigative interviews first and foremost, we are seeking an admission of guilt.

Another pair of words creating confusion are admission and confession. They are not the same. A confession is a statement that includes an admission satisfying all of the elements of a crime. In the private sector, obtaining confessions is not necessary. In order to discipline or take corrective action against an offender, in most instances, one needs only to prove the individual in question committed the offense. Generally, an employer or institution does not need to prove or demonstrate things like means, motive, and state of mind or intent. Those elements of the offense are inconsequential and generally have no bearing on the decision to impose discipline or corrective action. There are, however, significant exceptions. Organizational codes of ethics and honor codes sometimes stipulate that an offense must be premeditated and deliberately intended to harm, thus increasing or decreasing the burden of proof necessary to justify the intended discipline. Regardless, armed with a properly obtained admission, a decision-maker rarely needs anything more to take disciplinary or corrective action against the offender. The same is not the case for criminal prosecution.

Failure to select the proper burden of proof when investigating a suspected offense tends to cause fact-finders to over-investigate. Many fact-finders and decision-makers falsely believe they must prove their case beyond a reasonable doubt. This extraordinarily high burden of proof is reserved only for criminal prosecution. Thus, in pursuing it, the fact-finder expends more time and resources than necessary. Figure 4.3 below graphically demonstrates the relative strength (both quality and amount) of the evidence (burden of proof), which must be met to prove three general categories of offenses:

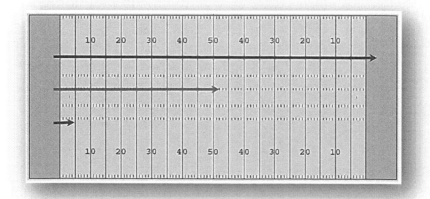

Figure 4.3

Overlaid on a facsimile of a one-hundred yard football field (aerial view), are three arrows. The longest, (uppermost) represents that which is necessary for proving a crime, *beyond a reasonable doubt.* The line beneath it represents proof needed to prevail in a civil action, *preponderance of evidence.* And the line beneath it represents that which is needed to justify imposing administrative discipline, *good faith investigation, reasonable conclusion.*[65] Essentially, to discipline an employee or student for a policy or code of conduct violation, all the decision-maker needs to do is get the ball out of the endzone! Clearly, incorrectly deciding the proof necessary to justify the administrative discipline of an individual, is costly and time consuming. Resultantly, the failure to select the proper burden of proof, causes many organizations to expend more time and resources than necessary. And in the case of the falsely accused, that's good news.

Conversely, because of the low standard of proof necessary to justify a disciplinary action, the converse of this dilemma is also true. It is my observation that many institutions of learning, both public and private, tend to over-react and resultantly, under-investigate allegations of misconduct. Whether forced by outside influences, or the lack of skill and sense of fairness, the rush to judgement is all too common. We will explore this issue more fully in the next chapter.

Like undercover, interviews are also interactive. They afford the fact-finder the opportunity to exchange information with the subject. Specifically, interviews afford the investigator the opportunity to determine who, what, where, when, how and why from the very person who was there and committed the offense. It also provides the fact-finder the unique opportunity to peek into the mind of the offender. This benefit, combined with the opportunity to obtain an admission, make the investigative interview the most powerful form of investigation available for those other than law enforcement. For that reason, it is often the go-to tool fact-finders select and use first.

The Timing of Investigatory Interviews

Returning to page 85 and 86 for a moment, you will note that which I call the *Seven Phases of Investigation.* As stated they are:

1. Assessment
2. Preparation and planning (goal and objective setting)
3. Information gathering and fact-finding
4. Verification and analysis
5. Decision-making
6. Disbursement of disciplinary and/or corrective action
7. Prevention and education

The verification and analysis phase is the phase in which investigative interviewing takes place. Appropriately, it follows the information gathering and fact-finding phase. This phase concludes the fact-finders information gathering. As such, it should *only* be initiated after all of the preceding phases of investigation have been completed. Successful investigative interviews are largely predicated on the amount of information the interviewer possesses before the interview. Bypassing the *information gathering and fact-finding phase* and going directly to investigative interviews rarely produces useful results, and can often create unnecessary liability for both the interviewer and his customer.

Deciding Discipline and Corrective Action

Following the third and fourth phases of the investigation, the project manager and his or hers fact-finders should assemble the results and present it to the decision-makers. This typically involves reducing the findings into a concise report and formally presenting it. To analyze, interpret and detail one's work is easier than it sounds if the project manager has the proper information management processes in place. At this phase of the investigation, it is important to access what has been achieved, and its value to the decision-makers. Effectively the process at this point should have yielded:

1. Significant factual information regarding the matter under investigation;

2. Information identifying at least some of those involved, and some idea of their intent and actions;

3. Corroborative information, obtained during administrative interviews, regarding the offender(s) from his or her co-conspirators or witnesses; and

4. Admissions from the wrong-doers regarding their transgressions.

Demonstrably, the investigative team has leveraged the initial information gathered during the fact-finding phase into two additional sources of information; that which was provided by the subject(s), and that which others said about him. Armed with this wealth of information, the decision-makers can then easily and safely determine the equitable disbursement of discipline and/or corrective action, if appropriate. Let's look closer.

In the instances in which admissions exist, decision-making is simple. However, lacking an admission, the decision-makers might have corroborative statements from those who witnessed the subject's behavior, as well as other evidence developed during the fact-finding phase. Regardless, lacking an admission, the decision-makers still have the results from the fact-finding phase. Even in the face of a denial by any particular subject, armed with sufficiently reliable incriminating information, the decision-makers are afforded the luxury to safely make a tough call if it applies a good faith investigation/reasonable conclusion standard. In other words, the process has engineered defensible fallback options even in the worst case scenario—the lack of an admission from anyone. This may all appear a bit esoteric, but I assure you these intricate machinations will not be missed on a trier-of-fact with any sophistication. At the very least, if challenged, the decision-makers and fact-finders will be able to demonstrate that they employed a well-conceived systematic process, one with structure, purpose, and fairness. It is one that epitomizes professionalism and separates it, and its principles from the typical bungling, incompetence that most judges and juries are accustomed. Plaintiffs claiming innocence and the attorneys who represent them, love decision-makers (and investigators) that lack process, fly by the seat of their pants, and make mistakes at every turn.

It should be emphasized that this phase of the investigation is strictly the responsibility of the organization's decision-makers. It is often best that the fact-finder is not involved in either the decision-making or discipline disbursement phase of the investigation. To do otherwise may create the appearance of bias or prejudice. Similarly, those who are not true fact-finders should not become part of the fact-finding process. Segregating these duties is critical to the protection of the investigation's integrity and those that conducted it.

Decision-makers should also keep in mind that an abundance of evidence and an admission don't make a minor offense a capital crime. Conversely, punishing all offenders equally is not necessarily equitable. The punishment must first fit the offense, then all similar offenses, must be punished similarly. The failure to do so, invites discrimination and disparate treatment claims. Successfully defending such claims can be embarrassing and costly.

While I make it a practice of not recommending any particular form of discipline or corrective action, I have made recommendations to my clients. When I believed it necessary, I have advised my clients to carefully consider the strength of the evidence I gathered, the appropriateness of the discipline contemplated, and how other decision-makers in similar circumstances chose to respond. I have also suggested the consideration of other options. They include allowing those guilty of an actionable offense the opportunity to quietly resign or quietly transfer to another school. Decision-makers and administrators that allow the guilty to simply resign or quit should consider a hold-harmless agreement in exchange for not opposing their application for unemployment insurance or releasing transcripts.

Prevention and Education

Tying the process together is the final phase, prevention and education. During this phase, the decision-makers, administrators, and investigative team join together to critique the effort, bench mark, review considered best practices, and analyze their performance. Additionally, this team should assess the damage the precipitating event inflicted, and attempt to sort out what went wrong in the first place. What was it that permitted the problem or event to occur and how can it be prevented in the future? This evaluation can be priceless. Clearly, if the organization or institution continues to use defective policies and practices, it is likely to get the same result again in the future. Such behavior is stupid, it may also be negligent. Under the legal theory of foreseeability, negligence is compounded when a party should have reasonably foreseen an event that could have been prevented had it taken appropriate corrective or preventative action. Organizations make the mistake often, and in doing so incur unnecessary additional liability.

With the approval of counsel, the team might consider reducing its determinations into some sort of recommendations. The recommendations often include altering or modifying policies, changing or imposing new procedures and/or practices, and finally, training for those who need it. Of all of the phases of investigation, this is the least utilized. In many instances, once the process has reached this phase no one is interested in doing anything further or expending more resources. However, experience has shown that if the lessons learned are not leveraged, problems and challenges tend to reappear and repeat themselves. As such, passing up the opportunity to learn from past mistakes and record best practices seems to be a heavy price to pay for simply wanting to close a file and move on to the next challenge.

Summary

It should now be clear, the foundation on which all successful investigative interviews rest is a quality investigation. All proper and useful investigations are driven by process and that process is called the *Process of Investigation.* It should also be clear that without a proper investigation an investigative interview is merely reduced to an administrative interview. Generally, administrative interviews yield useful information. However, only occasionally will they yield an admission. If criminal prosecution is not an objective, confessions are not necessary; instead, all that is needed is an admission. In order to discipline an offender, in most instances, the decision-maker needs only to prove the individual in question committed the alleged offense. The organization does not need to prove or demonstrate things like means, motive, premeditation, and state of mind or intent. Those elements of the offense are inconsequential and have no bearing on the decision to impose administrative discipline or corrective action. Instead, armed with a properly obtained admission, an organization needs nothing more to take disciplinary or corrective action against the offender, when appropriate. For those interested in learning more about the *Process of Investigation* obtain a copy of my book, *Investigations in the Workplace, Second Edition* (2012). It can be found through online retailers or wherever quality books are sold.

Frequently Asked Questions

During investigations, our HR department rarely asks those it interviews to provide a written statement. Shouldn't the organization be consistent regarding its fact-finding practices?

Yes. Not only should the organization's practices be consistent, to the extent possible, its practices should be those considered as best practices. The ANSI/ASIS INV.1-2015 Investigations Standard encourages the taking of written statements, particularly from the subject of the investigation. At Appendix F you will find checklists for taking written statements and an assortment of forms useful during administrative interviews and investigatory interviews.

My organization does not have an established investigative process. Do you recommend it have one?

Yes. Almost every organization should have an established investigative process. For larger organizations, an investigative policy or written protocol is also appropriate. A protocol differs from a policy in that it is not as prescriptive, thus more flexible and easier to amend than a policy. Regardless, the document should establish how, and under what circumstances the organization should undertake an internal investigation. Furthermore, every written investigative policy or protocol should stipulate that the accuser and the accused must cooperate and that his or her failure to do so is a violation of the policy or protocol. Thus, failure to cooperate may be considered an actionable offense, which in and of itself, may result in disciplinary action, up to and including termination or expulsion.

How big are the legal risks for the fact-finder and why should the fact-finder be concerned?

The risks can be enormous, both to one's career and pocketbook. Moreover, litigation will consume time and money even if the claims are frivolous. The best way to avoid these risks is to use an investigative process to pursue well-considered objectives, obey the law, and treat all people with respect and dignity regardless of the circumstances.

Is there a process for the proper conduct of investigatory interviews, and where can one learn more about that process?

Indeed there is process for the proper and **safe** conduct of investigatory interviews. All that one could possibly want to know about investigatory interviews can be found in my book entitled, *Investigative Interviewing: Psychology, Method, and Practice.* The book is published by CRC Press and can be found on Amazon. The other authoritative resource on the topic is the *ANSI/ASIS INV.1-2015 Investigations Standard.* Whether you are interested in improving your interviewing skills or challenging the interview skills and practices of another, these two works are a must read.

As a fact-finder, I always reduce my handwritten notes to some form of a clean electronic document and then destroy the original notes. Should I continue that practice if my electronic versions are in fact exact copies of those which were handwritten?

J. Edgar Hoover, the first Director of the FBI memorialized your practice of note destruction in the early 1930's. Fearing, sloppy note taking could embarrass the fledging FBI and himself, he instituted the policy of reducing his agent's notes to a formal report. Identified as Interview Report Form 302, once completed and approved, the agent's notes are destroyed. Because the destruction of evidence (and one's notes are indeed evidence) may be considered spoliation, it is difficult to understand why this practice continues. Regardless, it is my long-standing opinion that all notes should be retained. The destruction of one's investigative notes is easily characterized as spoliation. Spoliation is actionable, and for it, sanctions can be imposed. It also looks bad. It creates the appearance that the fact-finder is attempting to exclude or hide something. Moreover, if the electronic version is "identical" to the handwritten version, why would one waste the time and create an electronic duplicate if all one had to do was scan the original?

What is wrong with an organization choosing prosecution as an investigative objective?

First, prosecution is surprisingly expensive and time consuming. Because the standard of proof is so much higher, the organization performing the investigation will have to invest more of both to achieve that objective. Moreover, show me an organization with a mission statement that includes something regarding the prosecution of its members. I have yet to see one. Why? Because it does little to further the goals of the organization nor is it consistent with its purpose. Secondly, organizations don't prosecute law-breakers—prosecutors prosecute law-breakers. So unless a prosecutor decides to file the case, no prosecutions will occur. This obstacle is particularly valuable to the accused. However, the falsely accused should not feel safe because HR or the IX office is driving the investigation. Law enforcement is not likely to raise its head until all covert means of investigation have been completed. So just because the accused or his defenders haven't seen a badge, does not mean that one is not in the next room, listening in on a private telephone call or seeing every text he sends.

The question, "What will happen if I tell the truth" is an admission disguised as a question, whereas the response, "If I did it, I don't remember" is a lie offered as a conditional admission. Nevertheless, both are often needlessly accepted without challenge or further inquiry.

---

[45] Substantially derived from the definition provided in the ANSI/ASIS INV.1-2015, p. xiv.

[46] For the purposes of this book, the term private sector shall mean, the part of the national economy that is not under direct government control or jurisdiction.

[47] https://nypost.com/2013/03/12/sandusky-scandal-has-cost-penn-st-41m-8-1m-for-freeh-report/

[48] According to the Association of Certified Fraud Examiners, most frauds are first disclosed by a tipster. In its most recent *Report to the Nations 2018*, 40 percent or more of all frauds are first discovered (and resultantly reported) by a tipster. https://acfe.com/report-to-the-Nations/2018/

[49] In order for an idea to be patentable in the U.S., the "invention" must be novel, useful, and non-obvious.

[50] Of the many patent applications I filled, three patents were ultimately granted by the U.S. Patent and Trademark Office. Issued were patent numbers 8250025, 9135598, and 9588944, of which the last was issued in early 2019. Today my inventions are still in use and cover significant aspects of the whistleblower technology, which is currently used by Convercent, Inc.

[51] This is not to say, there are no other reliable resources other than Littler available. However, this book is not about whistleblowers or hotlines. My point is merely that tips, regardless how they are communicated, are often the means by which organizations discover internal problems. Those who represent the falsely accused should at least have some familiarity with them and how they work, for not only can an alleged victim offer tips, so can the accused.

[52] Not surprisingly, Birkenfeld returned a little more than a third of the reward to the IRS in the form of taxes. It is unknown how much his lawyers received.

[53] It is my experience that unless specifically directed, even when an account is moved from one vendor/provider to another, the former retains copies of all reports and associated data in its possession.

[54] Since the mid-1990s the author has provided trainings and courses on the topic of proper internal investigations, both publicly and privately for organizations of all sizes. Those clients have included the U.S. Treasury, Department of Energy, and many of America's largest public and private organizations and institutions.

[55] The term, *Process of Investigation* is an unregistered trademark belonging to the author and was coined by the author more than 25 years ago. Today the term, and methodology behind it, is widely used in the United States and elsewhere. The author frequently provides instructor-led training on the topic in either a two or three-day course. Contact the author directly at Gene.Ferraro@InDefenseofthe Innocent.com for more information.

[56] The ANSI/ASIS INV.1-15 Investigation Standard can be purchased online from ASIS International (https://www.asisonline.org/publications/sg-investigations-standard/ or Amazon (where both print and eBook versions are available).

[57] An investigation according to the ANSI/ASIS INV.1-15 Investigation Standard is defined as a "fact-finding process of logically, methodically, and lawfully gathering and documenting information for the specific purpose of objectively developing a reasonable conclusion based on the facts learned through this process."

[58] https://en.wikipedia.org/wiki/PDCA

[59] ASIS International (ASIS) is the largest membership organization for security management professionals that crosses industry sectors, embracing every

discipline along the security spectrum from operational to cybersecurity. Founded in 1955, ASIS is dedicated to increasing the effectiveness of security professionals at all levels. With membership and chapters around the globe, ASIS develops and delivers board certifications and industry standards, hosts networking opportunities, publishes the award-winning Security Management magazine, and offers educational programs, including the Annual Seminar and Exhibits—the security industry's most influential event. Whether providing thought leadership through the CSO Roundtable for the industry's most senior executives or advocating before business, government, or the media, ASIS is focused on advancing the profession, and ensuring that the security community has access to intelligence, resources, and technology needed within the business enterprise. To learn more go to: www.asisonline.org

[60] To learn more about standards and how to obtain a copy of the ANSI/ASIS INV.1-2015, go to https://www.asisonline.org/publications--resources/standards--guidelines/

[61] A standard is a written document, created by consensus, that provides rules, guidelines or characteristics for products, services, and activities or their results. Standards play an important role in everyday life. A standard may establish the size, shape, or capacity of a product, process or system. Standards can specify guidance regarding the performance of products or personnel. They also can define terms so that there is no misunderstanding among those using those terms while attempting to implement a particular standard (see https://www.ansi.org/about_ansi/faqs/faqs?menuid=1). While a standard is a technical expression of how to make a product, activity, or process safe, efficient, and effective, a standard alone cannot guarantee performance or outcomes. It is up to the organization that adopts a standard to ensure its guidance is properly implemented and its benefits are maximized. Depending upon the technical specifications of the standard, *conformity* is determined by means of formal audit or structured examination and evaluation. Thus, conformity assessments, increase consumer confidence by providing assurances that products, systems, processes, or services are evaluated against the requirements of a relevant published standard. ANSI (American National Standards Institute) coordinates the U.S. voluntary consensus standards system, by providing a neutral forum for the development of standards and serves as a watchdog for standards development and conformity assessment programs and their functioning. Alternatively, conformance is a state of general conformity and may be determined by simple observation. To conform is to be in conformance, and in the world of standards, such is not considered conformity.

[62] Throughout this book, the reader will find italicized words and terms that unless noted otherwise have conveniently been compiled as a glossary and appear as Appendix A in the back of the book.

[63] Some outlaw motorcycle clubs can be distinguished by a "1%" patch worn on their *colors* (a sleeveless denim jacket with their club patch on the back). This is said to be a response to a public comment by the American Motorcyclist Association (AMA) that 99% of all motorcyclists were law-abiding citizens,

implying that the last one percent were outlaws. Sadly, many 1%'ers seek to live up to their name and reputation.

[64] If you are eager to learn more about undercover and how this powerful investigative tool can and should be used, obtain of copy of my book, *Undercover Investigations in the Workplace*. Though published in 1999, the information it contains is invaluable to those who are interested. Used copies are readily available from book sellers with offerings on Amazon.com.

[65] Not until the California Supreme Court case in Cotran v. Rollins Hudig Hall International, Inc., 17 Cal. 4th 93; 69 Cal. Rptr. 2d 900 (2002), was it clear what standard of proof employers would be held to in determining whether disciplinary action could be taken in conjunction with such allegations. Since Cotran, the decision has been followed by courts throughout the United States. In Cotran, the Court was faced with the issue often called, "he said, she said" allegations and how an employer must decide whom to believe. The Court recognized that employers were caught between a rock and a hard place if they sided with the victim, they were subject to a possible wrongful termination action brought by the accused; if they sided with the accused, they faced the likelihood of being sued by the accuser for failing to take appropriate action to address the misconduct. In this significant ruling, the Court determined that an employer in such a situation was not required to establish that the ultimate decision it made was the correct one, only that it was based upon a *good faith investigation and a reasonable conclusion*. Cotran established for the first time that HR executives must have competent and well-trained investigators, whose investigations must be thorough and complete and the conclusion must be based upon logic and reason. This decision demonstrates the importance of ensuring that every employer have at least one individual who has been properly trained on how to conduct these investigations. As a result, if an investigation meets this standard of care, and a lawsuit is brought by either the accused or the accuser, it is unlikely that a plaintiff's claim will result in liability.

CHAPTER FIVE

HOW TO RESPOND
WHEN FALSELY ACCUSED

W hat if upon arriving at work, you were to find a prioritized email from the Director of HR indicating she wanted you in her office immediately? Her message indicated that it would not be necessary to make any changes to your planned schedule, for she had already done it for you. You'd be a fool to not be concerned, for this may be the beginning of a living nightmare.

Few things can be more frightening than being falsely accused of a serious offense. Being falsely accused of sexual assault can shake one to their core. Our founders knew that sort of fear well, and fully recognized the need to provide the innocent a means to defend themselves. As mentioned in Chapter 3, on December 15, 1791, as representatives of the newly created United States carefully drafted, debated, and ratified one of the most remarkable documents in human history. With care and precision, they codified the universal rights of the American people and the limitations of their government. That document, known today as *The Bill of Rights*, among other things provides an assortment of inalienable rights to all citizens, particularly those who have been accused by the government of an offense. Among the ten rights comprising The Bill of Rights, were six simple and very clear, yet carefully interconnected

125

protections to which every American was, and to this day is, entitled.

In order, those six amendments can be summarized as:

IV. *Protection against unreasonable search and seizure.*

V. *No unlawful imprisonment; double jeopardy, self-incrimination; or taking of private property without just compensation, and trial by jury in criminal matters.*

VI. *Speedy and public trial, opportunity to confront witnesses and know the charges that one faces.*

VII. *The guarantee of trial by jury in federal court for civil matters.*

VIII. *No excessive bail, no cruel or unusual punishment.*

IX. *Assurances that the individual rights, that are not enumerated in the Constitution, are secure—that is, that these rights should not be automatically infringed upon because they are omitted from the Constitution.*

Also in Chapter 3, the importance of the Fourteenth Amendment was examined, for it further addresses the right of Due Process. However, its *Due Process Clause* additionally prohibits state and local government officials from depriving persons of life, liberty, or property without legislative authorization. This clause has also been used by the federal judiciary to make most of the amendments contained in the Bill of Rights applicable to the states, as well as to recognize substantive and procedural requirements that state laws must satisfy. The Equal Protection Clause requires each state to provide equal protection under the law to *all people*, including all non-citizens, within its jurisdiction.

Quite intentionally, the Constitution places significant restrictions on the government, thus protecting the people *from the government* and the intrusions it might impose on them. To protect citizens from each other and govern our civil behavior, *laws* and *regulations* have been created by our elected lawmakers and rule makers. Some of these we have already examined in detail. Considering all of the aforementioned, and no small quantity of my professional experience, for the remainder of this chapter we will examine how and when one should respond when falsely accused. I will also provide an assortment of valuable tools that can be used to delay, disrupt, and defeat an unfair and improperly conducted investigation.

The Obligations of the Organization

During the Brent Kavanaugh confirmation hearing in late 2018, many of his defenders demanded his accuser, Christine Blasey Ford should have done this or that, provide the names of her witnesses and disclose an array of details that she claimed she could not remember. From both sides, many of the demands made by their defenders and detractors, were unrealistic and arguably unfair. The fault was not that of the accuser or the accused, it was the fault of the Senate's leadership.

While glued to my television watching the spectacle unfold, I repeatedly asked myself *why the hell didn't the Senate have established policies and procedures for handling and managing this mess?* Both sides, though loud and demanding, were clueless. The press and network news commentators provided no real insight or authority either. Instead, they collectively added to the confusion by lecturing and pontificating on matters and *procedures* that either did not exist or that they knew extremely little about. One would have thought that after the Robert Bork and Clarence Thomas embarrassing confirmation hearings, the Senate would have been more prepared and certainly, have had better processes. The only people who should have been more embarrassed than appointee Kavanaugh and Dr. Blasey Ford were the hapless fools who were running the show.

Foundationally, those who are responsible or tasked with the management of investigating such matters should have well-considered and articulated policies, procedures, and practices. As discussed at length in the preceding chapter, a proper investigation of any allegation of serious misconduct that is fair and impartial is not possible without the architectural foundation of a well-designed *process*. In the absence of a defined process, how can anyone be assured that the investigation is or was performed properly and fairly?

Before agreeing to cooperate, the accused and his defenders should demand to know the policies, procedures and practices of any inquiry that may guide the fact-finders and their process. If denied such, or it is disclosed the organization hasn't anything in writing, or is unwilling to provide those that they have, such should be witnessed if possible and the very least, documented. The accused's refusal to cooperate under such circumstances places the fact-finder(s) *and* decision-maker(s) in a challenging position. Short of established policies, procedures, or past practices to rely upon, they must now decide what to do next. Adding to their dilemma is that the accused's refusal to cooperate may be justifiable, and arguably defensible under such circumstances. But before we go there, let's go back to the organization's possible options should the accused refuse to participate.

In place of a process, some organizations simply rely upon past practices and precedence in conducting their investigations and deciding corrective action. In principle, it is not a bad thing. However, if the practices are unfair or otherwise lacking, it doesn't matter how long they have been in use. It is unlikely they will eventually become good practices simply because of their repeated use. Alternatively, inconsistency poses another problem for the organization. For example, if in the past an organization allowed the accused to have a witness of his choice accompany him during his investigatory interview, then suddenly discontinued the practice and disallowed the participation of a witness, the practice could be challenged on the basis of its inconsistent application. The inconsistent practices can give rise to the accused's claim of *disparate treatment.* A disparate treatment claim alleges that the accused was treated differently than others who were similarly situated, and that the difference was based on a protected characteristic. Those protected characteristics include age, race, gender, religion, sexual orientation or any other protected class(es) that he may belong and jurisdictionally recognized.

Alternatively, if factually supported, it could be asserted that he was denied a witness because of the *witness's* age, race, religion, gender, sexual orientation or any other protected class that he or she belonged. Thus the foundation would be laid for the charge of unfairness and disparate treatment but additionally, the legal claim of discrimination.

However, remember that in the private sector, the privilege of a having a witness (or an attorney), present during any proceeding or investigation related interview is not a legal right. Instead, it is a privilege of which the organization chooses to voluntarily provide.[66] In part, this is the reason that the *Process of Investigation* restricts investigatory interviews to the *verification and analysis phase* of the investigation. Adherence to the *Process* prevents the premature interview of the accused, and when justified, it permits discipline or corrective action in the absence of an admission with a significant reduction of legal risk. At the end of the day, an organization is obligated to apply its practices consistently. The failure to do so is often unfair but reckless as well, and again may give rise to the claim of disparate treatment. See Appendix F for more guidance.

However, deviation from the policies, procedures, and past practices are sometimes defensible. Not all allegations or fact-patterns are alike. Flexibility in both the application and execution of established practices and procedures are sometimes appropriate if not necessary. The privilege of being flexible however, must be used judiciously. In the world of HR we have a mantra that goes—*document, document, document everything.* The failure to document the justification for any significant deviation from established policies and past practices can be extremely difficult to defend. Similarly, the failure to have any policies and consistent past practices may also be indefensible. As an expert witness encountering such deficiencies, if given the opportunity, this is a moment that allows me to circle back and look at the organization's mission, vision, and values statements. If these statements and the resultant policies and past practices in use are not properly coupled, it may be possible to characterize those mission, vision, and values statements as mere window dressing. When supported, pointing out the inconsistency may make the organization look insincere and damage the credibility of its fact-finders and decision-makers. I have found that jurors dislike defendants who say, "yes, but" more than once.

At the same time, many organizations and those responsible for investigating and adjudicating allegations of inappropriate behavior or misconduct often don't know the extent to which the rights of the accused may be limited. As such, an astute and informed individual can sometimes demand, and often obtain benefits and protections that are not otherwise available had they not been requested. As mentioned earlier, this shift of power can make the difference between one receiving punishment or a humble apology. Regardless, information is power. He who has the most of it has a decided advantage. I will discuss all of the reasonable demands of the accused shortly.

The organization also has the obligation to ensure that the fact-finders it deploys have the education, training, and experience necessary to perform their job properly. The mere designation of fact-finder does make one a fact-finder. The fact-finder should have both formal and informal education, training, and on-the-job experience as well as an assortment of core competencies necessary to perform their job properly. He or she also has the responsibility to continue their education and training once designated as a fact-finder. Numerous organizations such the Society of Human Resources Management (SHRM), ASIS International, state and local bar associations, and others routinely provide continuing education opportunities for fact-finders at every level.

To demonstrate their qualifications and skills, fact-finders should also seek out and possess the relevant professional certifications and designations of a qualified fact-finder. As proof of such, fact-finders should have some presentable form of documentation. That documentation is often reduced to a short biography or a simple curriculum vitae. As an example, I have provided my curriculum vitae (commonly identified as a CV) that can be found as Appendix G in the back of this book. A quick examination of it should put to rest any questions one might have about my qualifications as an author and that of a qualified and specialized fact-finder.

An organization's failure to field qualified and experienced fact-finders is also unfair and reckless. The career of an innocent man, a manager, teacher, coach, corporate titan, or a promising young college athlete could be at stake. I have given testimony at deposition and trial regarding the quality of the education, training, and experience of fact-finders and their suitability as such. Using my testimony, plaintiff attorneys have successfully argued that the fact-finders in question were NOT qualified to have performed the investigation they did, thus bringing into question the quality of their effort, but most importantly, the reliability of their findings.

Organizations must also have a fair and impartial method of determining the guilt of the accused. The method should contemplate not only the means by which guilt is determined, but the type and amount of corrective action appropriate for the offense. Assuming a presumption of innocence, negates the need to the accused to prove his innocence. However, in our new #MeToo world many decision-makers and the organizations that employ them, quietly embrace an automatic presumption of guilt, thereby necessitating the accused to prove his innocence. They know that memorializing such a practice in a policy or code of conduct would draw embarrassment and criticism. So instead, their requirement that the accused prove his innocence goes unmentioned and kept as an internal secret. In some cases the doctrine is so embedded into the organization's psyche and culture that there is no need to hide it, it just is!

Resultantly, such organizations avoid considering the implementation or use of a standard of proof, or the presumption of innocence. However, that mindset doesn't make for a respectable and healthy culture. Nor is it consistent with institutional best-practices and standards such as ANSI/ASIS INV.1-2015. When confronted properly, such practices simply don't hold up. In Appendix H, I have listed the most common elements I have found contained in the student codes of conduct. Having read this far, it should be fairly easy for you to identify a few elements that are missing.

And finally, organizations that perform internal investigations should have policies and/or procedures that address retaliation. Preceding any investigation an organization should have some means to identify, address and prevent retaliation. The policies and procedures imposed should address any form of retaliation and protect both the accuser and *accused*. But sadly, most don't. Instead, ample attention is typically given to the "victim" and little to the accused. Unlike some corners of our criminal justice system, where the accused are fawned over and praised for their courage to fight a cruel and unfair system, in corporate America and for many of our institutions of higher-learning, the same cannot be said.

The Obligations of the Accuser

Not surprising, the obligations of the accuser are limited. If any, they would likely be found in an employee or student handbook/Code of Conduct, or in the organization's written investigation policy and/or its procedures. Some private sector organizations have a published code of conduct or honor code in addition to policies. The obligations of an accuser are sometimes found there as well. Regardless, if not in writing, most organization are able to rely upon their past practices as a source of guidance in identifying an accuser's obligations to the organization (if any), and its fact-finding process.

That said, I think it is reasonable to expect the accuser to:

1. Be truthful and not exaggerate or embellish either her claims, accusations, facts, or any aspect of her recollection;

2. Not slander or libel the accused, or otherwise attempt to damage his reputation;

3. Have no contact with the accused, his associates or witnesses who are likely to support or corroborate her allegations;

4. Identify, preserve, and produce any and all evidence, whether it be direct, corroborative, or exculpatory;

5. Not fabricate, destroy, alter or embellish any evidence she may have in her possession or under her control;

6. Correctly identify all possible and reliable witnesses;

7. Not intentionally mis-identify, recruit, enlist, intimidate or threaten witnesses;

8. Cooperate fully with the investigation, its fact-finders and decision-makers; and

9. Not perform her own fact-finding or engage someone to do

it for her.

The sum of these expectations amount to an assurance that the accused stay to himself and remain out of the way and the accuser, so as not to interfere with any investigation which may be performed on her behalf.

The Obligations of the Accused

The obligations of the accused are typically greater than those imposed on the accuser. However, like the complainant, his obligations would also likely be found in an employee or student handbook, code of conduct, or in the organization's written investigation policy or procedures. Nevertheless, if not entirely in writing, most organizations will likely claim their past practices as a source of guidance in identifying the accused's obligations to the organization and its fact-finding process.

That said, the accused has no obligation to incriminate himself. If a fact-finder or any of the references mentioned above insist he does, he should immediately seek the advice of a competent attorney while judiciously asserting a constitutional right to remain silent.[67] But before we examine that advice further, here a few things that will likely be required of him:

1. Be truthful, and do not exaggerate or embellish the proof or evidence he believes proves his innocence;

2. Not slander or libel the accuser, or otherwise attempt to damage her reputation;

3. Have no contact with the accuser, her associates, or witnesses who are likely to support or corroborate her allegations;

4. Identify, preserve, and produce any and all evidence, whether

it be direct, corroborative, or exculpatory;

5. Not fabricate, destroy, alter or embellish any evidence he may have in his possession or under his control;

6. Correctly identify all possible and reliable witnesses;

7. Not intentionally mis-identify, recruit, enlist, intimidate, or threaten witnesses

8. Cooperate fully with the investigation and its fact-finders; and

9. Not perform his own fact-finding or hire someone to do it for him.

Notice that the two lists above are very similar, thus suggesting an element of fairness by holding the same expectations for both parties. But you should also notice that I qualified these expectations as to *expect* them of the accuser, but require them of the accused. The astute and those with a legal mind will also notice that the failure to honor some of these expectations could be considered a tortious act. Accordingly, giving rise to a tort claim against the offending party, thus making them a defendant in a civil action. For that reason alone, the complainant, (as the accuser is more properly identified at this stage), and the accused are better served by voluntarily assuming these obligations, regardless if mentioned or not in a policy or code of conduct.

Additionally, the accused should expect to be instructed to return all property in his possession, or under his control, which belongs to the organization or institution, including all things physical and electronic. Such things include: all work or course related materials, parking passes, access cards, keys, specifically identified proprietary documents and records of all varieties, electronic devices, files, tools and anything else the requestor thinks belongs to the organization he or she represents. He should also be expected to be placed on administrative leave or suspension. In the case of administrative leave, in all likelihood it will be with pay. Alternatively, suspensions rarely come with pay or continued benefits. Further impacting the accused is the likelihood of being barred from physically setting foot on his employers premises or any premises, under the control of his school or institution…including housing and dining facilities!

The blunt force of these administrative actions can be emotionally devastating and disruptive. For a student, it could mean missing class, practice or a big game, the ability to remain in campus housing, or the inability to take his final exams. For the employed, it means sitting home and waiting in solitude. Administrative actions are also likely to impose enormous financial consequences. Lawyers, professional or specialized investigators, consultants, experts and counselors may need to be hired. Computers, phones and electronic devices of all sorts might require replacement. Then, of course is the detachment from friends, colleagues, co-workers and clients.

Collaterally, these actions and impositions preclude the accused's defenders from performing a timely investigation of their own or collecting and examining fungible evidence that might exonerate their client.[68] These consequences can be minimized if the organization is thoughtful enough to consider them. However, most organizations, particularly those in the world of education, are focused on the allegation(s) and its duty to protect the accuser and *her interests*, not those of the accused, or so it appears. I will forgo the stories and examination of media frenzies these practices and their misapplication have intentionally and unintentionally wrought. Instead, we will turn our full attention to the title of this chapter and examine *how one should respond when falsely accused!* That journey typically begins with the notification of the accused, quickly followed by an interview.

Notification of the Complaint

In the workplace, notifying the accused that a complaint has been made against him, often takes the form which I began this chapter. The accused, called the *subject* by professional fact-finders, is notified by email or phone to contact or report to HR. By whatever means, the accused is typically told that a complaint or accusation regarding some prior behavior has been received and followed up with, "as you know Bob, we have the obligation to look into it." With a huff, the investigation begins!

With little or no predication or disclaimers, the accused is often cornered and crudely confronted with the allegation(s) against him. Unless properly trained, his inquisitor(s) will seek a quick admission of guilt by informing the accused that denying the truth will only make matters worse. To move the process along a little faster, the accused might be told that unless he comes completely clean and tells the entire truth, there will be no need to tell anyone else about his offense or will there be a need to involve the police. So as to not inform nor educate any ham-fisted, clumsy HR professionals or Title IX officers any further than I already have, I will simply state that this is not the way to treat someone or find the truth. But then again, these sort of investigations are often not about finding the truth. Sadly, they are about vindicating victims, and polishing the organization's reputation as a defender of women. As an HR professional who has mopped up the mess left behind by such clumsiness, I can speak with some authority. Throughout my career, my clients have largely been HR professionals and the law firms they hire to represent their organization in such matters. I have seen much, and regretfully often left somewhat disappointed. At the same time, there are many HR professionals, Title IX officers, civil rights advocates, lawyers, and professional investigators who are fair, impartial, and extremely conscientious. They are good people and have the best intentions.

However, the response of schools and higher-ed to a complaint can be equally discouraging. Typically, upon receipt and preliminary review of a Title IX complaint, a designated representative will issue a "notice of charges" and the obligatory, "no contact order" to the now, "Respondent." Though, the communication to the accused student is often identified as a *notice of charges*, rarely does the document provide any meaningful information about the allegation or actual charges. Instead, with or without even identifying the accuser, the accused is merely informed he has been accused of a Code of Conduct violation and is now under investigation.

Inducing more anxiety and confusion, the "notice" might stipulate "interim sanctions." Though intended to protect the accuser and prevent the respondent from interfering in the investigation, it instead, often heightens his anxiety. Such sanctions include, changing his on-campus housing arrangements, rearrangement of his class schedules, temporary suspension of access to the school library, dining facility(s), gym, bookstore, student center, or his participation in any sports, even if receiving a scholarship requiring him to attend practice.

The U.S. Department of Education's Office of Civil Rights ("OCR"), which issued the "Dear Colleague Letter" (see pages 41 through 45), required the swift and formal investigation of allegations of both sexual harassment and sexual violence by institutions under its purview, as well attending to the "resolution" of such matters. And while it stipulated schools should "minimize the burden [of proof] on the complainant" it lowered the standard of proof to justify the discipline of the accused, to merely proving the allegation(s) were "more likely [true] than not." The OCR didn't stop there. It informed covered entities that because a school's Title IX *panel* cannot order incarceration, "the same procedural protections and legal standards [present in a criminal investigation] are not required."[69]

138

Imagine your eighteen year-old son or friend being cornered behind closed doors and told, "Sit down and answer my questions or else, and no you can't have a lawyer, nor may you leave until you tell me the truth!" To effectively confront such tactics, the accused must *request that the accuser's complaint be provided in writing prior to any face-to-face meeting or the answering of ANY questions*, period.

Your First Priorities

That which I am about to offer is not intended to protect the guilty, nor disrupt a fair and impartial inquiry. It is intended to assist the innocent and those who defend them. Acknowledging my fondness for lists and checklists, I will start with some foundational do's and don'ts for the accused as he steps into the Colosseum's arena:

1. Upon notification of a complaint and responding to it in any fashion, *insist that the complaint be provided to you in writing*;

2. If possible, do not agree to any face-to-face meeting to discuss the matter until you have been provided a copy of the complaint. But if left with no choice but to participate in a meeting, be sure to read my advice on the next page first;

3. As quickly as practical, hire a lawyer with expertise in handling #MeToo allegations, employment law, or if appropriate, Title IX investigations. Should that not be possible, seek out a lawyer with both criminal defense and civil litigation expertise;

4. Don't fall for a polite request to join a call or email chain to discuss the matter or "answer just a few questions" without your attorney's authorization. If that is not

possible, insist that a witness of your choice participate in any and all communications;

5. DO NOT contact the accuser or any of her associates, even if given permission to do so, it could be a trap;

6. DO NOT text, email, or call anyone who might be associated with the complainant, her complaint, or has knowledge of it;

7. DO NOT destroy anything in your possession or belonging to someone else, which later may be considered evidence; and

8. Take a deep breath and don't panic.

It is likely that during his ordeal, the accused will encounter individuals of various skills and levels of professionalism. Regardless, the accused and his supporters should seek and hold the high ground. There is no room for dirty tricks or unethical behavior. So as you examine the following lists and advice, do not misinterpret them as offering schemes or underhanded tactics. Instead, they include tools and tactical actions intended to enable a proper and lawful defense of the innocent.

Following notification of the accused, the next likely step involving him, will be inviting him to a face-to-face meeting. In all actuality, there will be no meeting, the event will likely take the form of an interrogation. The date, time, and place will be provided or communicated. If time permits, obtain a copy of the employee handbook or student code of conduct, (or whatever its equivalent might be), and read it. If the organization has promulgated an investigation policy or protocol, seek a copy and familiarize yourself with it as well. In addition to the obvious benefits of doing so, familiarity will allow you to recognize whenever the organization or institution is not following its own policies or guidelines.

Here are your preparatory actions before the meeting:

1. If you are a student, *immediately* obtain at least three certified copies of your transcripts;[70]

2. If you are an employee, *immediately* obtain a copy of your personnel file if possible. Note that many employers will provide such or will allow access to it. However, the person who controls your file is likely to be the one performing the investigation;[71]

3. Print and save in a safe place, clean copies of the employee or student handbook, and any relevant guidelines, rules, or other directives associated with the matter at hand, whether they be in paper form or electronic;

4. To the extent it is prudent and in your interest, follow the rules and guidelines therein;

5. If the accuser has been identified, do not communicate with her, or have someone communicate with her on your behalf;

6. Do not delete or destroy anything that might be considered evidence or may be evidence, whether it may be used against you or in your defense;

7. If possible, and without making a scene or alerting others, remove from your place of work or school housing and securely store off-site, your personal:

    a. Files, records, documents, and personal items; and

    b. Your computer and ALL other electronic devices,

including your personal phone;[72] and store them someplace off site and safe;

8. Do not discuss your matter with anyone while in your workplace office or dorm room. Should the allegation against you constitute a crime, it is possible that law enforcement is already involved and has obtained search warrants and authorization to electronically monitor you while in your office or dorm room without your knowledge or authorization;

9. If you have not done so already, purchase a new phone and transfer your existing number to the new device. Put the old phone in a safe place and do not allow others to access it unless instructed to do so by your attorney;

10. Do not delete any social media accounts you have or use. However, if possible lock them down so others cannot access them or communicate with you using them (see warning below):

11. Do not initiate our own investigation or recruit others to do so for you; and

12. BEGIN THE SEARCH FOR A QUALIFIED ATTORNEY IF YOU HAVEN'T ONE ALREADY.

Let me repeat, DO NOT DELETE ANYTHING ON YOUR ELECTRONIC DEVICES, whether the information resides in the cloud or on social media accounts, unless told to do so by your attorney. The intentional or negligent destruction or alteration of potential evidence could be a crime for which you could be criminally prosecuted. The offense is commonly called *spoliation* and is criminally and civilly punishable as such.

The First Meeting

The time has arrived. You have received and acknowledged the invitation to appear and address an issue that has come to the attention of the organization or institution of which you are a member. Your meeting place will likely be a secluded conference room somewhere in HR, the principal's office, Dean's office, the office of the President, or Title IX Coordinator, or wherever the fact-finders decide to question you. Accompanying you hopefully, is a witness or your lawyer. Regardless, such sessions are conducted in spaces controlled by people who, at that moment, are not your friends. In deference to them, whoever is driving the process and/or asking the questions, we'll call the *fact-finder*. He or she may be accompanied by a witness or an additional fact-finder. Upon arrival, and after the formality of introductions, you and your witness (or lawyer) will be offered to sit. Accept the offer and remain alert and silent. Be sure to take a writing instrument, note pad and your new cell phone to the meeting.

Your fact-finder will likely have with him or her: files, papers, documents, copies of polices, and other items they will identify as their working documents and files. The less trained and skilled they are, the cheesier their presentation and performance will be. Following introductions, if not already in your possession, request a notepad and writing instrument in order to take notes. Immediately, document the date, time and the name and position of everyone present in the room. Note who is sitting closest to the door and who appears to control who may enter or leave the room. To the extent you can, document everything that is said to you or asked you.

Next, unless otherwise instructed by your attorney, immediately breakout your phone, place it in plain view, and begin audio recording. Do not record anyone without their knowledge unless told to by your attorney. Note, I said *knowledge*. You do not need permission to openly record anyone UNLESS the organization or school has a policy or established practice to the contrary. If no policy or practice prohibits recording, but you are simply told to stop, clearly state your intention to record the meeting and continue to do so. If told you may not record and doing so without permission of those present, will result in some form of disciplinary or corrective action, you must make a decision. You may acquiesce, turn off the recording app, or without saying a word, stand up, turn around, walk out of the room, and leave the building. Understand, that in all likelihood, if you leave under such circumstances you will be immediately suspended and your access to the building, your place of employment, or your campus will hastily be terminated.

In my experience, the employer or school should not have any legitimate reason to not allow you to take notes, and it is my experience that most organizations will permit and if necessary, facilitate note-taking by providing a note pad and a writing instrument. However, that is not the case with audio-recording. As such, the accused must decide for himself whether to stay or walk out if his request to record is declined. To no surprise, fact-finders often record their interviews and many do so surreptitiously. Thus, regardless of what you are told, proceed with the belief you are being recorded. Both federal and state law regulate surreptitious audio recording, with state law controlling. If you decide to participate in spite of not being allowed to record the meeting, you should state audibly and very clearly at both the start of the meeting and near its conclusion, that you were told you could not record and did not. If told the interviewer(s) intended, or alternatively the interviewer(s) said they did not intend to record the meeting, state such loudly and clearly as well. Regardless, I would not submit to an investigatory interview during which the interviewer(s) did not allow me to have a witness of my choice, or alternatively record the entire interview. More on this topic later.

In the meantime, let's look at what happens next. Typically, once everyone has settled in, the fact-finder will make his or her *introduction*. The introduction, sometimes called *pitch*, includes a disclosure of their title, role, and purpose. They will likely discuss the allegation and some details regarding it, and maybe a little bit about what they think or know "really" happened. It is common for inexperienced and poorly trained interviewers to lie and minimize the seriousness of the alleged offense while exaggerating the amount and quality of evidence in their possession. Most typically, amateurs who lie about the quality and quantity of the proof they have will hold up a document, file, or some other physical thing and claim it to be evidence. If the accused requests to examine the item, undoubtedly his request will be denied. Using this technique, the accused can feel trapped and confused. Overwhelmed, the accused is likely to say something or reveal information that the fact-finder doesn't have or know. The accused can also anticipate a request that he allow the fact-finder to examine his phone, notebook computer, email and Twitter account or his private Facebook page. The accused will be told, that if he is innocent, he should have nothing to fear. Of course these are all lies. More than likely the only evidence the fact-finder has is the allegation of the accuser, a few screen captures off her phone, and the promise she will produce witnesses as soon as she has their permission to do so. If the accused continues to resist making an admission, the frustrated fact-finder will begin to threaten the accused with termination, expulsion, humiliation, and jail. Asserting he knows exactly what happened, he will likely insist the only thing he wants to know is why the accused did what he did?

Because of a lack of proper training, amateurs generally rely on their experience when interviewing. Should that experience be law enforcement, one might generally expect the fact-finder will be tempted to rely on using lies, making promises, or threatening the accused. But these techniques are unacceptable in the private sector, and depending upon how they are deployed, their use may be tortious.

Here is an overview:

	Public Sector	Private Sector
Lying	Generally acceptable to the extent the falsehood merely embellishes the quantity or quality of evidence.	Unacceptable and widely considered unethical.
Making promises	Generally unacceptable if relied upon by a defendant in making a confession. Some promises, however, are acceptable (see Dempsey, page 191 for several examples).	Unacceptable and widely considered unethical.
Threatening	The use of threats is considered inherently coercive and their use may render a confession as involuntary.	Unacceptable and widely considered unethical — may even be unlawful if threat is used for the purpose of extortion.

Figure 5.1

Another indicator that an interviewer is inexperienced and poorly trained is the arrangement of the meeting room and where the interviewer sits relative to the interviewee. Inexperienced interviewers will typically sit behind a desk or table when interviewing. Mistakenly, they think that sitting behind a large barrier projects authority and power. It is my suspicion they have seen too much television and have recognized that the size and height of a judge's bench projects power and authority. Impressed, and desiring to project similar power, the fact-finder believes the larger the table or barrier he sits behind, the greater his power. Experienced interviewers know better. They have learned that it is best to have no barrier between him and the subject. He or she will unlikely sit in a large chair or sofa, or casually have a small coffee table or something similar between himself and his interviewee. Here is what the room may look like:

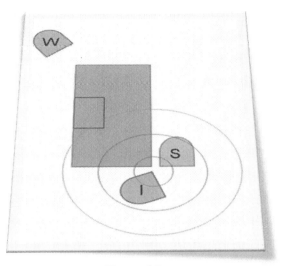

Figure 5.2

Notice the proximity of the interviewer (I) at the corner of the desk to the subject (S) near the same corner. Should the subject back away, the interviewer can casually move toward him. What's more, using proxemics, the interviewer can indicate his approval or disapproval of an interviewee's response without any verbal communication. Should he believe the subject's answer, he inches slightly toward the subject. If he disbelieves his response, he moves away. The further and faster he moves from the subject, the more he is able to silently indicate the strength of his disapproval of the answer provided. Note also that the witness (W) is positioned such that she is out of the subject's view. So while taking notes, she will neither distract him or reveal any clues as to the importance of anything the subject offers. In mere minutes the subject will forget anyone else other than he and the interviewer are in the room.

To avoid revealing more tactics or further educating the untrained and inexperienced, I will not tell you much more about investigative interviewing methods and practices. However, I would be remiss to not share what to expect from a well-trained and experienced fact-finder at this point. His or her opening will be carefully prepared and professionally presented. Should the organization be a anything other than a school or institution of higher learning, it will likely go something like this:

"As you know, this organization has had a long standing policy regarding sexual harassment and the means by which we address improper behavior in the workplace. It has come to the attention of our organization's management team that recently that policy had been possibly violated. First, Human Resources received anonymous reports that something was going on. Then, several employees came forward and made complaints. One of those employees went so far as to submit their complaint in writing. As such, management decided to undertake a formal investigation. Today I am going to share with you some of the things we learned during that investigation."

At the expense of sounding as if I am hawking my books, for those desiring to learn more about the proper way to conduct such an interview, I suggest they obtain a copy of my book, *Investigative Interviewing* as mentioned previously on page 120.

Following the interviewer's *presentation*, his questions will begin. Before answering a single question or volunteering any information, stop take a deep breath, and insist you be provided a written copy of the complaint. Unless it is the organization's policy or practice, it is unlikely a copy of the complaint will be provided and you will be so informed. Immediately document the fact-finder's response and ask what the organization fears in allowing you to examine the complaint. If your request is still refused, in a calm and professional manner ask to see the policy or rule that states you are not entitled to see or have a copy of the document. Be firm and hold your ground. An experienced fact-finder will have anticipated the request and have been prepared to properly respond. Because it is possible the fact-finder is covertly recording the conversation, at this moment and throughout the meeting, attempt to keep the fact-finder talking and busy with answering your questions, while limiting the number of questions he is able to ask you.

On the other hand, if you are shown a copy of the organization's policy or practices relative to the matter in question or any other document, insist on being provided copies you may keep. If refused, ask why. Upon receiving the fact-finder's response, ask for a break, and without waiting for a response, stand up while grabbing your phone and note pad and move toward the door. Unless told to not leave, (a directive which might constitute false imprisonment), without saying anything more, tell the fact-finder you are taking a break and will return in 15 minutes. Briskly leave with your witness or lawyer. Unless in police custody, you needn't anyone's permission to take a break or discontinue the meeting.

Let's recap some the decisions and obstacles you will likely confront at this point. Upon receiving an invitation (or directive) to attend a meeting, you should prepare as to whether you:

1. Accept or decline the request to attend a meeting;

2. Insist on having a witness of your choice;

3. Audio-record the interview with or without your fact-finder's permission;

4. Answer the fact-finder's questions;

5. Surrender evidence in your possession;

6. Allow the fact-finder to inspect your phone;

7. Permit the search of your dorm room, office, desk, locker, or vehicle;

8. Admit to some form of guilt (if in fact guilty);

9. Provide a written statement of any type;

10. Agree to another meeting if requested to do so;

11. Agree to talk to the police if asked;

12. Resign and terminate your employment or transfer to another school; and

13. Tell your spouse or parents about the allegations against you and hire an attorney to assist you.

As if that's not enough, there will likely be other difficulties with which to contend. Some employers hire professional investigators such as myself to perform their internal investigations. Though expensive, doing so increases the quality of the investigation performed, and it reduces the likelihood of unnecessary and costly mistakes. Using the Process of Investigation, a properly trained and experienced investigator will be familiar with the ANSI/ASIS INV.1-2015 and industry best practices. He or she will have performed a proper and thorough gathering of information, and will be fully prepared to confront and interview the accused without making clumsy or unnecessary mistakes. Reflecting back to our examination of the *Process of Investigation*, you might remember that the verification and analysis phase of the investigation comes only *after* the investigation is complete. Thus, the experienced fact-finder will have already completed his or her fact-finding and interviewing, and all that is left for them to accomplish is interviewing the subject and obtaining his side of the story and, if appropriate, an admission.

Alternatively, having accepted a meeting, the accused might instead find themselves confronting a lawyer. Lawyers have become the leading competitor of professional investigators such as myself. Typically being driven by the need to find ever-more billable hours, law firms have convinced employers and schools to hire them to perform their internal investigations. With few exceptions, most lawyers are not good investigators. I have found that most are resistant to the rigors of detailed and tedious processes. Many have difficulty appreciating the gentle art of investigative interviewing and treat their interviewees as a hostile deponents. To gain cooperation, the clumsiest will resort to instilling fear, using intimidation, and making threats.

But for the accused, being interviewed by a lawyer instead of a professional investigator has advantages. The two most common mistakes investigator-lawyers make are: 1) expressing opinions and memorializing them in their written investigative reports; and 2) accidentally becoming a witness in their own case. Theoretically, lawyers sell two things, their time and advice. Professional investigators sell their time and the ability to find facts. Lawyers also like to write. So I find it very common, that investigations performed by lawyers are overwrought and very sterile. Most common however, is their reports are often littered with opinions. Overworking a case generally causes little harm, but it does increase the overall cost of the investigation. However, putting one's opinions in an investigative report diminishes its value and exposes its author to a challenge of his objectiveness.

What's more, there exists the *lawyer-witness rule*. The rule prohibits an attorney from serving as an advocate and a witness in the same case. However, the lawyer-witness rule has two notable exceptions:

1. In cases in which testimony is about an uncontested matter; and

2. In cases where a disqualification of an attorney would create a substantial hardship for the client.

151

The lawyer-witness rule, also known as the advocate-witness rule, insists that a lawyer cannot continue the representation of his client if he knows or believes that he is or may be, a witness necessary to establish an essential fact on behalf of the client. [Juan Carlos Ayus, M.D., P.A. v. Total Renal Care, Inc., 48 F. Supp. 2d 714 (S.D. Tex. 1999)].

Putting aside the above, lawyers tend to enjoy opining. As an expert witness, hired by plaintiff's counsel, I often see matters in which the defendant's counsel performed the investigation in question. In such cases, contained in the report that followed that investigation, its proud author will sometimes begin a paragraph with the sentence, "It is our opinion....". Of course the fact-finder(s) has an opinion, but his investigative report is no place to offer it. In offering an opinion, the fact-finder is attempting to influence the decision-maker who reads it. Why else would it be offered? Where such a practice appropriate, why would an organization need decision-makers? Moreover, as mentioned in the prior chapter, the practice may create the appearance of bias or prejudice on the part of the fact-finder. In doing so, it tends to diminish the fact-finders' claim she performed a fair and impartial investigation.

The First Meeting May Not Be What You Expected

While the goal of ending discrimination in institutions of higher-learning is admirable, Title IX investigations of allegations of sexual assault or other serious misconduct can be quite different than previously described. Here we will examine what a Title IX hearing is, the many problems related to these hearings, and the steps you can take to protect yourself and your civil rights.

Title IX requires institutions of higher-learning that receive federal aid to prevent sexual discrimination and its affects. Title IX requires universities to undertake a credible investigate of any accusations of sexual harassment and maintain a safe environment on campus. Thus, Title IX hearings are used to investigate and remediate accusations involving sexual assault or harassment. In such hearings, it is common that the accused is brought before a panel. Generally, the hearings involve faculty-sourced panel members reviewing the evidence and allegations brought against the accused. Rarely is the complainant asked to testify while the accused is present and more rarely, is the accused or his representative allowed to question the complainant or cross-examine her. When the panel has decided it has "learned" enough, behind closed doors, it decides the fate of the accused. By any reasonable measure rarely, can this form of justice be considered fair.

The most common deficiencies the accused and his representative will likely encounter, include:

1. Unclear or opaque rules: Because Title IX hearings are not criminal proceeding, the rules are often unclear and inconsistently applied. It is common that a panel decides to expel the accused and then undertake its investigation. More often, the accused is questioned without being informed of either the identity of his accuser or the precise allegations against him. Quite typically in such instances, the accused's failure to self-incriminate is considered proof of guilt;

2. Panel member bias: While Title IX panel members are required to be unbiased adjudicators, it is not always the case. As demonstrated in the Kavanaugh hearings, it is possible that some panel members may be incapable of putting aside unpleasant personal experiences from their past, or they are sufficiently so agenda driven that they are incapable of impartial decision-making;

3. Very loose or nonexistent rules of evidence: Both criminal and civil law have clear and strict rules regarding that which constitutes evidence, how it is gathered, examined, and stored, and when and how it becomes admissible. Absent such rules, things such as hearsay, rumors, one's intuition or suspicion can be considered evidence;

4. The failure to recognize that which constitutes consent and that which does not: Both criminal and civil apply tests to determine things such as capacity, intent, state of mind, and motive to assist in the determination of guilt. Unfortunately, some members of a Title IX panel find the application of such tests too tedious or time consuming; and

5. Psychological and coercive pressure: While the identity of panel members might not be confidential, not always is it public. Regardless, pressure from peers, community activists, school administrators, trustees, alumni, parents, and the press can easily influence panel members and the decisions they make.

Remember, if it is believed by enough influencers that the accused is truly a predator, what responsible panel member or university would allow him the chance to attack and destroy the life of another victim? What kind of educator or administrator would ever jeopardize their opportunity to achieve tenure or retire comfortably by making an unnecessary mistake simply for the sake of fairness and impartiality?

Complicating matters further is the issue of which evidentiary standard of proof the panel should use. Under former existing federal guidance the standard of proof for the determination of guilt was preponderance of evidence, a carry-over from the Obama administration. However, as mentioned in the second chapter, on September 22, 2017, US Secretary of Education Betsy Devos rescinded the Obama-era guidelines. The rescinded guidelines had prodded colleges and universities to more aggressively investigate campus sexual assaults and swiftly punish those responsible. Current guidance (the final rules are pending), has encouraged schools to elevate the standard to clear and convincing, a threshold closer to a seventy-five percent probability of guilt. The final rules published by the Department of Education now allows institutions to use either one.

While institutions of higher learning are required to notify the accused if they intend to investigate accusations of sexual assault or harassment, it seems clear the practice is not uniform. The best source for determining such is likely the school's student code of conduct or its equivalent. But think about it, wouldn't it be to the accused's advantage to know sooner than later? Of course it would, and it is precisely why schools are tempted to delay the notification until it has decided the accused is guilty. But wait, training for panel members is on the way.

Education and training have been far behind a crisis or new problem. I know because among other things, I am in the education and training industry. A quick Google search will produce dozens of training opportunities for panel members and the newly appointed. Here is a quick look at what such training may offer:

Assault & Title IX Training for
Campus Hearing Panels

PROGRAM OVERVIEW: The overall goal of this training program is to provide each participant with a sufficient amount of knowledge, understanding, and practical skill to serve as a hearing examiner, panel member or decision-maker in student disciplinary proceedings involving sexual violence. This program will provide participants with an overview of the topic of sexual violence as it relates to conducting student disciplinary proceedings on college campuses. Participants will receive a basic understanding of federal laws and guidance in regard to sexual violence on a college campus. Participants will also be trained on the definitions of sexual violence, the cultural myths and misperceptions of sexual violence, and how a traumatic event can impact the behavior of a victim of sexual violence.

Finally, participants will be provided with the opportunity to serve as a hearing panel member and engage in the process of reviewing evidence and issuing a determination in a student disciplinary proceeding for sexual assault. A roundtable discussion will be scheduled at the end of the program to allow participants to share their previous experiences and collaborate on this topic.[73]

Notice, the term *sexual violence* appears six times in this marketing blurb. Yet, the words innocent, fair, impartial, or balanced do not appear once. I will let you draw your own conclusions. However, I offer this not to insult the organization that offers this training or the instructors who provide it, but merely to make the point that apparently there is a demand for panel member training. Another example suggesting the need to raise the bar and improve the quality of panel members, is the University of Alabama at Birmingham. The university offers a two-day *Hearing Panel Certification* course for those seeking an "interactive opportunity to develop (their) skills to serve on a campus hearing panel."[74] Knowing that some panel members have no training is not very comforting when one considers the authority they wield and the potentially life-changing consequences of their decisions.

What Can the Accused Expect Next?

Earlier in this chapter we examined what typically occurs during the accused's first meeting with the organization's fact-finder(s) and left off at the moment the fact-finder's introduction was completed. Remember, the introduction is theater. It provides the stage from which the fact-finder will attempt to extract information from the accused. To interrupt the momentum he gained during the introduction, I suggested the accused immediately take a break and temporarily leave the meeting, with or without the permission of the fact-finder. Should the fact-finder refuse to permit a break or disallow the accused to leave the room, the stage has been set for the tortious claim of false imprisonment.

False imprisonment occurs when a person intentionally restricts another person's movement within any area (i.e. an office or small meeting room) without legal authority, justification, or consent. Actual physical restraint is not necessary for false imprisonment to occur. Under common law, false imprisonment is both a crime and a tort. Thus, not only can the accused potentially make a civil claim for false imprisonment, he can seek criminal charges. To prevail under a false imprisonment claim, a plaintiff must only prove: (1) willful detention in a bounded area; (2) without consent; and (3) without authority of lawful arrest. Helpful in proving this claim, is a voice recording of the event. A careless statement such as "you cannot leave this room until you tell me what happened," is more than enough to prove false imprisonment and justify potential monetary damages.

It is not difficult to imagine that a poorly trained or frustrated fact-finder not only tell the subject he may not leave the room and block his exit, but without thinking touch, grab, hold, or physically detain him or in some fashion come in physical contact with the accused. Should the fact-finder lose control of himself and thoughtlessly do such a thing, the accused may bring the additional claims of assault and battery. Battery is, in many ways, the completion of an assault. Battery is defined as an intentional offensive or harmful touching of another person that is done without his or her consent. Since an assault is the threatening of harm, and a battery is the actual act of harm, the two crimes are often charged together. As a reward, the fact-finder may find himself fired for such a careless mistake, but sued by the accused, and charged with the crimes of assault and battery. And by the way, in most states assault and battery are also torts. Torts which cannot only attach to the offender, his employer as well. The fact-finder's employer might later ask itself, *"Is this any way to advance our organization's reputation, and demonstrate our intent to protect victims against violence?"*

Assuming the taking of a break is permitted and causes no difficulties, the accused should use the break to refresh, collect his wits, and consult with his witness should he have one. However, because most workplace investigations begin just as I described at the beginning of this chapter (see page 125), the likelihood of thinking fast enough, or having enough time to grab a witness while on the way to HR is small. Regardless, most employers do not allow just anyone to be a witness. Least likely to be allowed would be a co-worker or one's superior. Instead, you will likely be alone and remain on your own for the duration of the meeting.

Again, I will forgo educating the untrained or poorly skilled fact-finder, and not disclose how the fact-finder should proceed.[75] Instead, there are some things you can expect following his introduction. In no particular order, the fact-finder may:

1. State his investigation is complete or conversely, it has not yet fully begun. Should he state his investigation is complete, he'll follow with a statement containing something to the effect, "We already know what happened, what we don't know is why it happened." Alternatively, he

might state the investigation has just begun and he knows very little of what took place. For what should be obvious reasons, both statements ought to be treated as untrue;

2. State that he is merely following up on a minor complaint and the accused has nothing to worry about, for the purpose of the meeting is "simply to tie-up a few loose ends…a mere formality of sorts";

3. Claim the amount of evidence in his possession or under his control is substantial, and any untruthfulness or omissions on the part of the accused will only make matters worse;

4. Alternatively, state that lying for any reason will make matters worse, which in fact may be true. However, to drive the point home he may add, he knows the answers to all of the questions he intends to ask, as such lying is pointless;

5. State that in his possession is an abundance of evidence, both physical and testimonial, to include affidavits, written statements, images, text messages, video, and audio recordings;

6. Claim time is of the essence and any hesitation to cooperate or allow the search of his office, desk, work area, personal vehicle, locker, backpack or personal phone would imply gilt and may result in the accused's immediate termination;

7. Claim law enforcement is not yet involved and the decision to involve them will be based upon the amount of cooperation the accused provides; and most deceptively,

8. State his role is to assist the accused and protect him, his employment, and reputation.

These tactics are unconscionable and surely violate the mission, vision, and values of any organization and its code of conduct. Unless true, their use is not necessary nor should they be used. But sadly they are the go-to tools of the untrained and dishonest fact-finder. For the accused to survive such tactics here are some critical dos and don'ts. First, the dos:

1. Using your phone's audio recording app, audio record everything said during the meeting. Start the recording by stating your name, the date and time, and identify everyone else in the room. If told recording is not permitted, demand to see the written policy or procedure prohibiting such. Regardless of what you are told, record anyway. But don't lie and say you are not recording when in fact you are;

2. Make a sketch of the room's layout and who and where those present are sitting;

3. Take notes. To the best of your ability document the questions you are asked, as well as your responses;

4. Refuse to allow the fact-finder or her witness to read your notes or make copies of them. If they insist it is necessary, ask why and demand to see the written policy or procedure mandating you do so. If necessary, force your position and threaten to leave the meeting. Remember, your notes belong to you and no else;

5. At the end of the meeting when leaving the room ask to have copies of any notes created by the fact-finder and those of anyone else in the room. Document the response;

6. Request copies of any and all evidence disclosed or in the possession of the fact-finder;

7. Do not say you don't remember, when in fact you do. Instead say something to the effect, "In order to answer that question accurately, I need more time to reflect";

8. Document the start time and finish time of your breaks as

well as the comings and goings of others in the room;

9. Remain professional and retain your dignity;

Here are some things you should not do. DO NOT:

1. Lie, mislead, or be rude;

2. Agree to empty your pockets or allow a body search;

3. Provide access to any personal property under your control or belonging to you, to include your desk, locker, file cabinet(s), wallet, backpack, phone, vehicle, personal computer, files or papers, etc. Keep in mind however, most organizations have "search policies" and in all likelihood the organization may conduct a search with or without your permission in most instances;

4. Make suggestions as to who else should be interviewed or speculate why you have been falsely accused;

5. Make suggestions as to where or how the fact-finder may find "real" evidence or the guilty party;

6. Identify another suspect or others who may have information valuable to the fact-finder;

7. Make jokes, taunt, or be disrespectful; and

8. Don't lose your temper, raise your voice, or say anything that you may regret later.

Remember the fact-finder's purpose is to find facts and gather evidence that can be used *against* you. I use the word evidence loosely. The fact-finder may not be looking for evidence at all, he or she may instead be seeking a scalp. Many fact-finders are taught to be aggressive and use their authority to dominate and intimidate the accused. Thus, anything that comes out of your mouth can and will be used against you, as will body language, facial expressions, and aloofness. And in many instances, the entire interview is merely theater. It may be performed for the sole purpose of allowing the organization the ability to hide behind a poorly conducted or unfair investigation. Offering the accused the opportunity to provide his own version of the event(s) in question diminishes the accused's ability to argue he was never allowed to tell his version of the events in order to prove his innocence. Remember, the accused will very likely be dealing with people who believe, *men should be considered guilty until proven innocent.*

It is very likely the meeting will end with the fact-finder asking the accused to provide a written statement. The request or "offer" should be declined. Even if told that the refusal to provide a written statement is of itself, a policy or code violation, DO NOT do it. Put nothing in writing if requested. Only at the direction of counsel, that is your counsel, should anything regarding the matter be put into writing. Do not sign anything, do not agree to reflect on it, or provide anything in writing without the approval of your lawyer. Written statements, *whether signed or unsigned* are evidence. Written statements, emails, computer generated documents, or any other communication created by you or acknowledged as true or truthful by you, is evidence. And at the end of the day, that evidence will be used against you. Even a written statement or explanation you create and destroy before signing, is evidence. If a shredded or destroyed document can be successfully recovered, and still readable, will be allowed to be used as evidence. Even a written statement claiming your innocence is evidence and can and will be used against you.

How? Should you later change or modify your story or add additional details, the original document can be used to impeach you and discredit you. Ah yes, what about the notes you took during the meeting, aren't they evidence as well? Yes, that is why I suggested that you create them. That evidence however, was created for the purpose of capturing what occurred during the meeting and all of the who, what, where, and when that went with it.

Following the meeting, gather your things and quietly leave. Shake hands only if you wish. Don't offer a thank you or good bye, simply leave. However, before leaving you will likely be placed on administrative leave with or without pay (if employed). If receiving a directive to leave, you will likely be told you cannot return to your office, desk, locker, or work station. You may even be walked to your vehicle and told to leave the property. Students can expect anything ranging from the receipt of a thank you to immediate suspension and orders to leave the campus until told otherwise.

Should your employer place you on administrative leave, do as you are told. Do not contact your accuser or any other employees. Do not perform your own investigation and for heaven's sake, do not start trashing people or colleagues on social media. In all likelihood, evidence of any of these behaviors will lead to more complications and difficulties. What you might consider is spending your new found leisure time searching for a job search and finding a good attorney. Remember, in spite of your innocence, your organization may still conclude you committed an actionable offense and it is time to part ways.

You should also expect being told not to contact any clients, customers, vendors, or suppliers. Sternly, you will be informed that any contact with the organization, its affiliates, or members will be considered actionable and may result in your termination. Similarly, your access-control card, organizational email, internal network, and similar employer provided essentials will be shut down and will be made, "unavailable until further notice." For some, the sense of isolation and exclusion will quickly become unbearable. The silence will be deafening. But don't weaken and violate any post-interview directives you are given.

163

Possible Good News for the Accused

In spite of bold pronouncements and elaborate codes-of-conduct, many organizations are timid and their decision-makers, unsure.[76] Thus it seems, students are not the only snowflakes. For such organizations, sometimes the best decision is to make no decision. The resultant procrastination creates the appearance that the offense in question may not be as serious as proclaimed. I have had instances of employer-clients sitting on my investigative result for up to sixty or more days. All the while, the accused was left hanging waiting anxiously for a decision regarding his continued employment. The message sent was that the employer was unsure of the seriousness of the offense and feared making a mistake. However, the longer the accused waited, the angrier he became. In two notable instance, the accused took matters into his own hands, hired an attorney, and sued. They not only sued the employer, but sued the decision-makers and their accusers. We will examine this as a strategy in the next chapter in detail. In the meantime, carefully consider what took place. The accused struck first and added additional complexities and cost to the employer's already unpleasant circumstances. Not only would the employer have to defend its investigation, it now had to defend itself, and however many fingers were in the decision-making process.

Under such circumstances I have typically observed, the *defendants* find the most economical solution is settlement. Yes, some organizations cannot resist a fight and chose to litigate. But why? Employment litigation rarely ends with a trial. More than nine out ten times, the parties settle. For the accused-plaintiff the outcome may include reinstatement and monetary recovery of lost wages and benefits, and legal expenses. If not reinstated, the plaintiff may recover all of the above and some sort of cash sweetener. Depending on the circumstances, the sweetener could be in the hundreds of thousands of dollars.

Frequently Asked Questions

What is the purpose of insisting a break be taken immediately after the fact-finder's opening statement or pitch?

The purpose is to break the tempo and interrupt the interview or proceeding. No one, especially those with authority, likes being interrupted when they think they are in control. In all likelihood, the fact-finder will attempt to discourage a break, suggesting, "Why don't we continue a bit longer, I think there is something you should know before you leave." Nonsense, take the break and smartly leave the room without looking back at anyone. Use the break to confer with your witness or attorney and collect your thoughts.

If innocent, wouldn't it be better to fully cooperate and attempt to sort things out?

Yes, in a fair and perfect world. But that is not where the accused will likely find himself. In a perfect world, the accused will not be confronted or questioned until the fact-finder(s) have completed all of the fact-finding they think is necessary or reasonably possible. It is my practice, and that of other sophisticated investigators, that the accused is not confronted until the fact-finding is complete and I have a very high level of confidence that the accused is in fact, guilty. Not so for the untrained and unskilled. If by chance, the accused cooperates in an investigation in which the fact-finding is largely incomplete, the puzzle pieces provided by the innocent may be misidentified as evidence of guilt. Thus, turning what was believed to be an incomplete or unsolved matter, into a slam-dunk finding of guilt.

What if my school's code of conduct requires that I cooperate and provide any and all information and evidence in my possession to the Title IX officer conducting the investigation or a panel, and I refuse their request?

You will likely be found guilty of violating the code of conduct. But the decision to not cooperate deserves additional information and a cost/benefit analysis. If the school's Title IX panel is known to be fair and balanced, cooperating might be a good decision. On the other hand, if the panel is known for its lack of transparency and an aggressive smack-down of *sexual violence* wherever it can be found, choosing to cooperate could be dangerous and costly.

Upon reporting for my meeting, what if the fact-finder turns out to be a complete stranger and identifies himself as a police officer...should I cooperate?

You will be faced with a difficult decision. Whether taken into custody for questioning or placed under arrest, you have no duty to cooperate or answer any questions posed to you by law enforcement, or under any circumstances, incriminate yourself. However, as discussed in considerable detail on pages 31 and 32, if a suspect makes a spontaneous statement while in custody prior to being made aware of his Miranda rights, law enforcement can use the statement against the suspect, provided that police interrogation did not prompt the statement. Knowing this, the officer may say that all he wishes is to talk and that at any time, the accused may discontinue the meeting and leave. Without a credible and cooperative witness present, anything can happen (go back and read pages 31 and 32 again). The best you can do for yourself, is stand up and walk out. As Martha Stewart learned, never talk to the police unless you are reporting a crime.[77]

Courage is to think out loud when no one else is talking. Thus, while finding anger is so easy, courage often hides in plain sight.

---

[66] Organizations that are parties to a collective bargaining agreement are often contractually obligated to allow a witness. That obligation is the product of a 1975, United States Supreme Court case (NLRB v. J. Weingarten, Inc. 420 U.S. 251) in which the Court upheld a National Labor Relations Board decision that employee members of a collective bargaining agreement (a valid labor agreement), have a right to union representation during investigatory interviews. These rights have become known as the Weingarten Rights.

[67] As mentioned previously, the constitutional right to remain silent does not exist unless one has been accused by the government. However, it is not likely that his questioner will clarify his purpose or authority, nor is he likely to disclose with whom he intends, or may share that which is told. Thus, the safest path at this stage of the inquiry, is for the accused to remain silent and no answer any questions until he is more informed or engages proper representation.

[68] Fungible evidence is evidence that has the capability of mutation, alteration, substitution, or degradation.

[69] Office of Civil Rights, "Questions and Answers about Title IX and Sexual Violence," U.S. Dep't of Education, April 29, 2014.

[70] It is a common practice that colleges and universities put a "hold" on the release of any transcripts of a student under investigation for a suspected code of conduct offense. I strongly suggest that upon notification of a suspected offense, the first thing the student should do is obtain certified copies of his transcripts so that he may have them in the event he wishes to transfer to another school.

[71] In some states (California for example), the law requires an employer to provide a copy of any document in one's personnel file, which the employee has signed.

[72] If practical, rent a safe-deposit box at a nearby and convenient bank and put your electronic devices in it. The bank should provide two keys. Hide one off-site somewhere and give/or mail the other to someone you trust (possible your parents or lawyer should you have one). The other stuff can be boxed and stored someplace safe off-site. DO NOT DELETE ANYTHING ON YOUR ELECTRONIC DEVICES unless told to do so by your attorney. The intentional or negligent destruction of evidence could be a crime for which you could be criminally prosecuted.

[73] http://www.riselinggroup.com/files/images/RG_T-IX_Program_Overview_Objectives_Schedule.pdf (April 19, 2020)

---

[74] https://calendar.uab.edu/event/title_ix_hearing_panel_certification #.Xpx5BchKiUk (April 19, 2020)

[75] For more information about proper investigative interviewing, see the previously mentioned, *Investigative Interviewing: Psychology, Method, and Practice,* E.F. Ferraro, Routledge, Boca Raton, FL, 2014.

[76] While Chuck Palahniuk is frequently credited with coining the metaphor, having used the term in his 1996 novel *Fight Club*, which contains the quote, "you are not special, you are not a beautiful and unique snowflake", two decades later, the metaphor has achieved celebrity status among students to celebrate their individual uniqueness https://en.wikipedia.org/wiki/ Snowflake_(slang), (April 30, 2020)

[77] In 2004, Martha Helen Stewart, an American retail businesswoman, writer, television personality, and former model was convicted of charges related to the ImClone stock trading case. According to the U.S. Securities and Exchange Commission (SEC), Stewart avoided a loss of $45,673 by selling all 3,928 shares of her ImClone Systems stock on December 27, 2001, after receiving material, nonpublic information from Peter Bacanovic, who was Stewart's broker at Merrill Lynch. The day following her sale, the stock value fell 16%. Later she was found guilty of felony charges of conspiracy, obstruction of an agency proceeding, and *making false statements* to federal investigators, and was sentenced to serve a five-month term in a federal correctional facility and a two-year period of supervised release. https://en.wikipedia.org/wiki/Martha_Stewart (April 30, 2020)

CHAPTER SIX

IN DEFENSE OF THE
INNOCENT

Good attorneys are hard to find. They can also be expensive. Today, billing rates for a specialized and talented attorney can easily reach $400 per hour and rates of $1200 per hour are rare, but not out of the realm of possibility. But if there is a service for which one typically gets what they pay for, it is legal services. In the practice of law, one size fits all does not exist. As the accused, you may find yourself in need of both a criminal defense attorney *and* another with plaintiff litigation and trial experience. In some instances an employment law attorney is desirable. While many employment attorneys have defense employment experience, that is experience defending employers, you must seek someone with explicit plaintiff expertise...attorneys that have experience suing employers on behalf of their clients. The reason is simple. Should you be innocent and have avoided criminal charges, you may still be facing termination or other unwarranted punishment. Thus, you may want to sue your (former) employer, your accuser, and/or those who performed the investigation of the allegations against you, or at least create the appearance you intend to do so. Similarly, should you be a student and in similar circumstances, you will also likely need specialized assistance.

Returning for a moment to the topic of fees, there are

alternatives relative to fee arrangements. Depending on a host of variables, some attorneys will take a case pursuant to a contingency agreement. A contingency agreement is any contract that depends on one or more events which may or may not take place. If the specified events occur, the parties may have a binding contract or the contract will be invalidated depending on the nature of the contingency. In such arrangements, the client only pays his lawyer if his case is won. It is typical in such arrangements that plaintiffs pay a percentage of the damages awarded against the defendant(s). Because of the financial risk taken by the attorney, it is not uncommon that she receives more than 50% of the total award, PLUS costs.

Recently, litigation funding, also known as legal financing and third-party litigation funding, has become another alternative. It enables a party to litigate or arbitrate without having to pay for it, whether they are unable to pay for it or because they do not want the risk. A third party professional funder can pay some, or all, of the costs/expenses associated with the litigation in return for a share of the proceeds of the dispute, if it is successful. If the litigation is not successful, the funder bears the costs it has agreed to fund. Litigation funding is still evolving. Currently, it can be broadly split into four forms: conditional fee agreements, damages based agreements, fixed fees and general third party funding. Research these alternative very carefully before entering into any agreement.

The Benefits of Legal Representation

An attorney puts space between you and the opposing party, be them the accuser, your employer, or school. Once represented by counsel, the opposition must communicate with you through your attorney. While your employer or school has likely already issued a "no contact/communication" order, the order does not preclude your employer or school (and their investigators) from contacting you. However, if represented by counsel, they may not contact you directly, in any fashion or for any reason, if related to the allegations against you. Thus, once represented, all communications from the other side must go through counsel. No one on the other side, whether directly connected with the organization or school, or any one they hire, may contact you. The resultant imposition will frustrate their fact-finding and Title IX effort while buying you time to think, plan, and mount a legal defense.

Once represented, not only is your employer or school not permitted to contact you regarding the allegations brought against you, law enforcement may not contact you either. Law enforcement tactics, like the one I mentioned on page 32, may be impossible. No tricks, no games, no contact. Furthermore, any meetings or interviews they wish to conduct, allow you to have your attorney at your side throughout. For the inexperienced organization or fact-finder this is both intimidating and inconvenient. While the attorney may not be allowed to ask questions or interfere with the interviewer, she is certainly allowed to confer with her client and provide him counsel.

In the role of fact-finder on behalf of my clients, it is my practice to allow the accused's attorney to ask me questions if my client approves. I have found that by doing so, counsel will often demonstrate his or her legal skills and sometimes reveal insights into their strategy. Even an attorney's sporadic or hasty note-taking reveals something about what he is thinking and what he believes is important. On the other hand, an untrained or poorly skilled fact-finder will often answer questions posed by counsel, and on occasion, even allow her to examine that which the fact-finder claims to be evidence. How naive.

Another benefit of having counsel, is that she can offer encouragement and uplift one's spirit. Though not her job, emotional support can emanate from knowing she is on one's side. Her mere involvement can inspire confidence and hope. Counsel will also likely impose some rules. Those rules, guidance really, will be intended to prevent mistakes and missteps on the part of her client…you. Here are a few things you will likely hear from your attorney:

1. Respect those with authority, even when they don't deserve it;

2. Play by the rules, even when others don't;

3. Pay attention and listen when others speak;

4. Consider that sometimes good people say and do bad things, and conversely, bad people sometimes say and do good things;

5. Don't talk to the press unless given permission;

6. Trust me, and follow my instructions, I am your lawyer, for I likely know a lot more than you;

7. At all costs, maintain your dignity and self-respect because at the end of the day, it may be all you have left;

8. Treat all people with respect and dignity, including your accuser and those that support her; and

9. Remember, not everyone is an enemy.

In the meantime, remember your accuser is likely receiving advice and counsel as well. While her fact-finders may be clumsy and lack experience, their lawyers will be nothing of the sort. Those lawyers will remind the accused and their client that the "matter" will not be concluded until the statute of limitations has run on all of the potential claims the accused might bring. Well known to them, increasingly common among plaintiff's claims, are assault and battery, false imprisonment, spoliation, invasion of privacy, and of course, defamation. Your opponents know they must navigate these potential hazards, just as you must navigate yours. Do not underestimate them. What's more, they will likely have more resources than you. But, at the end of the day, remember, the law is complicated, it is inefficient, and unlike you, it has no conscience.

Taking the Offensive

History is replete with stories of individuals, known and unknown, who stepped up when everyone else was looking down. George Washington was such an individual. Known for his leadership and the deserved honor as America's first President, he was also a military tactician known for taking the offensive—

"Frightfully, the war for independence was not going well. After having spent the winter holed up in Cambridge, General Washington was anxious to drive the British from Boston. His forces, battered after their losses at Bunker Hill, were eager to fight and expel the British once and for all. Washington was no less anxious and was hoping for a decisive solution. That solution was delivered to him by a 25-year-old bookseller-turned-soldier, named Henry Knox.[78]

Months earlier in November 1775, Washington had sent the young Knox to bring to Boston the heavy artillery that had been captured during battle at Fort Ticonderoga. In a technically complex and demanding operation, Knox brought the valuable cannons to Boston and delivered them to Washington in late January 1776. In March 1776, these artillery had been secretly positioned and now fortified Dorchester Heights (which overlooked Boston and its harbor), thereby threatening the British's one and only remaining supply line, the sea.

Upon waking up on a frigid morning of March 17, 1776, the British commander, Sir William Howe saw the hills surrounding him bristling with cannon. At once he knew, Washington had thrown down the gauntlet and was prepared to destroy him and his army. Howe knew the British position at the foot of the hills surrounding him was indefensible, and if he chose to fight, he and his army faced certain destruction. What Howe did not know was that Washington's display of force was just that, a display. Washington's men and weapons were more than ready to destroy the British, but lacked enough gunpowder to fire a single shot!

Having concluded surrender was not an option, Howe ordered the withdrawal of all forces in Boston and hastily sent them to the British stronghold at Halifax, Nova Scotia. Following Washington's siege, the port-city of Boston effectively ceased to be a military target, but became a center of revolutionary activities, including the fitting ships of war and privateers. Many of its leading citizens would eventually play an important roles in the development of the future United States. To this day, Bostonians celebrate March 17th as Evacuation Day."[79]

While history is replete with lessons of all sorts, Washington's return to Bunker Hill in 1776, and subsequent victory vividly demonstrates that the weak and seemingly powerless can prevail over a stronger and more capable opponent. By merely creating the appearance of a willingness to take the offensive, the accused can potentially convince a more powerful force to retreat. To survive, the falsely accused must control his fear, hire a good lawyer, and prepare to take the fight to his opponents.

To that end, we are beginning to see attorneys who have started to expand their existing practices to include this new area of law. Among them, notably is Andrew Miltenberg, a name partner in the

New York firm, Nesenoff & Miltenberg, LLP, Harmeet K. Dhillon, of the Dhillon Law Group Inc. in the San Francisco Bay Area, and Lisa M. Wayne, in private practice in Denver, Colorado.[80]

In a recent interview, talk radio host, Rich Zeoli asked Miltenberg what it's like to be a young man on today's college campuses if you are accused of sexual assault or sexual harassment?[81] Expressing frustration, Miltenberg responded—

"The way these cases are handled is that it starts with believing the victim, and that is a mantra of what's known as the victim-centric investigative technique, which is employed by all colleges when it comes to sexual assault. So the mere fact that someone is making the claim or making the allegations makes it true in the mind of an investigator." The interview continues:

Rich (Zeoli): You know, it was the Obama administration, really led by Joe Biden, who did this by stripping away the due process protections that people should be afforded at colleges and universities. It was really them who took the step of saying, a simple accusation is enough. They create these kangaroo courts, the kids are thrown out of college. And by the way, we've talked about this too, Andrew. It could be something where a woman revokes consent that she had given weeks earlier, right?

Andrew (Miltenberg): It could be that and it could be a woman revokes consent that she gave moments ago. So it's sort of the Wild West if you're a young man and you are alone with a woman at your own risk.

Rich: You defend a lot of these students and you've had a lot of success defending feminism. It's wonderful that you've been able to do that. What are some of the cases that really stand out for you?

Andrew: Well, some of the cases that stand out most recently is a former NFL player who lost his job with the Houston Texans as a wide receiver and had been there for two years and was moving up the depth chart, because a young lady, two years after he graduated, made a claim to the university that she had been sexually assaulted by him. The university held an investigation and a hearing without him present, revoked, retroactively took back his degree, and it was picked up by a newspaper that he was found responsible for sexual assault and was waived the next day by the Houston Texans. And that's a very dramatic, but very real indication of how deep these allegations can go and how much they can affect you even when you're no longer in college."

The interview continues, but Miltenberg closes following Zeoli's observation, "It's really, really amazing, and it undermines women who are actually raped by people who, you know, deserve to be prosecuted. This kangaroo court makes a mockery of that in my opinion" with this...

Andrew: It absolutely does. Women sexual assault is a real issue, and it's very dangerous, and it's tragic. And I have two daughters, and I speak to it not just as a lawyer but as a father. But much of what I see is borderline ridiculous. The allegations are ridiculous, and you shake your head at them and you think to yourself, "Seriously? These are the real allegations that someone's making, and this is going to impact a young man's life forever and ever." And it does denigrate women who really need it and men who are subject to sexual assault, attacks, and rape.

Attorneys such as Miltenberg, Dhillon, and Wayne are now taking the fight to the accuser and the machine behind her. Not only defending the falsely accused, lawyers are now beginning to bring suit against the accuser and in some cases, the organizations that may be blindly defending her. Here are some of the potential claims that may be available to the accused, whether employed or a student.

Due Process

Having read this far, you should have now learned there are a host of civil claims that can be brought against those seeking the scalp of the falsely accused. While of course, there are no assurances that any claim regardless of the evidence supporting it will survive a defendant's challenges, it is also true that bad facts make their defense more difficult. The term *bad facts* is commonly used by attorneys to describe evidence that is unfavorable to their client's case. Clearly, no sane business executive, HR professional, college president, or Title IX panel member wishes to be sued or have their reputation jeopardized merely because of bad facts. Thus, there is often pressure on defendants, (the accuser, her defenders, and the organization supporting the accused) to settle in lieu of a trial.

In the legal arsenal at the disposal of the accused, first and foremost, are those addressing the right of due process and procedural fairness. Within the last several years, a number of courts have recognized that the processes and procedures used by some schools for investigating and disciplining students accused of sexual misconduct fail to comport with basic notions of procedural fairness and due process. In Doe v. Rector & Visitors of George Mason Univ., 149 F. Supp. 3d 602 (E.D. Va. 2016), the court ruled that the University failed to afford *constitutionally adequate process* and did not provide the accused with notice of the full scope of the charges against him. As such, his opportunity to be fairly heard was adversely impacted, as was his ability to provide evidence that addressed the context in which the charges arose.

So it appears that while private universities (those that are privately funded or receive little or no government funding), may believe they are excluded from the requirements of due process and fairness, which publicly funded or supported institutions are clearly not, federal courts have found that disciplinary hearings or adjudications at private institutions involving Title IX accusations must still be conducted with "basic fairness." In March 2016, a federal district court in Massachusetts held that a complaint plausibly alleged a violation of basic fairness where a private university failed to provide a party accused of sexual misconduct with "a variety of procedural protections…many of which, in the criminal context, are the most basic and fundamental components of due process of law." Among those basic and fundamental components included the right to a notice of charges, counsel, confronting of the accuser, cross-examination of witnesses, examination of evidence or witness statements, or an effective mechanism for appeal.[82]

Thus, given the seriousness of the accusations and the consequences from such accusations, more importantly false ones, it only seems fair that before a school requires the accused to participate in an investigative interview or hearing, the university should provide proper notice in advance. This holding is not insignificant. The courts are saying, that in spite of the organization's private status, the accused enjoys at least some constitutional protections. What is not fully known is what remedies (and monetary damages) will future courts put on such procedural shortcomings or failures?

How far these due process rights can be pressed remains to be seen. Is it not possible, these small victories can be expanded or at least argued in matters involving non-government employers in cases where an employee is similarly accused of sexual assault by a coworker falsely or otherwise? Let's hope so.

Defamation

While claiming procedural unfairness and the failure to provide some semblance of due process, the accused can further complicate the life of the accuser and her supporters by raising the issue of defamation. Defamation, (sometimes known as calumny, vilification, libel, slander or traducement), is the oral or written communication of a false statement about another that unjustly harms their reputation. In addition to being a tort, defamation in some jurisdictions is a crime.

Under common law, for an act to constitute defamation, an assertion or claim must generally be false and must have been made to someone other than the person defamed (meaning a third party). Some common law jurisdictions also distinguish between spoken defamation, called *slander*, and defamation in other media such as printed words or images, called *libel*. In the United States, false light laws protect against statements that are not technically false, but are misleading. Another important aspect of defamation is the difference between fact and opinion. Statements made or stated as "facts" are frequently actionable defamation. Statements of opinion, or pure opinion, are not generally actionable. Interestingly, some jurisdictions decline to recognize any legal distinction between fact and opinion.

To be awarded damages in a libel case, the plaintiff must first show that the statements were represented as "statements of fact or mixed statements of opinion and fact," and second, that these statements were false. Conversely, a typical defense to defamation is that the statements were in fact opinion and not intended to be considered factual. One of the major tests to distinguish whether a statement is fact or opinion is whether the statement can be proved true or false in a court of law. If the statement *can be* proved either true or false, then on that basis, the case will be heard by a jury to determine whether *it is* in fact true or false. If the statement cannot be proved true or false, the court may dismiss the libel case without it ever going to a jury to find facts in the case.

So let's briefly recap. First, the accused claims depravation of his due process rights. He then charges both his employer (or school) and accuser of defamation, claiming slander and/or libel. Of course, attached to these claims must be supporting facts. But if the impact of these initial shots across the bow are not enough to get attention, a cacophony of the following claims very likely will.

Invasion of Privacy

To further his challenge of his accuser's false allegation, he and his attorney might next raise the prospect of the additional claim of invasion of privacy. Invasion of privacy is the intrusion into the personal life of another (sometimes described as intrusion into his seclusion), without just cause.

The claim can give the accused whose privacy has been invaded, a right to bring a civil claim for damages against the person or entity that intruded. For employees, generally what one does on his or her own time, while off the clock and away from work is his business, and no one else's. Thus, the employer cannot discipline or take action against an employee for what he does *off duty*, while off premises or while on property not controlled by his employer. An employer's violation of this principle likely constitutes an actionable tort for which the employer may have liability.

Classic examples of these sort of privacy claims include matters in which a school or employer placed hidden cameras in places where the accused had a reasonable expectation of privacy. Examples include, a dorm room, locker room, private office, dressing or change areas, and, of course a restroom. Invasion of privacy could exist if one secretly audio-recorded another person or persons in situations where the party (or parties) had or should have had a *reasonable expectation of privacy*. Both federal and state law impose limitations on surreptitious recordings of private conversations and the conditions under which do so is lawful.

Some might recall Linda Tripp who played a prominent role in the Clinton–Lewinsky scandal of 1998. Tripp's action to secretly record Monica Lewinsky's confidential phone calls about her relationship with President Bill Clinton caused a sensation with their links to the earlier Clinton v. Jones lawsuit and with the disclosing of intimate details. Tripp unsuccessfully claimed that her motives were purely patriotic. As a resident of Columbia, Maryland, at the time she made her surreptitious recordings, she was subject to Maryland law, which stipulated that all parties to the conversation must know their conversation was being recorded. Resultantly, Tripp faced two charges—illegally recording Lewinsky and then providing the recording to Newsweek. Each charge carried a maximum of five years in prison and a $10,000. She was ultimately able to avoid a criminal prosecution in exchange for surrendering the tapes to independent counsel, Ken Starr.

Thus, it is easy to imagine a careless fact-finder or HR professional whose investigation wanders too for may find themselves, their employer, and the hapless accuser on the wrong end of a lawsuit. In what would likely be a worst case scenario, the fact-finders are criminally charged, their employer is left defending multiple claims and multiple parties for believing it was doing the right thing for the right reasons, while they become defendants in a civil action in what may be federal court. With sufficient facts, a seasoned attorney in such matters can easily outline all of this for opposing counsel and cause the accuser and her defenders to quietly fold their tent and stand down.

Perjury

One would think that lying is also a tort. However, it is not. Instead it is the criminal offense of willfully telling an untruth in a court, or other formal legal proceeding, such as a deposition, after having taken an oath or affirmation. An individual who is falsely accused cannot sue the lying witness for civil (or monetary) damages.

In my state of Colorado, perjury is considered to have occurred when a person fabricates or states false information while under oath, whether in a courtroom or deposition. Thus, if the accused could prove that the accuser made the original underlying false allegation, then lied during a hearing or deposition, the accuser could find herself criminally charged for lying. By making this possibility clear to the accuser and those performing the investigation of her allegations, while simultaneously raising due process concerns and threatening tort based litigation, a pre-litigation settlement becomes increasingly possible.

Additional Tort Claims

To avoid getting too far over my skies and accused of teaching law, I will allow the lawyers to take it from here. However, I will offer the following in the form of a preliminary list of possible tort claims, which may be available to those falsely accused of sexual assault or other serious misconduct. Whether brought (sometimes quite creatively), by an employee or student, it should be noted that the selection, use, and prosecution of these claims should be the work of a competent and qualified attorney. In alphabetical order those claims, (loosely defined,) variously include but are not limited to the following:

Assault and Battery: The threat to harm another, or lawful attempt to cause an injury on the person of another; assault is often described as an attempt to commit a battery (and/or unwanted or inappropriate touching).

Breach of Contract or Breach of an Implied Contract: A broken promise, stemming from someone's failure to fulfill any term of a contract without a legitimate, lawful excuse. Generally speaking, there are four types of contract breaches: anticipatory, actual, minor and material. Some states such as Colorado, for recognize verbal contracts as well.

Breach of Fiduciary Duty: The law forbids a fiduciary, a party that acts on behalf another, from acting in any manner adverse or contrary to the interests of the other party to which they owe that duty, or from acting for his own benefit in relation to the subject matter.

Civil Conspiracy: An agreement between two or more parties to deprive a third party of legal rights or deceive a third party to obtain an illegal objective.

Fraud and Constructive Fraud: Theft of something of value by means of deception.

Defamation: the act of damaging the good reputation of an individual, typically brought as a tort of either slander or libel.

Discrimination: The unjust or prejudicial treatment of different categories of people or things, especially on the grounds of race, color, age, gender, or sexual orientation.

False Imprisonment: Detaining someone against their will. Actual physical restraint is not necessary.

Intentional Infliction/Negligent infliction of Emotional Distress: Intentionally or negligently behaving abominably or outrageously with intent to cause another to suffer severe emotional distress, such as issuing the threat of future harm.

General Negligence: The failure to exercise appropriate and or ethical ruled care expected to be exercised amongst specified circumstances. The area of tort law known as negligence involves harm caused by failing to act as a form of carelessness, possibly with extenuating circumstances.

Malicious Prosecution: The wrongful institution of criminal proceedings against someone without reasonable grounds.

Negligent Hiring: The claim of an injured party against an employer, based on the theory that the employer knew or should have known about the employee's background, which, if known, indicates a dangerous or untrustworthy character.

Negligent Investigation: A relatively new tort, asserting that the fact-finder and/or his employer's investigation was defective to the extent that the use of the investigation's results are sufficiently lacking or defective so as to constitutes negligence.

Negligent Misrepresentation: A material misrepresentation is an untrue or misleading statement of fact.

Promissory Estoppel: The legal principle that a promise is enforceable by law, even if made without formal consideration when a promisor has made a promise to a promisee who then relies on that promise to his subsequent detriment.

Wrongful Discharge/Termination: Also known as wrongful dismissal, is a claim arising from a breadth of an employee's contract of employment or a statute provision or rule according to employment law.

Wrongful Prosecution: The tort of initiating a criminal prosecution or civil suit against another party with malice and without probable cause.

Most obviously, the employment and application of these claims are fact driven and jurisdictionally controlled. Both the facts and the law will determine how and when these claims may be brought and under what circumstances. Additionally, is that little annoyance called that statute of limitations. Employment law attorneys will also note that in matters in which discrimination is claimed, the Employment Opportunity Commission, (as briefly mentioned in Chapter 3), plays a role as well.

The EEOC is a federal agency that administers and enforces civil rights laws against workplace discrimination. The EEOC investigates discrimination complaints based on an individual's race/color, national origin, religion, sex, age, disability, sexual orientation, gender identity, genetic information, and retaliation for reporting, participating in, and/or opposing a discriminatory practice. Given the breadth of the EEOC's reach, under the right circumstances and fact-pattern, it would appear one falsely accused of sexual assault or other serious misconduct must have an EEO claim of some sort! That is not to suggest I support falsely making a claim (of any sort) proper or even worthy of considering. What I am conveying is that no potential claim should be overlooked or categorically ignored.

Entrapment

Entrapment is an affirmative defense often made by those accused of serious misconduct. Entrapment is generally characterized as an intentional inducement, (by an agent of the government such as an undercover police detective), which results in an otherwise honest person committing a crime, that without the inducement, that person would not have committed. Entrapment is merely a criminal defense and not a crime, nor is it illegal if done in good faith. However, in order to use entrapment as a defense, *the accused must first admit they committed the offense.* Thus, the use of entrapment as a defense can be very dangerous for the accused. What's more, as a defense, it is emphatically unavailable to the falsely accused for it is only available to those that committed a crime and admitted it. For more definitions of legal terms and generally relevance, please see Appendix A.

Spoliation

Spoliation is the destruction of evidence and constitutes an obstruction of justice. Spoliation is also the destruction, or significant and meaningful alteration, of a document or instrument. The rules of evidence impose an obligation to retain and produce evidence deemed admissible and relevant in criminal and civil matters. The intentional and sometimes even the unintentional destruction of evidence may be unlawful and/or civilly actionable—and for good reason. The destruction of evidence very often provides one party an advantage at the expense of another. Recent cases involving the employees, and in some instances the agents (outside accountants and auditors), of public companies intentionally destroying documents and critical records demonstrate the consequences. Litigation and criminal indictments of both the organization and the responsible parties are not uncommon. Worst yet maybe is the damage to the organization's reputation and the loss of public confidence in its role as an organization capable of enforcing its sexual harassment and discrimination policies. Thus, the mere claim of spoliation against an organizations' fact-finders and decision-makers can be incalculable.

During an organization's investigation, should items such as e-mails, notes, and apparently extraneous documents be discarded, claims of spoliation may later arise. In emotionally charged cases such as those involving the claim of discrimination or sexual assault, accusations about the destruction of evidence are common. Furthermore, they are difficult to disprove. The mere fact the alleged document (which may have never existed) cannot be produced inferentially suggests that it was destroyed. Generally, only testimony can be used to prove the document didn't exist. Think of one's personal notes and how one would prove they or portions of them, didn't exist. If the credibility of the witness(s) used to prove the document didn't exist is in question, the charge of spoliation has a good chance of gaining traction. If so, the credibility of these witness(s) will suffer further damage.

Evidence Retention and Preservation

For many of the reasons stated earlier, evidence retention and preservation has become a popular topic. The mishandling and misplacing of evidence can be catastrophic and the intentional or negligent destruction of evidence may lead to claims of spoliation. The fact-finder's investigative process must contemplate this issue from the onset. Reconstruction of evidence is time consuming and expensive. It is best to handle it properly from the onset. However, one must consider that evidence comes in many forms. Most common of all forms of evidence is that which is testimonial and physical. But over the last decade, electronic evidence has become a significant and dominating evidentiary consideration in matters involving sexual assault and other serious misconduct.

It is now black letter law that information generated and stored on computers and in other electronic forms, (inclusive of the content found on or in websites, blogs, text messaging systems, social media, personal computers, and communication devices; the cloud; digital recordings, and images), are all now discoverable. It is estimated that 98 percent or more of all information stored on computers and other electronic devices is never reduced to printed form. Moreover, the electronic version of a document usually contains information that simply does not appear in the printed version. Meta data and document histories are good examples. As one would expect, finding the information stored on computers is becoming an important if not critical part, of the discovery process.

Many lawyers now ask for electronic evidence, especially e-mail, as a routine part of their discovery efforts. But, as a practical matter, most lawyers have little or no experience in collecting and analyzing the data they request. For them, here are few recommendations:

First: Immediately prepare and dispatch a preservation of evidence letter. Because some information stored on electronic devices is in volatile memory, such as RAM (random access memory), which is altered or deleted every time the device is used or repowered, time is of the essence. The parties should be placed on immediate notice that electronic evidence through discovery will be sought. The sooner the notice is sent the better. The notice should identify, as specifically as possible, the types of information to be preserved and explain the possible places that information may exist. If appropriate, consider obtaining a protective order requiring all parties to preserve electronic evidence and be sure to establish the proper protocols to do so.

Second: In your correspondence, include definitions, instructions, and specific questions about the existence and storage of electronic evidence as well the custodian's responsible management and proper storage of that information.

Third: Consider the use of interrogatories to get an overview of the systems used to create and store the information you are seeking. The interrogatories can then be followed up with a 30(b)(6) deposition of the appropriate party.

However, don't overlook the favored tool in private sector investigations to catalogue and preserve evidence. That tool is generally referred to as an evidence file. An evidence file may be nothing more than a manila folder in which evidentiary documents are placed for safekeeping. Accordion folders, corrugated boxes, file cabinets or safes may also be used to store evidence. On the extreme end of the spectrum is the evidence locker or compound. Regardless of its form or construction, the purpose is the safe storage of evidence.

In addition to containing evidence, the evidence folder should contain a document used to identify and track the evidence within it. Variations of this form are largely a matter of preference.

Chain of Custody

The transfer of evidence from one party to another should be carefully documented. Each person who handles or takes control of evidence must be recorded, creating what is called the chain of custody. The chain of custody, sometimes called the chain of evidence, is a document that at a minimum identifies each custodian, when they received it, and to whom they transferred it. The chain of custody must not be broken. That is, there cannot be gaps during when the evidence was unaccounted for or out of the control of a custodian of record. A chain of custody that is broken exposes it to challenge and jeopardizes the admissibility of the evidence.

The sloppy handling of evidence exposes both the fact-finder and the evidence to credibility challenges. Claims of evidence tampering, alteration, or contamination are possible when evidence is mishandled. Fact-finders should not handle or use originals during their investigation. Whenever possible, copies, photographs, or models should be used in lieu of the actual evidence. Never place an original piece of evidence in the hands of the subject. Knowing the value of the evidence and its implications, the subject may be tempted to not return it or destroy it.

Litigation

Unsurprisingly, in matters involving sexual assault or other serious misconduct, the results of an organization's investigation and that which follows it, rarely conclude happily for everyone. Almost always, one or both parties are displeased. The reasons for their dissatisfaction will drive that which follows. In many cases, ending with the termination of the falsely accused employee or expulsion of the falsely accused student, the accused are tempted to seek justice. And often that justice is sought via litigation.

Alleging one or more of the civil claims previously mentioned, suit is then brought against the alleged wrongdoers. Counsel for the plaintiff will carefully assess what allegedly occurred, the accusers credibility, the type and quality of evidence gathered against his or her client, the responsive actions taken against their client by their employer or institution, and an assessment of legal options available. Should civil litigation be the path of choice, counsel and client together will decide the path forward. Upon filing suit, the accused becomes the plaintiff and his accuser and her employer or school will be among the defendants. At the most fundamental level, these are the phases of civil litigation:

Figure 6.1

As any attorney with litigation experience will tell you, the process is slow and expensive. Unlike the movies and made-for-television series like *Bull*, civil claims are not litigated and brought to trial in days or weeks. In real-life, it is not uncommon for it to take three to four years to bring the case to trial, and longer if one of the parties appeals an outcome they dislike.

A common driver for plaintiffs in deciding whether to bring a civil action is the proportionality of the punishment they receive. Organizations frequently substitute process of fairness. They intentionally create elaborate, detailed processes, which add little value and merely complicate that which was simple. Such schemes provide the organization a curtain to hide behind in the event of mandatory mediation or litigation. Unlike the process and flow chart I provided as Appendix E, these schemes incorporate elaborate busy work for both the fact-finders and decision-makers alike. So elaborate and complicated, the machinations could be used to "indict a ham sandwich."[83] Looking closely at the product these processes systematically produce, it is not uncommon that the discipline and/or corrective actions they produce differ little from one case to another. It is in matters such as these, expert witnesses can be invaluable.

Expert Witnesses

Fundamentally, in the world of litigation and criminal law there are two types of witnesses, fact witnesses and expert witnesses. A fact witness is an individual with knowledge about that he or she said, saw, heard, observed, witnessed, or experienced firsthand. It is typical that a fact witness testifies to what occurred and the facts pertaining to it as he or she experienced or observed them. While there a several exceptions, typically for a fact witness to testify, their observations and/or knowledge must be firsthand. An expert witness is someone possessing specialized education, training, and experience for which the court finds valuable. As a result of the quality and quantity of their education, training, and experience, if approved by the court, a "designated expert" may offer testimony relative to their *opinions*. I have testified as either a fact or expert witness in more than 200 matters. One of those times, I testified in both capacities.

In order to qualify as an expert one must reveal their qualifications and submit to an oral examination by judge or counsel.

Pursuant to recent matters, I offered these qualifications prior to being allowed to offer an opinion (in part):

"I am board certified in both Human Resources Management (SPHR and SHRM-SCP designations) and Security Management (CPP designation). I have provided HR consulting and/or investigative services and tools with a specific focus on matters such as student safety, improper faculty and employee behavior, harassment, discrimination, and the management of whistleblower complaints for entities including Pennsylvania State University, University of Houston, Scripps, Florida Institute of Technology, University of Detroit Mercy, and the U.S. Olympic Committee's Safe Sport initiative.

I have also developed and/or delivered Human Resources management and internal investigation training to several hundred employers and their employees. These employers include Hewlett-Packard, Cardinal Health, Johnson & Johnson, Kraft Foods, Pennsylvania State University, University of Denver, Colorado Department of Human Services (and its Office of Early Childhood), and the U.S. Departments of Treasury, Energy and Homeland Security. I have been a member of ASIS International since 1987, and I currently serve as a member and Vice Chair of its Standards and Guidelines Commission."

You get the idea. In the matter for which I offered these qualifications as an expert, the following questions were put before me:

1.   What is the responsibility of an employer in the screening of employment applicants in public schools, and does there exist recognized best practices and/or guidelines that public sector employers should consider and follow when screening employment applicants?

2.   Should such best practices and/or guidelines exist, did _____ have published policies that were consistent with those best practices and guidelines, and did _____ comply

with its policies and fulfill its duty during its pre-employment screening of _____ prior to hiring him?

3. What duty, if any, did _____have when it became aware of the allegations against _____ and saw for the first time, (evidence described here), which appears to have corroborated those allegations?

Note the narrowness of these questions. Very intentionally, the questions were crafted with extreme precision. Appropriately, a lay witness would be unable to answer these questions. Only a qualified expert who had the education, training, and experience could address these questions with authority. In order to support an opinion, the expert must reveal how she formulated that opinion and be able to defend her methodology of doing so during cross-examination. As such, it is not uncommon for opposing counsel to attempt to draw an over-confident and talkative expert to speculate outside her area of expertise. Such traps can lead to the expert making horrible mistakes.

Generally, I do not think an attempt to be humorous is a very good idea. However, during a recent trial in which I was a witness, defense counsel held up a copy of one of my books. In bold print on the cover was my name, clearly visible to the judge and jury. Smartly, counsel demanded, "Is this your book?" shaking the book as she spoke. Without even thinking I answered, "No, it appears to be your book, mine is at home." A big smile instantly appeared on the face of the judge, who said with a chuckle, "I think he's correct, counselor."

In a similar vein, just for fun here is a little more humorous testimony. Allegedly given at trial or during a deposition, though I have not been able verify it:

ATTORNEY: How was your first marriage terminated?
WITNESS: By death..
ATTORNEY: And by whose death was it terminated?
WITNESS: Take a guess.

LAWYER: Now sir, I'm sure you are an intelligent and honest man--
WITNESS: Thank you. If I weren't under oath, I'd return the compliment.

ATTORNEY: What gear were you in at the moment of the impact?
WITNESS: Gucci sweats and Reeboks.

LAWYER: What happened then?
WITNESS: He told me, he says, 'I have to kill you because you can identify me.'
LAWYER: Did he kill you?
WITNESS: No.

LAWYER: Any suggestions as to what prevented this from being a murder trial instead of an attempted murder trial?
WITNESS: The victim lived.

Fact Witnesses and Depositions

Following the filing of the complaint and all of the responsive pleadings that go back and forth between the parties, witnesses are disclosed and depositions scheduled. A deposition is a part of the permitted pre-trial discovery (investigation) process. Depositions, or depos as they are typically called, are coordinated by counsel in order to obtain sworn testimony of the opposing party, whether defendant or plaintiff. Also deposed may be fact witnesses and experts intended to be called by either party at trial. The sworn, out-of-court oral testimony obtained during the depo is often reduced to a written transcript for later use in court or for discovery purposes. It is very common that both the plaintiff and defendant are deposed rigorously.

Intentionally, depositions are often intended to create stress and confuse the deponent. What is often sought is testimony that contradicts the facts and claims contained in the complaint or the opposition's answer to the complaint. Inconsistencies and contradictions may be used to discredit the witness and his or her claims and/or prior statements. As such, counsel will typically prepare her witnesses before the deposition and provide suggestions as to how one might handle difficult or trick questions. Not surprisingly, volumes have been written on the topic and the means by which to survive the *dreaded* depo.[84]

Here are a few suggestions for the perspective deponent:

☐ Know the facts/timeline and the names of those likely raised during the proceeding;

☐ Read and reread your notes and all of the materials available to you;

☐ Prepare your testimony and know the terminology you intend to use;

☐ Be mindful that opposing counsel is not your friend;

☐ Practice "Yes" and "No" responses, for they are the best responses one can give to a question;

☐ Dress for success and look the part;

☐ Show up on time;

☐ Remember that you will be observed even when not testifying; and

☐ Don't forget to smile

Be prepared to be asked to speculate, consider hypotheticals, and insisting you answer an impossibly complicated question with a simple yes or no. To avoid being forced to answer with a yes or no, you might consider answering the question with:

"Not necessarily...

"It depends…

"I would need to know more…

"Yes (or No), but the facts in this case are quite different…

"Yes (or No), but the facts in this case suggest…

"It may be possible, but the facts in this case suggest…

"Could you please restate the question and provide more detail?

Professional Investigators

Of the assorted members of the accused's defense and prosecution team, the dedicated team fact-finder, is often the most underutilized. But not all investigators are created equal. The best of the breed are specialists that narrowly focus their practice on specific services and client needs. There is, of course, crossover of skills and many qualified professional investigators have both multiple skills and specialties. Regardless, the outcome of his or her effort will largely be driven by the ability to bring to bear their specialized skill and prior experience in an orderly and effective fashion. Just as one would not ask an ophthalmologist to set a broken leg, one should not expect any particular investigator to perform every type of investigation skillfully. Instead, it is best that their skill be matched to the type and quality of information sought. One's attorney is the best person to make that determination.

Importantly, thinking experience trumps skill is a common error. Because of their education, training, and experience, lawyers tend to hire investigators with law enforcement experience. On its face this seems to make perfect sense, however confusing the experience of one responsible for the enforcement of public law with one that is required to investigate a claim of workplace sexual harassment or date rape is a serious mistake. Contrary to popular belief, the sad fact of the matter is that there is very little experience cross-over between the public and private sector. Yet this mistake is made every day. A host of organizations, large and small, intentionally seek out and hire those with prior law enforcement experience to support Human Resources or fill campus security positions. It is my opinion that the skill and experience of most law enforcement professionals does not match that needed by the private sector. Similarly, human resource professionals are often asked to perform investigative tasks of which they have no experience either. Here's a good example:

The matter began with an anonymous tip from a concerned employee. The employee, using his employer's anonymous incident reporting mechanism, in this case, a toll-free hotline, reported that a small group of female coworkers had been co-opted by a foreman and were recruited into what had become a prostitution ring. The concerned individual or CI also reported that the participants frequently drank on the job and that on more than one occasion the foreman had nearly wrecked a company vehicle when driving while impaired. The report was quickly passed up the chain of command and soon was on the desk of the CEO. He immediately called my office and requested assistance. As the reader might imagine, I suggested some fundamental fact-finding was in order. Work orders, time cards, and work schedules needed to be examined.

Once the investigation's objectives are agreed upon, the first order of business when allegations of this sort are received is to somehow substantiate them. I outlined for the CEO an appropriate plan and he instructed me to coordinate the effort through his director of human resources, a woman with whom I had worked previously. In a short time, together we were able to corroborate some of the allegations and uncover additional irregularities. We quickly packaged the results and recommended that my team interview the suspected transgressors. The CEO, however, balked. Concluding that his director of security, a former law enforcement officer knew the personalities involved and his organization's processes better than my

197

team, and directed her to conduct the interviews. Experienced as she was with routine traffic stops and highway accident investigations, she had never confronted or interviewed anyone suspected of such serious offenses. Reluctantly, she proceeded and resultantly failed miserably. Not a single individual made an admission. Instead, each accused her and the organization of a witch hunt. Inexperienced in conducting difficult investigatory interviews, she visibly demonstrated her uneasiness and lack of confidence. She was unable to overcome the meagerest of denials, and quickly found herself defending the investigation and all of the evidence it had produced.

Takeaway: when available, use only experienced fact-finders. Match both the skill and the experience of the fact-finder to the specifics of the investigation. Experience in law enforcement and human resources does not make one an experienced fact-finder nor an effective investigator.

All but several states require that investigators who sell their services be licensed and have some form of commercial liability protection. Accordingly, hiring and using an investigator who is operating outside law poses problems for both the person who hired him and his client.

Here is a list of some of the tasks a qualified investigator can perform on behalf of an attorney his client:

1. Economically, perform public record research, including driving histories, criminal records, driver histories, property ownership, litigation, and employment histories;

2. Gather, harvest, examine, evaluate, and properly secure both physical and electronic evidence;

3. Identify, find and interview witnesses or others possessing potentially valuable information;

4. Obtain written statements and declarations when appropriate;

5. Conduct both physical and electronical surveillance; and

6. Provide other lawful and useful services as directed by counsel.

Professional investigators almost always produce written reports. When prepared properly, not only might they contain very useful information, they can be used as evidence. As mentioned earlier, one's report should be factual and not contain opinions. By definition, a proper investigative report contains only facts.

For more information about internal investigations, consider reading one or both of my books, *Investigations in the Workplace, Second Edition*, or *Investigative Interviewing: Psychology, Method and Practice*. Both can be found on Amazon.

Detecting Bias and Other Anomalies

Experts can provide other assistance as well. In addition to preparing a report of my own I will occasionally prepare and provide a counter-opinion relative to the opinion of an opposing expert. On other occasions, as a professional investigator, I am able to analyze the investigation and its result, which gave rise to the present litigation. Among the things I like to do is evaluate the quality and content of the report generated following the defendants investigation. Without going too deep into the weeds, one of the simplest forms of analysis of an investigative report is a simple word search. After converting the report from a PDF to an MS Word.doc, and using Word's word search tool I able to selectively see how frequent or infrequent a particular word or phrase is used in the document.

As I did on page 156, where I searched for the term *sexual violence* in an advertisement and found the term had been used six times. However, the words *innocent, fair, impartial,* or *balanced* do not appear once! The same technique can be used on any document produced during litigation. Depending on the results, an expert such as I could opine on its significance. What would you think if the defendant's 50+ page investigative report contained the word sexual violence and/or guilty more than three dozen times each, yet not once contained the words *innocent, fair, impartial,* or *balanced?* And by the way, *sexual violence* has appeared 20 times at this point in this book and *innocent* 36 times, excluding its use in the title, the front matter, and the header of each even-numbered page. Were you to know nothing more about this book than that, what might you conclude about its theme or message and views of the author? Such analysis can often produce compelling insights into the ideology, mindset, and the existence of possible bias of the expert or the fact-finder's investigative report on which that expert is opining. Another tool sometimes useful in detecting bias, is a detailed timeline, like this:

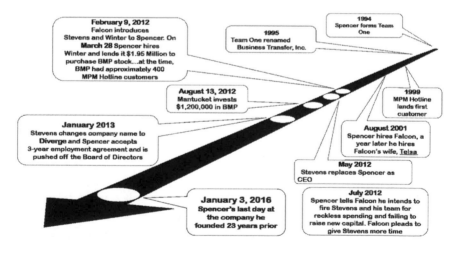

Figure 6.2

Good investigators and fact-finders frequently create timelines in order to better illustrate and understand the course of events. Simple and visually effective, timelines can also facilitate the existence and analysis of relationships. While difficult to read because of its size, you can see some of the possibilities:

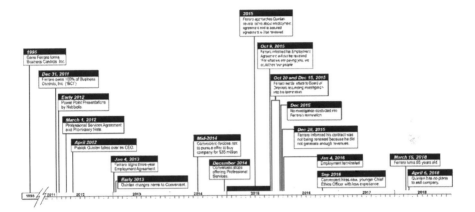

Figure 6.3

Here is an example demonstrating the progress of a simple project plan and completion of critical fact-finding tasks:

Case Number FP20096 Internal Investigation

ACTIVITY	PLANNED START DATE	PLAN DURATION	START DATE	ACTUAL COMPLETION	PERCENT COMPLETE
Project Green-Light	.	32	3-Nov	.	70%
Fact-Finding	.	7	4-Nov	8-Nov	100%
Internal Interviews	.	3	6-Nov	9-Nov	100%
Final Report	.	8	6-Nov	.	100%
Management Review	.	30	3-Nov	.	40%
Activity 06					
Activity 07					

Figure 6.4

I have found the use of graphics such as these to be very effective. Not only are these useful project management tools, they are an effective means of conveying the sophistication of one's processes and methods. Rarely are tools like these seen in either investigative or expert reports involving the topic of this book or the machinations thereof. Of course, depending on the information these visuals are intended to present, it is difficult to believe the fact-finder or expert using such tools is flying by the seat of his pants. Moreover, such attention to detail tends to make those that prepare them, pay more attention to detail and their proclaimed use of processes.

Some of the forensic tools available to both experts and fact-finders are rather interesting. One of the least familiar and more fascinating of them is Benford's Law, a powerful bias detection tool that predicts the frequency of numbers (digits) in some naturally-occurring, unmanipulated groups. Engineers and mathematicians have long known of this simple but powerful mathematical model that quickly predicts the distribution of numbers for pointing suspicion at frauds, embezzlers, tax evaders, sloppy accountants, and even computer bugs. Frank Benford, re-discoverer of this phenomenon, was a physicist for General Electric who in 1938 recognized that certain "non-randomly behaved numbers in non-normally distributed data sets" can be ordered in a very predictable fashion. Benford analyzed over 20,000 data sets of various categories and found that all of the seemingly disparate numbers followed the same first-digit probability pattern. Benford's probability distribution (expressed as a percentage) of the first digit of any database that meets the criteria described above can be visualized on the following page.

Thus, if we examined a data set composed of invoice amounts, Benford's Law, (which is scale invariant) predicts that 30.10% of the invoice amounts begin with the digit 1. Those amounts for example, might be $1.29 or $17,031.81. Regardless, approximately 30% will begin with the digit 1; roughly 18% will begin with the digit 2 and so on. A data set that does not conform, is thus suspect. My personal investigative use of this powerful forensic tool has consistently provided insight into corrupt data. In such a case, I was able to identify three dishonest vendors out of a group of over 1500, all working on single $300 million construction project.

So powerful is this tool, the IRS uses it to identify potential fraud in tax returns. I have been told that one of the reasons the IRS favors electronic filing of tax returns and other required filings is that it allows it to systematically run every electronic document or completed form it receives through a Benford analysis.

Benford's Probability Distribution of the First Digit in Non-normally Distributed Data Sets

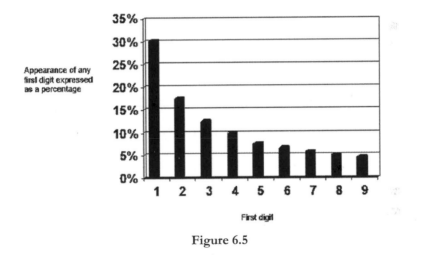

Figure 6.5

To easily demonstrate the power of this tool, next time you are in a group of ten or more homeowners ask how many of them have an address which begins with the number one (i.e. 13744 Benford Court). Because Benford's Law is scale invariant, you will find that 3 or more of the home owners will answer with the number 1! To use this tool one simply needs one or more data sets sufficiently relevant to the matter in question. In the case of detecting accounting irregularities it is simple. Payables, receivables, past dues, and daily/monthly or annual sales numbers can be easily tested. For detecting bias or other harmful behaviors impacting the outcome of an investigation, one must be a little more creative. Consider for a moment EEOC or DOE Title IX statistics. Even associations and organizations such as the Society for Human Resource Management (SHRM) have massive amounts of data. Depending on the fact pattern of the matter in question, say sexual assault in the workplace, one could possibly compare the analysis of large data sets, such as the above and compare them to that of an individual organization or a subunit of it. Going further, one could analyze subsets of these data and compare it to that of a particular organization or a subgroup of it. Not only would such an analysis identify possibly suspect data, but conversely benefit the organization in identifying trends and hotspots as well.

Forensic Science and Scientific Analysis

Forensic science, also known as *criminalistics,* is the application and use of science in criminal and civil investigation. Often overlooked in civil matters, forensic science or if you prefer, *forensics* can be a powerful tool. Those specializing in the field collect, preserve, and analyze scientific evidence during the course of an investigation. While some forensic experts travel to the scene of the crime to collect the evidence themselves, many allow others to bring the evidence to them. In addition to their laboratory work, forensic scientists testify as expert witnesses in both criminal and civil cases and can work for either the prosecution or the defense. While any field science could technically be forensic, certain sections have developed over time to encompass the majority of forensically related services for use in both criminal and civil matters. Be the evidence blood splatter, semen, saliva, fingerprints, tool marks, digital images, audio recording, or computer files and electronically stored information, there exist forensic experts capable of assisting the accused and his accuser.

My use of forensic experts has largely been with those able to find or recover electronically stored information. Because of the dynamic nature of electronically stored information, those wishing to capture and examine it should prioritize the collection of such material and obtain professional assistance in properly storing it.

Specialized forensic experts can assist in tracking the prior movement of a cell phone, notebook, or other handheld device. Under the right circumstances, even the data contained in a Fitbit could be valuable. According to Fitbit's dev.Fitbit.com website, "The Fitbit API allows developers to interact with Fitbit data in their own applications, products, and services.

The API allows for most of the read and write methods that you will need to support your application. If you have uses or needs that are not currently supported by the API, drop by the Dev Forum and let us know! We look forward to working closely with the development community to make the Fitbit API a system that enables you to do awesome, mind-blowing stuff."

The Lack of Rigor and/or Compliance

Depending upon their specialty, expertise, and experience, experts can also assist counsel in assessing the amount of rigor an organization and its fact-finders exercise in their fact-finding. They can also assist in determining whether or not their efforts met applicable industry standards and best practices. For example, a qualified expert might assess the organization's adherence to the ANSI/ASIS INV.1-2015 Investigations Standard and whether its investigation achieved conformance. Remember, *conformance* is a state of general conformity and may be determined by simple observation by those qualified to do so.

Similarly, on behalf of counsel an effort to determine whether a school is or was in compliance with the Clery Act and Title IX can be undertaken. Remember, the *Jeanne Clery Disclosure of Campus Security Policy and Campus Crime Statistics Act* is a federal law requiring United States colleges and universities to disclose information about crime on and around their campuses. The Act is enforced by the United States Department of Education, which is authorized to impose stiff fines for non-compliance. Similarly, DOE's new Title IX rules are also auditable. Unlike, the ANSI/ASIS INV.1-2015 Investigations Standard, Clery Act and Title IX compliance are demonstrable by means of audit. Given the opportunity, a qualified expert by means of review can identify gaps and irregularities, which used objectively, might be employed as levers in negotiating reasonable compromises when dealing with belligerent decision-makers. I am not suggesting extortion. What I am suggesting is simply pointing out that the organization's actions should match their expectations of others, including those involved in alleged misconduct. To do otherwise may suggest disparate treatment. The fact pattern in question and past practices would have to be considered. But at the end of the day, both employers and schools must apply their policies, procedures and practices uniformly.

As examined in detail in Chapter 4, an organization's mission, vision, values, polices, procedures and practices must be properly aligned as well. Inconsistent application of policies and procedures and an uneven application of standards and expectations are toxic to any organization.

The Role, Impact and Use of the Media

I have known Dr. Richard M. Carlton, M.D. for nearly thirty years. Among other things, social issues are something we have frequently discussed. A psychiatrist with 45 years' experience, including forensic evaluations in the Supreme Court of the City of New York, Dr. Carlton fully acknowledges that many women have suffered greatly as a result of male predatory behavior. However, he is also well aware that some women with personality disorders (typically either sociopathic or borderline personality disorder), will not hesitate to make false accusations of sexual misconduct against men they know or with whom they have had a relationship. Even when such cases are dismissed at trial, the men who were falsely accused are often left severely damaged. Though finding accurate information on the incidence of false allegations against men is difficult, what little there is tends to suggest that between 2 and 10 percent of all claims are indeed false.[85] Assuming the person being accused is guilty before conducting an investigation can be incredibly damaging to their career, reputation, future success, and emotional wellbeing.

It's easy to dismiss such low percentages. However, according to the EEOC, there were 7,514 charges of sex-based harassment filed in 2019. At the low range of possible false reporting, 2 percent of the 7,514 is 150 instances. At the higher end of ten percent, it's 750.

If one is able to depend on the numbers, the research suggests that somewhere between 150 and 750 people were falsely accused in 2019. However, EEOC data does not include the reports of harassment charges filed with state or local agencies or ones that never get reported through government channels. Potentially, the numbers could be even greater. So what? Well, having read the first few chapters, it is easy to recognize that the #MeToo movement has almost entirely been propelled by media. As a result, it has been brought into the forefront of the minds or our political leaders, our institutions, and those of big business. But it remains unknown, what is the role of media at on the ground level and its impact on false reporting?

"It can be easy to dismiss the concern, but famed lawyer Alan Dershowitz is no stranger to controversy. In fact, he often invites it with open arms. But being accused of rape and being lumped in with Prince Andrew and Jeffrey Epstein is a rare type of controversy that he finds himself uncomfortable with: "I welcome controversy about my ideas. I love having debates and controversy about my ideas. But having controversy about whether or not I'm a sex offender? That's not what I bargained for in my life.""[86]

Dershowitz has described the challenges of the false accusations against him. He has faced as an innocent, falsely accused. Including "the financial cost of fighting the accusation, to the embarrassment of having to tell every potential client of the claims while he is pursuing it in court, to the impact it has had on his family, including his grandchildren: "It's been terrible. No one who knows me believes it, none of my personal friends. Even those who are really upset at me about the Trump thing don't believe it because they know I'm not that guy. I'm not a player. But it has still had a terrible impact on my grandkids who are in school where people believe everything that's said, and on my children. It's had a terrible impact on us. I'm a victim, and no one wants to treat me like a victim."[87]

So, ought the falsely accused go to the press and if so, for what purpose? The question may not be answerable. At the very least, any answer should be qualified. But I tend to like guidelines instead. So here is my guidance:

1. Identify your purpose and agenda. Stick to them. Do not let an interviewer pull you from pursuing your agenda;

2. Communicate with the press only if your lawyer approves and agrees to be physically present and answer for you when appropriate. Alternatively, let your attorney earn his fees and answer all of the questions;

3. Don't slander anyone and don't mention the accuser by name;

4. Dress properly and be prepared for the unexpected.

Generally, judges do not like seeing their cases heard in the court of public opinion. Consider that, and your reputation, before allowing a microphone to be put in front of you.

Common Mistakes

Attorneys are human, and like everyone else, they are capable of making mistakes. Here are the five most common mistakes I see attorneys make regarding matters of alleged sexual assault and other serious misconduct when working for the accused:

1. Accepting a case that they either haven't the available time and/or experience to handle. For a host if reasons attorneys sometimes accept cases they should not. Because of the complexity, costs, and that which is at stake for the client, attorneys should accept a matter involving the allegation of sexual assault or other similarly serious misconduct;

2. Failing to fully inform their client of the seriousness and challenges regarding the allegations he is facing;

3. Failing to properly and efficiently use their experts and professional investigators;

4. Under-valuing their case and the strength of it various claims. Thus, resultantly demanding too little during settlement negotiations; and

5. Failing to be creative, take risks, or punch hard enough.

No organization looks forward to being sued and entrenched in litigation involving matters as distasteful as claims of sexual assault, harassment, wrongful discharge, discrimination, and defamation. Nor do they enjoy the publicity that can be associated with such matters. Sometimes an organization will be willing to do, or pay anything to get out from under such embarrassing and ever-increasingly expensive messes. I know, because I have been present when my client said that aloud with counsel present. An attorney's failure to be creative and communicate with their opponent is as wasteful as it is shameful.

I have witnessed plaintiff's counsel for whom I worked, fail to make simple evidentiary challenges because the defendant's organization's fact-finder was a former FBI agent! On other occasions, I have witnessed plaintiff's counsel fail to enforce subpoenas for documents and other evidence, which had been arbitrarily denied them or while lacking sufficient justification to not produce them. Responding with an "oh well," is hardly good lawyering.

But the most common shortcoming I have experienced, whether working for the plaintiff or defense, is the quality of his underlying investigation. It is difficult to exaggerate the poor quality and sufficiency of most investigations of which I have had involvement, as either a fact or expert witness, involving an alleged sexual assault or other serious misconduct. Bad facts can make for very difficult cases. But bad investigations can enable bad facts to win a case and good facts lose a case. Sadly, it is all too often it comes down to the quality of the investigation and which side of the case you are on. Imagine an investigative report in which the fact-finder confuses the identity of the accuser and the accused? Or a fact-finders report which failed to mention the date and place of the alleged event? But most memorable was a fact-finder who failed to interview the accuser and then mis-identified his client as the accused!

But attorneys and fact-finders are not the only ones who make mistakes. Employers and school administrators make mistakes also. Of them, the most preventable is substituting process for fairness. It has been my experience that the larger in size and greater in reach, the greater the likelihood that an organization succumbs to the substitution of process for fairness. Behaving like a machine, such organizations appear to chew people up and discard them. They impose strict procedures and protocols, which are unnecessarily inflexible and absolute in their application. With punishment, which is decisive and swift, that in the end serves little purpose and pleases no one, their identification as institutions fit them well. As a reminder to those I teach, I close every one of my investigations trainings with this simple but important advice:

- ✓ Remember, our work will affect the lives of those you investigate and interview, and those they touch;

- ✓ Treat the subject as you would wish someone treat you or a family member;

- ✓ Respect the rights of with those you interact and interview; and

- ✓ Treat all people with respect and dignity.

Frequently Asked Questions

What is the difference between a bench trial and a jury trial?

A bench trial is a trial without a jury. Instead the judge both hears the case and decides the outcome. A bench trial is usually a quicker way to complete a case because it can be scheduled sooner and does not require jury selection and jury instructions, which make the trial process last much longer. A jury trial is a trial for which the outcome is decided by a jury. A jury may be as large as twelve members and as few as seven.

Maybe I'm confused, how is it that Title IX panels and the codes of conduct they enforce, seem to so often ignore Amendment V and VI of our Bill of Rights (first mentioned on page 28 and elsewhere)…and appear to get away with it?

Your observation is noteworthy and has been asked many times. How is it that a school can investigate an allegation of the crime, of rape and find the accused guilty, and punish him? Why aren't such matters referred to the local authorities for proper investigation, and if justified, refer the case to the appropriate criminal prosecutor? Doing so would consume less time and fewer school resources. What's more, the accused would be afforded the constitutional protections he deserves. It is failures like this that cause me to think that today's understanding of Title IX and its enforcement mechanisms have become something that was not originally intended.

Returning to the prior question, in circumstances where constitutional rights may have been violated, hasn't the accused the opportunity to raise the issue of "agency"?

Yes. It has been variously established that institutions that receive federal government aid and/or financial support, may in fact be *agents* of the government. If held to be true, due process protections afforded by the Bill of Rights may very well be available to those who the *government's agents* might investigate. If agency can be established, and the institution fails to honor (or recognize) the accused's constitutional rights, the accused may have the opportunity to make a constitutional claim against the institution and its agents (those who performed the investigation). See page 37 for more details.

Is Clery compliance difficult and is the failure to be in compliance worth attacking by the falsely accused?

Yes and no to both components of the question. As it is often said (particularly in law), the answer depends on the totality of the circumstances. That said, if defending the wrongfully accused, I would suggest pursuing a school that is not in complete compliance with Clery. I would suggest counsel make the case about the school's failure to obey the law, not the "false and unfounded allegations" against the client. The more egregious the school's compliance failures, the harder I would push the attack.

By no means am I a passive individual, however your methods and techniques sometimes appear quite aggressive. Isn't it possible to achieve the same results without lawyers, litigation, and protracted tensions between the parties?

Yes. But the allegation of sexual assault or violence is no small matter. With it comes the possibility of criminal prosecution, imprisonment, and the loss of one's dreams and ambitions. Those who pursue the prosecution of such matters or heavy-handed enforcement of things like Title IX are purpose driven. You should be too. And when over, you can return to your kinder and more gentle self.

Why can't the accused perform his own investigation?

It is neither practical nor prudent. The accused should leave critical tasks to those best equipped to handle them. One should practice dental hygiene but leave root canals to the dentist.

It appears lawyers play a big role is such matters, is it practical for the accused to go it alone and defend himself?

As first uttered by Henry Kett, in his book, *The Flowers of Wit* (1814), "A man who is his own lawyer has a fool for a client." Don't be a fool, hire a good lawyer.

Honesty is more than not lying. It is being sincere and kind, thoughtful and thought-provoking. Honest people don't hide their deeds and often share their failures, for they know that to believe in something and not to share it, is dishonest.

78 Henry Knox, subsequently became the Continental Army's Chief of Artillery for the remainder of the Revolutionary War and became the country's first Secretary of War. A year before Bunker Hill, Knox, at age 25, had convinced Washington to proceed with the Christmas Eve 1776 crossing of the Delaware River. Accompanying him on the successful surprise attack on British and Hessian troops at Trenton, N.J. Knox, who had planned the crossing, was promoted to brigadier general and became one of Washington's most trusted advisors. Named in honor of the secretary, Fort Knox is a United States Army post in Kentucky, south of Louisville and north of Elizabethtown. It is also adjacent to the United States Bullion Depository, which is used to house a large portion of the United States' official gold reserves. The camp was later extended by the purchase of a further 40,000 acres in June 1918, and is still in use today as an active military installation.

79 Rose, J. D., *Lead, Follow, or Get Out of the Way*, with permission, AuthorVista, LLC, Denver, Colorado, 2019.

80 Harmeet Kaur Dhillon is an American lawyer and owns a law practice called Dhillon Law Group Inc. She specializes in high-stakes business, IP, internet, defamation & employment litigation.

81 https://nmllplaw.com/news/interview-rich-zeoli-show-1210am-wpht-trump-administrations-fight-due-process-rights-college-campuses/?utm_campaign=Title+9+-+Broad+-+NY+Office+%5BTitle+9%5D&utm_source=google&utm_medium=ppc&utm_term=title%20ix&utm_content=1860357xEAIaIQobChMI7MnZw7-V6QIVDb7ACh24FgMzEAAYASABEgK9_PD_BwE captured May 2, 2020.

82 Doe v. Brandeis University, 177 F. Supp. 3d 561,603 (D. Mass. 2016).

83 The phrase comes from Sol Wachtler, the former chief judge of the New York State Court of Appeals. Wachtler, who in 2014, became the state's top judge mused that district attorneys now have so much influence on grand juries that "by and large" they could get them to "indict a ham sandwich."

84 An excellent recourse on the topic is, *Nolo's Deposition Handbook: The Essential Guide for Anyone Facing or Conducting a Deposition* 7th Edition, Nolo Press, 2018. It can be found on Amazon.

85 Variously reported, however it is generally accepted that the incidence of false allegations tend to be somewhere between 2 and 10 percent. National Sexual Violence Resource Center, 2012 at https://www.nsvrc.org/sites/default/files/2012-03/Publications_NSVRC_Overview_False-Reporting.pdf

86 Holly Yan and Nicole Chavez, CNN at https://www.cnn.com/2018/10/03/health/sexual-assault-false-reports/index.html

87 Ibid.

CHAPTER SEVEN

RESOLUTION, RESTITUTION, AND RECOVERY

Attitude determines our altitude, say some motivational speakers. Others remind us that a half-filled glass is not half empty, in reality it is half full. Our perspective and world views are molded largely by our experiences. Yet every one of us knows or has met someone who has overcome a horrible tragedy or setback of devastating proportions who is happy, productive, and sometimes innocently inspirational. Four and half years ago my wife and I were dealt a tragic and devastating blow. Both in our late-60s, cruelly and barbarically taken from us was our dignity, self-respect, livelihood, and all that we thought to be our future. With vengeance, a small group of evil-doers intentionally attempted to destroyed us. Since that event, not a single day passes that each of us do not think about that which they so cruelly took from us. Yet, we have chosen to not seek vengeance or allow hate to consume us. Though, left deeply scarred, we choose to continue to live and remain thankful for that which we still have. The falsely accused can do so as well.

I have come to recognize that courage is not the absence of fear. It's not being completely unafraid. Courage is having apprehension and hesitation. Courage is living in spite of those things that scare us. Courage is the faith that some things will change and others never will. It is the belief that failure is not fatal, but to carry on when it is

215

almost certain.

Of the falsely accused with whom I've met or worked, not one has ever told me that they were unafraid. But somehow, they marshaled on and mustered the courage to survive, and most often— were in some fashion, thought themselves better for it.

Resolution

Matters involving allegations of sexual assault and other serious misconduct never simply vanish, nor are they wished away. Though the media continues to do that when the accused is one of their favorites. On May 3, 2020, Michigan Governor Gretchen Whitmer attempted to do just that during a CNN interview with Jake Tapper on the pitching mound:

Tapper: You have said that you believe Vice President Biden.[88] I want to compare that to 2018, when you said you believed Dr. Christine Blasey Ford after she accused now-Justice Brett Kavanaugh of assault. Kavanaugh also, like Biden, categorically denied that accusation. And Blasey Ford—to be honest, she did not have the contemporaneous accounts of her view of what happened that Tara Reade does. You have spoken movingly about how you're a survivor—survivor of assault yourself. Why do you believe Biden, and not Kavanaugh? Are they both entitled to the same presumption of innocence, regardless of their political views?

Whitmer: You know, Jake, as a survivor and as a feminist, I will say this. We need to give people an opportunity to tell their story. But then we have a duty to vet it. And just because you're a survivor doesn't mean that every claim is equal. It means we give them the ability to make their case, and the other side as well, and then to make a judgment that is informed. I have read a lot about this current allegation. I know Joe Biden, and I have watched his defense. And there's not a pattern that goes into this. And I think that, for these reasons, I'm very comfortable that Joe Biden is who he says he is. He's—and you know what? And that's all I'm going to say about it. I really resent the fact that, every time a case comes up, all of us survivors have to weigh in. It is reopening wounds. And it is—take us at our word, ask us for our opinion, and *let's move on*.

Of course, Governor Whitmer's choice of who to believe, or not believe, is hers to make. But it is hard not to recognize hypocrisy when one sees it. The falsely accused can and should expect hypocrisy among those who judge him. Anticipating such, is not only empowering, it provides us the courage to soldier on. So then what might the accused expect when falsely accused? Succinctly, there are three natural outcomes:

1. Not guilty of the alleged offense(s);

2. Guilty of one or more of the alleged offenses; and

3. A finding which is inconclusive, yet remains hanging over his head, thus continuing the suspicion of guilt.

Businesses tend to render one of the first two options, and schools and institutions of higher learning, are equally inclined to find any of the three. Yet ironically, the more autocratic the organization, the greater the likelihood it will render a finding of either 2 or 3. I haven't enough data or insight to know why, but I suspect that many decision-makers find outcome 3 the least difficult and the most palatable. You see, lacking clear objectives, sound policies, procedures, and practices it easy to declare one's effort inconclusive.

Few find it possible to successfully question a finding where the fact-finders simply claim, their findings inconclusive for the lack of proof! How brave, how bold, these morons.

Such a finding is unfair to everyone. And for that reason and others, I am so fond of the falsely accused aggressively taking the offensive. It is why I propose he hire a lawyer and, if justified, attack his prosecutors with a vengeance. As detailed in the prior chapter, the falsely accused should bring to bear every tool he has and take the fight to those who seek his scalp. But do the parties really need to get rough? I actually think not. While taking a firm position and defending his innocence, the falsely accused and his team might consider seeking a middle ground.

Litigation

As discussed in great detail in the prior chapter, litigation is expensive, and generally inefficient. What's more, litigation requires a cause of action. That is, there must be a *matter at issue.* There must exist a question of fact that is disputable. For that reason, the plaintiff must bring forth legally recognized claims, which must survive the defendant's effort to dismiss them. Resultantly, should there be no claims, there is no case, and thus, there can be no litigation. For these reasons and others, the falsely accused cannot simply claim he is innocent and sue his accuser and her employer or school.

If that is not enough, the plaintiff must also prove damages. That is, he must convincingly articulate the harm he suffered. Only after the harm is successfully articulated, can damages be determined. In most cases those damages translate into dollars. To do that, an array of experts (yep, they come again) are used to assist in determining how many dollars are justifiable. Economic damage experts are necessary to assist the trier of fact in determining the proper amount of dollars for the damages suffered. So again, it is possible the plaintiff can have a case and win, but have no damages.

Accordingly, good attorneys often tell their clients that litigation should be the path of last resort. I agree. But, the mere assertion that one has a case, is enough to open the door to his next option, that being mediation.

Mediation

Mediation is a dynamic, structured, interactive process where an impartial third party (often a former judge) assists disputing parties in resolving conflict or contested issues through the use of specialized communication and negotiation techniques. All participants in mediation are encouraged to actively participate in the process. Mediation is a *party-centered* process in that it is focused primarily upon the needs, rights, and interests of the parties. The mediator uses a wide variety of techniques to guide the process in a constructive direction and to help the parties find their optimal solution. A mediator is facilitative in that she/he manages the interaction between parties and facilitates open communication which otherwise may be impossible. Mediation is also evaluative in that the mediator analyzes issues and relevant norms using *reality-testing* while refraining from providing prescriptive advice to the parties such as "you should" or "you might consider."

Mediation, as used in law, is a recognized form of alternative dispute resolution, resolving disputes between two or more parties with concrete effects. Typically, a third party, the mediator, assists the parties to negotiate a settlement. Disputants may mediate disputes in a variety of domains, such as commercial, legal, diplomatic, workplace, community, and family matters. Having used mediation twice myself, I found it both fascinating and effective. However, to succeed, both parties must be willing to be reasonable and consider compromise. More specifically, mediation has a structure, timetable, and dynamics that other forms of negotiation lack. The process is private and confidential, and in some cases enforced by law. However, participation is typically voluntary. The mediator acts as a neutral third party and facilitates, rather than directs the process.

Mediators use various techniques to open, or improve, dialogue and empathy between disputants, aiming to help the parties reach an agreement. Much depends on the mediator's skill and training. As their use has gained popularity, training programs, certifications, and licensing has taken place in many states. Even when unsuccessful, it often permits each party to better understand the motive and drivers behind the other's position and needs.

But, short of a mandate or court order, mediation is only possible if the parties agree to come together. Either party may suggest it, but if either party is purely ideologically driven, success is rarely possible. Your lawyer is the best person to assist you in deciding whether to propose mediation or immediately go to the nuclear option...and litigate.

Arbitration

Like mediation, arbitration is a form of alternative dispute resolution (ADR), and like mediation, it is used as a way to resolve disputes outside the courts. Unlike mediation, the dispute is decided by one or more persons representing each of the parties. In countries such as the United States, arbitration is also frequently employed in consumer and employment matters, where arbitration may be mandated by the terms of employment or commercial contracts and may include a waiver of the right to bring litigation including class action claims. Mandatory consumer and employment arbitration are not consensual.

Typically, in employment matters, a labor contract between the employer and a collective bargaining unit (a union or its equivalent), requires all labor related matters including wages, benefits, and employee discipline be resolved by arbitrations. In consumer related matters, mandatory arbitration is used to avert class actions and coffer draining product liability litigation. But at the same time, some arbitrations are voluntary and typically nonhostile. Alternatively, non-binding arbitration is similar to mediation in that a decision cannot be imposed on the parties. However, the principal distinction is that whereas a mediator will try to help the parties find a middle ground on which to compromise, the (non-binding) arbiter remains totally removed from the settlement process and will only give a determination of liability, and, if appropriate, an indication of the *quantum* of damages payable.

Of course arbitrators are expected to be neutral, but like most people, they can have their moments and have been known in labor disputes to be openly tyrannical.

Here is a quick comparison of arbitration and mediation:

Arbitration vs. Mediation

The arbitrator decides the matter	With the aid of the mediator, the parties decide the matter
Proceedings are formal	Proceeding are informal
Less expensive than litigation	Less expensive than arbitration
Tensions can be high and emotional	Relationships likely to be maintained
Resolution is binding, upheld by the courts except in very narrow circumstances	Parties participate in the process and shape the resolution, or may reject it

As an option for the falsely accused, resolution to the conflict between he and his accuser, arbitration often makes sense, if the organization representing her is agreeable.

Restitution

The law of restitution is the law of gains-based recovery. It is to be contrasted with the law of compensation, which is the law of loss-based recovery. When a court orders restitution, it orders the defendant to give up his/her gains to the claimant. When a court orders compensation, it orders the defendant to pay the claimant for his or her loss or damages.

American Jurisprudence, 2nd Edition notes, the word *restitution* was used in earlier common law to denote the return or restoration of a specific thing or condition. In modern legal usage, its meaning has frequently been extended to include not only the restoration or giving back of something to its rightful owner and returning to the status quo, but also compensation, reimbursement, indemnification, or reparation for benefits derived from, or for, loss or injury caused to, another. In summary, therefore, the word restitution means the relinquishment of a benefit or the return of money or other property obtained through an improper means to the person from whom the property was taken.[89]

Restitution may be either a legal remedy or an equitable remedy, depending upon the basis for the plaintiff's claim and the nature of the underlying remedies sought. In matters where the particular harm at issue cannot be particularly identified, restitution is a legal remedy. This occurs, for example, when the plaintiff seeks a judgment imposing personal liability to pay a sum of money.[90]

The orthodox view suggests that there is only one principle on which the law of restitution is dependent, namely the principle of unjust enrichment. However, the view that restitution, like other legal responses, can be triggered by any one of a variety of causative events is increasingly prevalent. Thus, it appears it is possible one may be entitled to restitution for damages to his reputation. Some lawyers have proposed that there is a third basis for restitution, namely the vindication of property rights with which the defendant has interfered. But, again I am not a lawyer and such matters are well beyond my expertise. Nevertheless, damage to one's reputation as a result of a false allegation certainly exists if the false allegation is publicized and garners public attention. Among other things, the Duke University lacrosse team scandal in March 2006 is a perfect example of the reputational destruction a false allegation can inflict on an individual's reputation and almost one's associates…as well as the university that mishandled the allegations in the first place.

A less complicated form of restitution is a simple and unequivocal apology. Combined with back wages, reimbursement of legal fees, related costs, and a generous severance package (if appropriate), a simple apology could go a long way. In the case of a falsely accused student, the refund of all tuition, housing costs, incidentals and the release of all transcripts, along with a written apology with letter of recommendation might suffice. Alternatively, should the falsely accused student wish not to transfer and remain enrolled, he might be offered to continue his education tuition-free until graduation.

On the heels of internal investigations of employee misconduct that I performed, I have for years recommended my clients contemplate allowing the accused the opportunity to quietly resign and receive some form of severance in exchange for a release and hold-harmless agreement. In lieu of the undesirable effects of termination of employment by the employer, even those guilty of a serious offense can be permitted to move on with their dignity and self-respect intact. As the remarkably accomplished and wise employment lawyer, Bill Berger once told me, only angry and embarrassed employees sue their employer.

For the employers and school administrators who have difficulty accepting the guilty going unpunished as a result of such arrangements and agreements, they might be asked if harsh punishment was so effective and served as worthy deterrent, why are our prisons nearly full and criminal recidivism so high?

For the innocent, merely walking away with a check or a pat on the back may not be enough. And why should it? While the #MeToo movement seeks justice for women, ought there not be some form of justice and support for the falsely accused? Well there are, many of them actually. Most seek justice for the wrongfully accused and imprisoned. Organizations such as the National Center for Reason and Justice tell their supporters that:

> "Justice, community safety—and children themselves—are being gravely harmed, all in the name of child protection.
>
> Innocent Americans are wrongfully accused and imprisoned for sex crimes against children. Parents and guardians of children who die in accidents or fires are charged with homicide. In these cases, coerced testimony and junk forensic science sway judges, juries, and reporters, whose common sense is eclipsed by the mere suggestion of "harm to minors."
>
> [H]arsh post-incarceration restrictions prevent former sex offenders from reclaiming productive, law-abiding lives through work, family, education, worship, or civic engagement.
>
> In America's extraordinarily cruel criminal justice system, excessive punishment of sex offenders often is used as a wedge to impose similar practices on other offenders. Reforming sex offender laws and other statutes involving juvenile victims can help restore the human rights and dignity of all criminal offenders."[91]

Then of course is the Innocence Project., whose mission is to "Free the staggering number of innocent people who remain incarcerated, and to bring reform to the system responsible for their unjust imprisonment."[92] Its work and that of its many volunteers, is world renowned. But maybe the most interesting and relevant to the topic of this book is its work relative to forensic science. According to its website:

"Our efforts to free the wrongfully convicted and reform criminal justice policies require robust analysis of what has gone wrong and how these errors can be prevented....

A top priority is to improve the accuracy and reliability of forensic science. We work at the federal level to encourage science-based evaluation of validity of forensic disciplines, funding for research, development of national standards, and support for judicial training. At the state level, we work to address reforms needed to ensure consideration by the courts of new scientific evidence, including evidence discrediting previous expert testimony, and to strengthen the oversight of local and state forensic laboratories.

We also provide resources to assist researchers, lawyers, and others interested in learning about wrongful conviction. These resources include statistics about exoneration cases, systematic literature reviews of specific research questions, analyses of special topics, and ideas for future research."[93]

And for the criminally falsely convicted and imprisoned there is compensation available. The federal wrongful conviction compensation statute is the only statute that offers higher compensation for those who spent time on death row. Under the federal statute, a person can be awarded up to $50,000 per year of wrongful imprisonment and up to $100,000 per year on death row. Interestingly, many states have a version of the federal law. However, several states require that the person did not "contribute to their own conviction" in order to reap the benefits of the state's compensation statute. In other words, a person who falsely confessed or pleaded guilty to a crime he or she did not commit could be prohibited from receiving compensation. I will leave you to decide if that is fair.

Recovery

Allegedly, Alan Dershowitz, stated in his book, *Guilt by Accusation: The Challenge of Proving Innocence in the Age of #MeToo*, "I had someone say to me at a public event 'I know you're innocent but why don't you just fall on your sword in order to help the #MeToo Movement?'"[94] Whether true or not, to have even though such a thing, is remarkable onto itself. To have imagined that an innocent person should admit to something as serious as sexual assault so as to support and further the mission of a *movement* is stunning. Of course people lie in order to avoid punishment, but to be so committed to a social movement that one might even think men should sacrifice themselves to uphold a narrative is indeed worrisome.

But recovery from the experience of being falsely accused and subject to a trial by ordeal is not for the faint-hearted. In the third chapter, *Trial by Ordeal*, I described its origin and methods in detail. Used widely in the Dark Ages, the tactic held that death was the only proof of innocence. Equally worrisome is how rare it is that an accuser making a false allegation is held accountable.

Over six years ago in 2014, California became the first state to require university students to receive "active consent" before engaging in any sexual activity. Then governor, Jerry Brown signed into law a bill that imposed the new standard for consent at all colleges that receive state funding, including all public universities and many private institutions where students were receiving state grants or other financial assistance. The statute provides that consent can be conveyed by a verbal "yes," or signaled in a nonverbal way, but the lack of resistance or objection would not constitute consent. Advocates for victims of sexual assault have said that the new rules would remove the onus from victims to prove they said "no." Critics have since correctly argued the law unfairly shifts the burden of proof to the accused.

The law also provided other protections to include universities offer on-campus victims' advocates; victims who come forward to report a sexual assault may not be punished for under-age drinking; and all institutions are strictly required to teach incoming freshmen about sexual assault and consent during orientation. But one has to ask, what are the consequences of making a false allegation and how on earth might the falsely accused recover from such an ordeal? From where does he recover his reputation, dignity, and honor. Regretfully, I am unsure if I have a definitive answer or worthy suggestion.

What is clear, is that while the #MeToo movement, in its purest sense, embodies natural goodness and intent, in practice it has become a mercenary ethic that anyone can hire to fight for their cause. One's full emotional recovery is not possible until he understands that the false accusations against him were never really about him. Nor were they about defending human rights and gender equality. No, he was simply an unfortunate instrument used by others in search of power.

Things We Can Control

While there are some things we cannot control, there are many things we can. Throughout the ages, in spite of plague, famine, and war, much of humanity has sought peace and happiness. Eutychia was the Greek goddess of happiness. Her Roman equivalent is Felicitas and she was joined by Laetitia, the Roman goddess of joy and gaiety. Even in the English language we have names that convey happiness and joy. The name Carol represents the song of happiness, Gale was originally intended for those with a cheerful and boisterous nature, and the now rare name Winnifred, meaning happiness and simple joy.

While finding happiness and joy is a pursuit, maintaining it is the ability to control that which we can, and knowing that which we are unable. Here is a list of things most of us can control if we wish:

1. Our beliefs;

2. Our dignity;

3. Our attitude;

4. Our thoughts;

5. Our perspective;

6. Our purpose and pride;

7. Our willingness to forgive; and

8. Our enjoyment of life and shared happiness.

By releasing and accepting the things over which we have no control, we are given more time to control the things we can.

Here is a simple, but very unpleasant example. Imagine for a moment you are the victim of a false allegation involving sexual harassment or other serious behavior in the workplace. Following the embarrassment of a lengthy investigation by HR, you are then terminated. In need of employment, you begin a search and before even considering unemployment benefits, a friend makes a referral, and the next thing you know, an interview is scheduled. Good for you.

Appropriately you prepare. In doing so you realize that you will likely be asked why you left your former job. How might you answer it? Before you do, again read the list of eight things we can control shown above. Now consider how you would answer the question.

As a student of human behavior (all experienced investigators and HR professionals are you know [I'm smiling]), I am convinced that having read this far and having just re-read the list, your answer changed. Unless, you initially took a moment and reflected after reading the list the first time, and/or your spirit and courage is so strong that you had no need to read it the first time, the empowerment and courage you now possess should be enough to propel you and guide your response when asked such things.

An experienced HR professional (I am not smiling this time, I'm serious) knows well that not all investigations are created equal, nor are the allegations that precipitated them always true. As mentioned several times, it is not uncommon that some private sector investigations, whether work or school related, are driven not by facts, but by agenda. So upon hearing an applicant say with confidence and courage, he was falsely accused, and in spite of the truth, was fired, and the applicant knowing the possibility that such a disclosure might ruin his chance of being hired, would please the interviewer. Knowing that an informed prior employer, would never disclose that it had fired the applicant, no less reveal the reason for his termination, and yet the applicant courageously volunteered it, would necessitate moving his application to the top of the pile! By the way, the reason employers no longer reveal the reason an employee left them is because doing so could result in the former employee suing them. Knowing that a former employee merely claiming defamation or whatever the tort du jour might be at the time could be expensive to defend, why would any sophisticated employer want to help a likely competitor with a hiring decision?[95]

Understand also, employers and universities are competing for the best workers and students they can find. Of the attributes and qualifications sought in making decisions regarding employment and admissions, *character* is the most difficult to assess. Having been an employer and having offered pre-employment screening services to large employers for many years, I can attest that character can often trump skills and experience.[96] Skills can be taught and experience can be acquired, but character and integrity come from the heart.

Frequently Asked Questions

You've mentioned the possibility of damage awards several times in this chapter and elsewhere. Can you tell me more, and to whom and how they are awarded?

There are six different types of damages: compensatory, incidental, consequential, nominal, liquidated, and punitive. Damages are typically intended to return or restore that which belongs or is owed to the plaintiff. Of these, only several are applicable to the subject matter of this book. Compensatory damages are those that aid or directly compensate the nonbreaching party for the value of what was not done or performed. An example might be lost wages or backpay. Consequential damages are those incurred by the nonbreaching party without action on his part because of the breach. The taking-away or unnecessary loss of an athletic scholarship might be considered ripe for the award of consequential damages. And finally, there are punitive damages. Punitive damages are those awarded for the purpose of punishing a defendant in a civil action, in which criminal sanctions are of course unavailable. They are proper in cases where the defendant has acted willfully and maliciously and are thought to deter others from acting similarly. The facts of a case will determine the type of damages sought and the proof necessary to obtain those damages.

Given the complexity of the law and the array of claims a plaintiff might bring, is it often necessary to need more than one attorney?

Yes. As with many professions, lawyers too, specialize. In addition to specialties, some lawyers only take plaintiff cases with others accepting only defense cases.

Should I choose to litigate, will my attorney be able to make demands that the my former employer proved copies of the investigator's report and his notes?

Yes, of course. The process of requesting and demanding the production of evidence from the opposing party is called discovery. Your attorney should be reminded to request copies of the fact-finder's training file, CV, reports, and notes.

I am fearful that if I sue my former employer, word will get out and perspective employers might consider me to be a troublemaker. Is my concern valid?

Yes and no. It does appear at times that we live in a small world. But applicants with the right qualifications and experience are often difficult to find. As such, employers tend to consider all suitable applicants regardless of their litigation experience. Moreover, most HR professionals know the act of disqualifying an applicant who has sued a former employer because of age discrimination, could itself constitute age discrimination.

Hope is the strength in your moment of weakness, the light in the dark, the fire when it's cold. Hope is more powerful than fear, and is the only antidote to despair. For when we have hope, we can face even the most difficult challenges in our path. Like courage, hope offers us the belief that failure is not fatal, but the strength to carry on when it is almost certain.

---

[88] At the time of the interview, former Vice President Biden appeared to be the likely democratic candidate in the 2020 presidential election.

[89] American Jurisprudence (Second Edition is cited as Am. Jur. 2d) is an encyclopedia of the United States law, published by West. It was originated by Lawyers Cooperative Publishing, which was subsequently acquired by the Thomson Corporation. https://en.wikipedia.org/wiki/American_Jurisprudence captured, May 12, 2020.

[90] Quantum meruit is a Latin phrase meaning "what one has earned.". In the context of contract law, it means something along the lines of "reasonable value of services".

[91] https://ncrj.org/why-we-exist/

[92] https://www.innocenceproject.org/about/

[93] https://www.innocenceproject.org/Educate/

[94] https://www.forbes.com/sites/karlynborysenko/2020/02/12/the-dark-side-of-metoo-what-happens-when-men-are-falsely-accused/#e03f8864d85f
Note: I attempted to verify the attribution of this quote, but did not find it in his book. By the way, the book was exceptionally well written and quite the read.

[95] By the way, the Fair Credit Report Act, as amended, precludes perspective employers from inquiring about criminal arrests or matters for which the applicant was not convicted. Even in cases resulting in a criminal conviction, a perspective employer MUST limit their inquiries to the last seven years, commencing on the date of his or her application. See Appendix I for more details.

[96] To learn more about pre-employment screening does and don't see Appendix I

CHAPTER EIGHT

PREVENTION

A recent survey conducted by the HR consulting, case management, and service provider, *HR Acuity*, reveals that while in-house lawyers are routinely involved in their employer's internal investigations, the use of outside counsel is becoming more frequent. It appears that not only is outside counsel advising clients, they also are becoming active participants in their client's internal investigations, most often in the role of lead investigator. The survey also indicated that internal investigations have recently become more formalized, but only one-third of the respondents had "required processes", which utilized forms and templates for conducting investigations. Not surprisingly, large organizations were more likely to require the use of forms and templates than smaller ones. Another 45 percent of the respondents claimed to encourage the use of "investigation templates" and 14 percent had "no specific guidelines" or templates whatsoever.[97] Good news for plaintiff employment lawyers I suppose, but very bad news for the accused. But having read this far, I would think you now know why.

While I think lawyers can best serve their clients as counselors, internal investigations, whether conducted in the workplace or on campus, are more efficient and easier defended when driven by processes. As far back as I can remember, to squeeze opportunities for improvement out of our investigations, at the conclusion of a project or consultation, my team and I prepared what we came to call an *after-action report* for our client. Because our project report contained only facts and what we learned during the engagement, it contained no opinions or recommendations. But almost invariably, during the course of the engagement, we identified opportunities that could improve our client's organizational policies and procedures, if not our own. Only when having our client's permission, we memorialized our post-project review and findings in the form of an *after-action* report.

During this effort, our client and our investigative team joined together to critique the effort, bench mark, identify and/or validate best practices, and analyze the quality of their performance. Additionally, the team would search to understand how the original problem came about while attempting to identify points of failure. Together we attempted to determine what allowed the problem to occur and how it might be prevented in the future? The results can prove to be priceless. Clearly, if the organization continues the same practices, it is likely to get the same result again in the future. Such behavior is worse than pointless, it may also be negligent. Under the legal theory of foreseeability, negligence is compounded when a party *should have reasonably foreseen* an event that could have been prevented had it taken appropriate corrective or preventative action. Organizations often make this mistake and in doing so, incur unnecessary additional liability and distractions.

Effectively using the Plan-Do-Check-Act (PDCA) model as a process improvement tool, the team's findings can often be acted upon to effect process changes or improvements. The team's output can include suggestions to alter or modify policies, change or impose new practices and finally, training for those who need it. Of all of the phases of investigation and internal inquiries, this is the least utilized, and *HR Acuity's* research appears to verify it. In most instances once the project or undertaking has reached its completion no one is interested in doing anything further or expending more resources. But for those organizations with whom we undertook a formal postmortem, here are some of the more common opportunities we discovered:

1. **The need for more realistic policies and better procedures and practices**: Policies that make mandates using words such as must, shall, always and never are generally problematic. Like mandatory deadlines, these requirements confine the organization and reduces flexibility. Similarly, to the extent possible, processes should be flexible. Take a look at Appendix E, THE PROCESS OF INVESTIGATION FLOW CHART. Though detailed, notice that for nearly every action, the fact-finder and decision-maker(s) are provided options. Thus, the process is dynamic. And because the process conforms to the ANSI/ASIS INV.1-2015 Investigations Standard, one's investigation and use of the flow-chart are not only more defensible, they are more efficient. Contrarily, an organization where such processes and procedures are not in place is vulnerable to criticism and potentially legal challenges;

2. **Inconsistent policy enforcement practices**: It was not infrequent to have found inconsistencies regarding the disbursement of disciplinary and corrective actions. Common was the practice that hourly employees (and students) were held to a different standard than salaried employees (or faculty members); and

3. **Inconsistent standards of proof used in determining guilt or innocence**: Frequently, we observed that the standard of proof to discipline an hourly employee was lower than that of a salaried employee. In rare cases, we found that

235

the standard of proof necessary to discipline a senior executive was so high, it wasn't possible to achieve. The best example is a standard or practice that requires the executive to admit to the offense in order to be disciplined for committing it.

The result of these irregularities tend to make the organization's decision-making process more difficult to enforce and defend. They can impose an adverse effect on employee/student morale and the organization's reputation. For a vivid example look no further than Steve Wynn. At the beginning of January 2018, Wynn was a 75-year-old billionaire and chairman and CEO of Wynn Resorts. He had built and owned the property he named, The Mirage in Las Vegas, and was working on developing a $2.6 billion resort in Massachusetts. But by the beginning of February, Wynn would be unemployed and facing public shame and an uncertain future. Complicating his life was a January 26, 2018, *Wall Street Journal* article that had disclosed disturbing and graphic allegations regarding Wynn's sexual misconduct involving Wynn Resorts' female employees over decades. Accusations included sexual harassment, coercion, indecent exposure, and an alleged sexual assault case, which he ultimately paid $7.5 million to settle. Many of the allegations were made by salon and spa employees at his Wynn Las Vegas property, the luxury resort where Wynn primarily resided.

Though to this day, many facts remain unclear, the allegations destroyed Wynn and his reputation and damaged that of many others inside and outside of his organization, including outside counsel. Based on the little information available, it appears Wynn Resorts may have had failures in all three of the areas mentioned above.

Clearly, an organization's failure to properly align its mission, vision and values, with its policies, procedures, and practices cannot only lead to ruined lives and reputations, it is expensive. The thought that frequently runs through my head after such disasters is again and again, *what were these people thinking?* With jury awards in the millions of dollars in matters with similar failures, I suspect many jurors have thought the same thing.

However, alignment of an organization's mission, vision, and values, with its policies, procedures, and practices is not enough. Organizational members must also be equipped with the tools that enable them to make better decisions regarding workplace behavior and the means by which they uphold their values. Drivers generally know the speed limit of roads on which they travel, yet some drivers choose to speed. While the decision to speed is often the product of a simple risk benefit analysis, in many cases so is workplace behavior. Subjecting others to intimidating remarks, sexual propositions, and unwanted physical contact has no place in a civilized society, no less a workplace. Employers who tolerate an atmosphere of harassment and permit uncivil behavior, yet are champions of women's rights and equality are hypocrites. Sadly, there are many such employers.

Employee hotlines and helplines enable employees to anonymously speak out and report inappropriate behavior. But unless the organization is willing to address complaints, their mission, vision, and values are merely window dressing. To further fluff their image, some employers offer their employees unlimited paid time off, paid family leave, wellness bonuses, stock options, well stocked kitchens with hot cocoa and treats, and free cold beer. I know, I worked for such an organization not long ago. But at the end of the day what matters is the character of the organization's leadership, the honoring of its promises, and doing the right thing when no else is looking. Such attributes are rare. True leaders are not judged by their words, but by their actions.

Another post-investigation tool we found useful were surveys. Let's take a look and see why?

The Art and Science of Employee Surveys

Employee surveys have been in use for decades. But only in the last twenty years have they become sophisticated management improvement tools. Whether used to control an organization's employee or student experience, or assist management make policy decisions or mold their cultures, these tools are inexpensive and easy to use. Even tools like SurveyMonkey allow quick, easy to deploy surveys, without training or programming skills.

Key to their successful use is the styling of questions. Variables in question design include:

1. Number and sequence;

2. Length and wording;

3. Permissibility of closed or open answers; and

4. Whether the questions demand factual or attitudinal insights.

Questions that are vague or, use technical jargon, are relevant to only a segment of survey-takers. Those that use phrasing that is interpreted differently across audiences sabotage survey effectiveness and can frustrate employees. Multiple choice answers, likewise, are a concern when there are missing plausible choices, or when choices are too wordy or too numerous. In my use of employee surveys, short, direct and relevant questions produce the most valuable information.

Surveys also assist organizations in identifying systemic or operational failure points. They can also measure members' trust in management and the need for improvement. Because of their prevalence in today's public and private institutions, those organizations that do not use them can create a perception of disinterest and disregard for its employees or students. Boring questions are not particularly helpful either. According to Survey Monkey here are the top seven questions customers ask their

238

organizational members:

1. What changes would most improve our new service, specify new service?

2. What do you like most/least about our (service offering; benefit; product; etc.)?

3. What changes would most improve our new (service offering; benefit; product; etc.)?

4. What do you like most/least about our new (service offering; benefit; product; etc.)?

5. Overall, are you satisfied with your experience using our (specify product), neither satisfied or dissatisfied with it, or dissatisfied with it?

6. Which category below includes your age?

7. Are you male or female?

Rather boring don't you think? These questions, though possibly serving a purpose, are uninteresting and impersonal. For fun, try answering this survey question, which was allegedly used by a national hair styling chain: A stylist styles only the hair of those who do not style their own hair. Does she style her own hair? While the paradox may be entertaining and serve no apparent purpose, arguably it could serve as an introduction to a very serious and useful short survey.

In addition to identifying organizational attitudes, surveys can identify hotspots in need of attention. While one would hope the that the organization's mission, vision and values are consistent across all regions and subunits, we know from experience it is not always true. Surveys can quickly and economically identify divisions, units, groups, and teams that need attention, or assistance.

Do you agree?   ☐ Yes   ☐ No

For a few more ideas to improve employee relations and demonstrate appreciation for one's employees visit my website InDefenseofTheInnocent.org.

Student Discipline Best Practices

Like businesses, many of our schools and institutions of higher learning have procedural and process shortcomings as well. The first place to find their shortcomings are in their Code of Conduct. Like employee handbooks and workplace policy manuals, schools need foundational guidelines regarding schoolplace behavior and expectations, which are memorialized in writing. Only by developing and implementing a comprehensive and lawful Code of Conduct can a school expect to effectively and responsibly manage the environment it controls. That code should address the health and welfare of all parties, including the students, their family members, guardians, faculty, employees, advisors, assistants, volunteers, campus security, and anyone else directly associated with the school.

Here are some of the activities and practices I recommend attention be given:

1. Define infractions and consequences with specificity. Include a section on special education considerations that track federal law and requirements. Make sure all students and their parents or custodians, as well as any other student influencer, receive the Code and any revisions that are released;

2. Consistently and uniformly implement the Code of Conduct. The ignorance of disciplinary practices and sloppy execution can negate a strong Code. Annually train all staff and those that it effects on the Code and its expectations;

3. Create template letters that effectively communicate suspension status and information regarding scheduled disciplinary hearings. Such letters should advise students of alleged violations of the Code of Conduct and their due process rights. These communications should make a student's current suspension status clear and address any alternative educational services that the school will provide to a suspended student;

4. Ensure that students with disabilities are disciplined in accordance with applicable federal and state law. Students with disabilities should be afforded due process protections such as a manifestation determination review in advance of any proposed long-term suspension or expulsion;

5. Understand that federal protections apply to students who may be in need of special education and related services but do not yet have an Individualized Education Program (IEP). School policies and practices should direct staff to abide by special education due process protections when disciplining students whom they believe may be eligible to be identified as having a disability;

6. Provide appropriate and legally sufficient alternative educational services to students who are suspended. State laws vary on the nature and extent of alternative educational offerings;

7. Follow lawful practices when disciplining a student who brings weapons or drugs to school, or whose behavior constitutes a danger to themselves or others, to place them in interim alternative educational settings for up to 45 days in accordance with federal and state law.

8. Establish a clear, lawful process for conducting disciplinary hearings. Make it detailed and explicit in order to provide maximum clarity, fairness, and efficiency. Ensure all due process rights. Make evidentiary rules clear and properly documented;

9. Appoint neutral, capable hearing officers who have no conflicts of interest. Avoid appointing a staff member or other person who has been involved with the incident(s) at issue. Consider appointing a person from outside of the school community to serve as hearing officer; and

10. Establish a clear, lawful process for conducting disciplinary appeals. Make it detailed and explicit in order to provide maximum clarity. Notify students and families appealing a disciplinary ruling of any additional appeals or challenges allowed by state law,

Student discipline mistakes, which can be easily avoided:

1. There should not be substantial suspension (e.g., more than a few school days) in advance of a hearing determining whether or not a substantial suspension is warranted. If a hearing cannot be quickly scheduled, consider allowing the student to return to campus and attend class until the hearing date;

2. Avoid creating practices that limit student access to class, but fall outside of the Code of Conduct. Ill-conceived suspension policies or practices can skirt due process;

3. Do not engage in practices that impermissibly limit student access to the campus or class;

4. Do not overlook basic due process even for short-term suspensions. In Goss v. Lopez, the U.S. Supreme Court

established the minimum process for any suspension: The student has the right to be confronted with the charges and tell his or her side of the story; in some states, courts have determined that parents have the right to have the circumstances explained to them and to ask questions. Suspensions that fall short of this standard may be unlawful. A more formal hearing is required for longer suspensions and expulsions;

5. Avoid scheduling a disciplinary hearing either too quickly or with too much delay. If appropriate, parents should be given several days to seek an attorney and to arrange to attend the hearing. But especially where the accused student is suspended pending the hearing, the school should try to hold the hearing without delay;

6. Once a hearing officer or Title IX panel has been identified or empaneled, the hearing officers should not be made aware of the school's preparation of its case, unless policy dictates otherwise. In order to maintain impartiality, the hearing officer should not be made aware of either party's perspective, evidence, or intentions in advance of the hearing;

7. Do not misuse the interim alternative educational setting for students with disabilities. Federal and state laws may require students to be placed in an interim alternative education setting for up to 45 days in instances involving weapons, drugs, or dangerous behavior. The threshold for dangerous behavior is high, and must be extreme to trigger this emergency practice. Students must present a genuine threat to themselves or others;

8. When the combative behavior of a student warrants it—or he is known to be at risk and linked to a violation necessitating disciplinary action, exercise appropriate

precaution. For the safety of the student and others, a Functional Behavioral Assessment (FBA) should be considered and a Behavioral Intervention Plan (BIP) created to address the potentially challenging behavior, while preserving the dignity of the student and his accuser;

9. Do not fail to create a clear record of communications with families during disciplinary matters, and if appropriate during the investigation. Letters and emails should attest to a school's efforts to ensure that its policies and due process requirements are followed. Misunderstandings, disagreements, and other problems often arise when communications are informal or inconsistent; and

10. Do not fail to treat the accused with respect and dignity. Sadly, it may be the only thing of value they have left.[98]

How to Properly Handle a Termination or Separation

Experience has shown that if the lessons learned are not leveraged, workplace problems and school place issues tend to reappear and repeat themselves. As such, passing up the opportunity to learn from past mistakes and implement best practices seems to be a heavy price to pay for simply wanting to close a file and move on to the next project. Of the areas needing the most attention during our postmortems are employee terminations and separations, and student expulsions.

In the world of HR and employment law, the termination of employment is considered the equivalent of capital punishment. The same might be said for a for-cause expulsion. As such, it should be the choice of last resort. For this reason and others, the termination of employees and the permanent expulsion of a student in any one or more protected classes (age, race, color, gender, etc.) should be very carefully decided and orchestrated. Additionally, sophisticated decision-makers always consider alternatives to termination or expulsion. Barring past practices or court orders, only when alternatives are not available or have been tried and failed, should employers chose to terminate, or schools expel a student.

Alternatives might include:

1. Change of classification, duties, schedule, responsibilities, worksite, or other reasonable accommodation(s). In the case of a student, he or she might be transferred;

2. One-on-one coaching and counseling; and

3. Sensitivity, skills or technical retraining that may be beneficial to the organization.

When none of these options are available and the decision to terminate still seems too harsh, a common option is offer continued employment at a reduced pay rate or salary. Unethical employers sometimes use this option and over time reduce the employee's compensation to a level it is no longer economically possible for him/her to stay. Thus the employee will quit of their own accord. A "bleed-out" is a form of constructive discharge and is typically litigated as such.

According to HR generally accepted best practices, all terminations should be carefully considered, and around the decision to terminate should be a strategy that preserves the dignity of the individual, while closely following the organizations policies, past practices, and precedents. Equally, the rights of the employee should be carefully considered and protected. Once the decision to terminate an employee is made and vetted by the appropriate organizational authorities (including counsel), it should be communicated to the employee both verbally and in writing, in a timely fashion. Best practices dictate the termination of employees at the executive level should be particularly carefully handled as they pose significant litigation and reputational risks to the organization. It is common in such cases, legal counsel is used to provide guidance to ensure both the decision and action are handled appropriately and in accordance to the law. Rarely, is counsel used to communicate the decision to the employee in question.

In instances where the employee chosen for termination raises the issue of discrimination and/or retaliation, an investigation of the allegation is required. Title VII and various aspects of EEOC federal law require employers who knew, or should have known of possible harassment, discrimination, or retaliation to investigate.[99] A delay to investigate may be used as evidence that the employer condoned or even ratified the unlawful conduct. Also supporting "an employer's duty to investigate" are an assortment of EEOC Informal Discussion Letters, which address the general duty to investigate. Moreover, an employer's failure to investigate:

1. May be used as a basis to show the organization failed to prevent discrimination from occurring or condoned/ratified the unlawful conduct;

2. May be used by the aggrieved employee as an independent cause of action; and

3. May create an inference of malice, which could be basis to award punitive damages.

Additionally, it is well established that an employer's investigation be "timely and proper." HR best practices suggest that the investigation begin with an interview of the complainant. Doing so benefits the employer in several ways:

1. It demonstrates that the employer considers the allegation(s) serious and that it recognizes its duty to prevent/address

discrimination, harassment, and retaliation when it suspects (or should suspect) it has occurred;

2. It assists the employer in identifying the full nature and scope of the allegation(s); and

3. It provides the employer an opportunity to contain or establish boundaries around the complainant's allegations preventing them from expanding or morphing later.

According to the EEOC's website, "An employment policy or practice that applies to everyone, regardless of age, can be illegal if it has a negative impact on applicants or employees age 40 or older and is not based on a reasonable factor other than age (RFOA)."[100] On the same page is this, "The law [ADEA] forbids discrimination when it comes to any aspect of employment, including hiring, firing, pay, job assignments, promotions, layoff, training, fringe benefits, and any other term or condition of employment."

Employment attorneys often advise employers involved in terminations of employees who pose a risk of litigation to not provide a reason for the termination. Instead, they typically suggest the employer hold firm to its "at-will" prerogative and communicate such to the employee. This is a mistake. For every decision to terminate, there is obviously a reason. Though not required by law in most states, the failure to communicate a reason suggests that the employer's motive is either not easily defendable or unlawful, thus encouraging the litigation it is attempting to avoid. Similarly, using counsel to communicate the decision to terminate to the employee in question suggests the employer is hiding something and is not confident that the decision can be properly communicated by a member of the organization without revealing damaging information. Triers-of-fact typically see through these schemes and judge employers that use them accordingly.

To ease the emotional consequences of termination for the employee and life-disruptions it creates, there are several common HR tools, which thoughtful employers use. When justifiable, the most common include:

1. A generous severance package in exchange for a release of liability and another claims the employee might bring;

2. Outplacement services and job search assistance;

3. Actively referring the individual to other employers it knows or thinks may be hiring;

4. Coaching and counseling;

5. Use of organizational office space and/or equipment as a place to work while job seeking;

6. Reference letters or letters of recommendation; and

7. A thank you letter to the employee for his/her service. As hard as it might be to swallow, this rather simple gesture demonstrates the character of the organization and its leadership. It needn't be over-done, nor should it appear insincere. But consider for a moment, has an employer ever provided you a thank you letter...for any reason? How would you feel if having received one?[101]

Parting Thoughts

I mentioned in one of my prior books, that the famous jurist, Oliver Wendell Holmes thoughtfully mused almost 100 years ago, "We need education [of] the obvious more than the investigation of the obscure." The son of an accomplished physician, philosopher, and poet, Supreme Court Justice Holmes is considered one of the greatest legal minds in U.S. history. During the end of the 19th Century he witnessed the birth of the secular progressive movement and the rise of modern science, which helped advance it. Civilization's infatuation with self-actualization and social experimentation was so obsessive, world leaders embraced the metaphysical and even thought they could obsolete war simply by outlawing it. Justice Holmes was more pragmatic. He reasoned that without a fundamental understanding of the fundamental, nothing complex was thinkable, no less attainable.

I suspect the same to be true when dealing with people. I mentioned in the prior chapter that I was once told, "only angry and embarrassed employees sue their employer." I think it's true, and something similar is probably true as well when it comes to schools expelling students. While I have never been soft on crime and strongly disapprove of indecent and boorish behavior, I believe that one's punishment should be proportional to the offense committed. At the same time, I believe not all offenses deserve punishment. Sometimes the offer of an apology and a corresponding acceptance can be enough. Not all crimes deserve capital punishment, and not all transgressions deserve the loss of one's employment or scholarship.

Maybe it's time we all sit back, take a deep breath and ask "how did we get here?" Isn't it possible that all men are not filthy pigs? Isn't it possible in our new #MeToo world where men are guilty until proven innocent, that some of them are truly innocent? I think so and I hope you now think so too. Because, *without a fundamental understanding of the fundamental, nothing complex is thinkable—no less attainable.*

[97] https://www.hracuity.com/resources

[98] Substantially developed using guidance provided by https://charterschoolcenter.ed. gov/

[99] See Bator v. State of Hawaii (9th Cir. 1994) 39 F. 3d 1021; Nichols v. Azteca Restaurant Enterprises, Inc. [9th Cir. 2001] 256 F. 3d 864; and Fuller v. City of Oakland [9th Cir. 1995] 47 F. 3d 1522.

[100] www.eeoc.gov/age-discrimination

[101] To learn more about the proper way to handle an employee termination, see Appendix K.

AFTERWORD

S hould you have read this far, you are aware that I am of the mind that the #MeToo movement has done significant damage to our culture and what little confidence we had in our system of justice. If one needs more proof, Hawaii Senator Mazie Hirono has eagerly provided it. Nearly hysterical, she confidently instructed those who cared to listen, "Just shut up and step up. Do the right thing for a change."[102] In full support of the Supreme Court nominee Brett Kavanaugh's accuser, Senator Hirono went on to inform us, "Not only do women like Dr. Ford, who bravely comes forward need to be heard, but they need to be believed...They need to be believed!" So important was her message, Senator Hirono chose not to disclose that it was in fact fellow Senator Dianne Feinstein who had leaked Dr. Ford's identity, violating her promise to not involve her or disclose her name to anyone.

Not only has the movement been selective in choosing the victims it celebrates, it has brought to our campuses the foolishness of safe-spaces, speech codes, and the introduction of the use of hot cocoa and cuddly stuffed toy animals to comfort our distraught and defenseless victims. With remarkable and seemingly seamless efficiency, it shifted the burden of proof from the accuser to the accused. In many ways, having done so, it rebirthed a mindset last experienced in America in the mid-19th century, when women were widely considered defenseless and powerless. Though that movement gave way to the Progressive Era along with calls for temperance, women's education, suffrage, and moral purity. The Dress Reform movement called for emancipation from the "dictates of fashion," freeing not only the body, but the mind, and one's choice of dress.

Cultural changes have never been easy. Looking back, many of those changes were necessary and appropriate. Who today, would oppose a woman's right to vote, wear pants, or ride a bicycle? But not all shifts and cultural changes are healthy, nor do they all produce good. If one is truly rational, shouldn't he or she still ask *should all victims be believed and is our society better when we insist the accused must prove his innocence?* Who gains from such ideas and why must we trust those who embrace them? Remember it was in the 1960's we were introduced to bra-burnings and free love. So convinced of the women's liberation movement's momentum, America's largest corporations joined the charge. In 1967, Virginia Slims cigarette commercials reminded women, "You've come a long way, Baby!" And a mere five years later, Title IX became the law of the land.

From 1973 to today, women have made great advances. At times against terrific resistance and discrimination, however, they marshalled on, opened doors, and penetrated or brought down countless barriers. Our children, our society, and our country is better for it. But I believe that there can always be a bridge too far.

On March 23, 2006, forty-six of forty-seven members of the Duke University Lacrosse team complied with a judge's order to provide DNA after a young woman told Durham, North Carolina police that she was forced into a bathroom by three men and beaten, raped, and sodomized during a party at which she was a dancer. The sole black member of the team was not tested, because the accuser said all of her attackers were white. Though the DNA testing failed to identify a single attacker, a grand jury indicted the three the victim had identified as her assailants. After a year of agony, uncertainty, and soul-searching, on April 11, 2007, North Carolina Attorney General Roy Cooper dropped all charges against the three innocent young men.

In light of AG Cooper's unequivocal declaration of innocence, a handful of journalists who had rushed to judgment, issued apologies. The most heartfelt came from ESPN reporter/commentator, Jemele Hill. In an open letter to Reade Seligmann, Collin Finnerty, and David Evans posted on the news service's website, Hill acknowledged an apology was, "not enough...For the last year, your lives and those of your families have been more difficult than any of us can possibly imagine. I'll never know what it was like walking around normal society labeled a rapist. I'll never know what it's like to lose everything—your school, your program, and your life—because of one unproven accusation...I can't deny that your race, gender, and class [had] everything to do with how you were treated then...Some people believe white men are exempt from sympathy and incapable of being maligned, so they will not swallow their pride and offer you the decency you should have received in the first place."

Though she had never advanced the idea that the players were guilty, Hill admitted that she had "felt it", believing it was, "just as bad." Sadly, many of District Attorney Mike Nifong's enablers in the media and the elites who had invested in their guilt, simply refused to accept their innocence. To this day, nary a murmur or apology they gave the young innocent men. Must we believe someone simply because of their gender? Must we always side with the accuser? What is it that we gain when we fail to consider the possibility that the accused may be innocent? Must everyone join Ms. Sheryl Sandberg and Senator Hirono? Or may those who believe *IN THE DEFENSE OF THE INNOCENT* continue to hold onto a world where we are all innocent until proven guilty?

Few things can take the place of perseverance.
Talent will not; nothing is more common than unsuccessful people
with talent. Genius will not; the world is full of educated derelicts, nor
will beauty or brawn. Perseverance and its companion determination,
together determine our fate. Combined they are omnipotent
and when seized, they can be ours forever.

---

[102] https://www.cnn.com/2018/09/18/politics/senator-mazie-hirono-men-shut-up-brett-kavanaugh-sexual-assault/index.html

APPENDIX A
GLOSSARY OF COMMON TERMS AND TERMINOLOGY

Note that these terms and definitions are those of the author and not necessarily the legal or common definition used for other purposes.

Accomplice   Criminal cohort or conspirator. One who aids and abets others in the commission of a crime or offense.

Accused   Originally used to identify someone who is charged with an offence or a defendant in a criminal case. More recently the *accused* describes anyone to which blame is or can be attached, whether charged and proven guilty or not.

Action   A lawsuit brought in court.

Actionable   Alleged conduct or behavior which may be subject to a legal action or intervention.

Addendum   A statement prepared by an interviewer on behalf of himself, not the interviewee. In it, the interview should include information not contained in the interviewee's statement (if one has been provided) or elsewhere during the investigative process.

Adjudicate   To legally resolve and bring to formal closure.

Administrative interview   Interviews conducted for the purpose of gather information, versus *investigatory interviews* which are conducted for the purpose to obtain *admissions*.

Admissibility   The legal authority permitting the entry of evidence into a legal proceeding.

Admissible   Evidence which may be formally considered in a legal proceeding.

Admission   The simple admission to the commission of an offense, work rule or policy violation, or violation of the law. Differs from a confession in that it may or may not contain all of the elements of the offense or crime in question. Not to be confused with *confession*. A properly obtained admission is a valuable piece of evidence in most workplace and private sector investigations.

Affirm   To uphold or establish.

Agency   A legal doctrine in which the legal duties and responsibilities of a government actor (i.e. the police) are conferred to its agent (a private fact-finder). The result often imparts rights to an individual (subject) not otherwise available.

Answer   A response to a formal legal allegation, normally in writing.

Appeal   An application to a higher court or correct or modify a judgment rendered by a lower court.

Assault   In most jurisdictions assault is defined as the threat of bodily harm that reasonably causes fear of harm in the victim. Often it is confused with battery which is unwanted physical contact with another person. If the victim has not actually been touched, but only then the offense is more properly called an assault.

Arbitration An informal means of alternate dispute resolution without the use of a judge or jury. An arbitrator presides over the proceedings and at its conclusion renders a decision in favor of one party or the other.

Arrest The taking of a person into custody in a manner provided by law for the purpose of detention in order to answer a criminal charge or civil demand.

Attorney Client Privilege A legal doctrine that protects certain communications between a client and his or her attorney and keeps those communications confidential.

Attorney Work Product Evidence which a party to a lawsuit does not have to reveal during the discovery process because it represents the thought process and strategy of the opposing attorney preparing for trial.

At-will-employment A policy (public or private) which allows an employer to terminate one's employment for any lawful reason or no reason at all. Such policies also permit the employee to quite with or without at will.

257

Beyond a reasonable doubt	The standard of proof necessary to obtain a conviction in a criminal proceeding.
Case file	The tool used by fact-finders to organize and maintain their records, documents and reports during an investigation.
Chain of Custody	A record detailing those who handled or possessed a piece of evidence. Synonymous with chain of evidence.
Chain of Evidence	See Chain of Custody.
Circumstantial evidence	Indirect evidence which in and of itself does not prove a material fact. Often gathered and used cumulatively to prove a fact.
Client	The individual or entity for which an investigation is performed. Note: A customer is a more general term used to indicate the recipient of a tangible or intangible service of product.
Coercion	To compel by force or deception.
Commercial fraud	Any type of fraud committed against a business or organization.
Compensatory damages	Damages awarded to a plaintiff that are intended to compensate for a loss or other hardship.

Confession A comprehensive admission to the commission of an offense or violation of the law that contains all of the elements of the offense or crime in question. Not to be confused with *admission*.

Corporate investigations Investigations performed at the direction of the organization, for the organization. Usually involves the investigation of crimes and offences committed against the organization. Differs from workplace investigations in that the subject of the investigation may not be an employee or former employee of the organization.

Covert surveillance Surveillance which is intentionally covert or undetected.

Credibility The reliability or trustworthiness of an individual.

Custodian of record The person or entity responsible for record retention and preservation.

Decision-maker The member of the investigative team responsible for making decisions regarding discipline and corrective action.

Defendant The accused. The party whom the plaintiff opposes.

Direct evidence Evidence which proves a material fact.

Discovery The legal process of obtaining information and/or evidence from a legal opponent.

Disparate treatment	Unfair or unequal treatment of an individual or group.
Double-hearsay evidence	Testimony from a person who has third hand knowledge.
Due process	The collection of rights principally arising from the Bill of Rights which provide criminal suspects protections against abuses by the government.
Electronic surveillance	Any form of surveillance which uses electronic technology and does not require constant human monitoring.
Embezzlement	The unlawful appropriation of property or assets of another of which one has been entrusted.
Entrapment	Entrapment is generally characterized as an intentional inducement which results in an otherwise honest person committing a crime, that without the inducement, that person would not have committed. Entrapment is an affirmative criminal defense and not a crime.
Ethics	A collection of "accepted principles that govern" a particular group or profession.
Evidence	Evidence is any type of proof that when presented, is materially capable of proving or disproving a contention or fact. In order to be used or admissible, the evidence must be material to the matter in question.

Exculpatory Evidence	Evidence favorable to the defendant in a criminal trial that exonerates or tends to exonerate the defendant of guilt. It is the opposite of inculpatory evidence, which tends to present guilt.
Fact pattern	The collection of known facts associated with or directly related to the matter in question.
Fact-finder	A person engaged in the systematic collection, analysis and preservation of information and/or facts related to the matter in question. The fact-finder is often a member of an investigative team and typically works under the direction of a project manager.
False imprisonment	The criminal or civil offense of improper arrest or detainment without confinement, of a person without proper warrant or authority for that purpose by force, intimidation or coercion.
Fidelity insurance	Commercial insurance coverage against employee theft and dishonesty.
Fraud	Theft by deceit and deception.
Fungible evidence	Evidence that has the capability of mutation, substitution, or degradation. For example, drugs and blood have been considered to be fungible evidence.

Good faith investigation   A fair and impartial investigation conducted by an employer on its behalf. When used to make a *reasonable conclusion* it becomes the standard of proof needed to justify employee discipline.

Hearsay evidence   Testimony from a person who has secondhand knowledge.

Helpline   Historically called a hotline, is an internal or externally managed resource allowing users (employees, students, etc.) to report issues adversely impacting them or their organization. Typically, helplines allow users the option of remaining anonymous.

Immunity   Protection against prosecution. Typically granted in order to obtain some form of cooperation.

Impeach   To render one's testimony useless or diminish their credibility.

Inadmissible   Evidence which cannot be formerly considered in a legal proceeding.

Intent   A state of mind which if proven, demonstrates the intention to commit a criminal act.

Interrogation   A highly structured and formal interview intended to yield a confession.

Interrogator   One who conducts interrogations.

Interview	A conversational exchange for the purpose of collecting information.
Interviewer	One who conducts interviews.
Investigation	A fact-finding process of logically, methodically, and lawfully gathering and documenting information for the specific purpose of objectively developing a reasonable conclusion based on the facts learned through this process.
Investigation findings	A result or conclusion reached after examination or investigation. NOTE: The term as used in the ANSI/ASIS Investigations Standard should not be confused with the word findings when used as a term of art by the legal profession. Generally, when used as such, the word describes the result of the deliberations of a jury or court following a judicial proceeding or investigation.
Investigation process	A structured and sometimes scientific approach to investigation. Sufficiently structured to provide uniformity and consistency yet, fluid and flexible enough to accommodate any situation or fact pattern.
Investigation team leader (ITL)	The person designated as leading the investigation team. The ITL is typically the point of contact through whom those outside the investigative team communicate with it.

Investigator	A person engaged in the systematic collection, analysis and preservation of information and/or facts related to the matter in question. Note: The investigator may be a member of an investigative team working under the direction of an investigation team leader and/or investigation unit manager.
Investigative interview	A highly structured interview intended to obtain an admission.
Investigative unit (IU)	The entity within the organization tasked with conducting or overseeing investigations.
Investigative unit manager (IUM)	The person responsible for managing the investigation program and assuring the necessary financial, human, physical, and time resources are committed to conduct an effective investigation.
Judgment	A legal finding of responsibility.
Jurisdiction	An area or subject over which a party has authority.
Kick-back	Money or something of value improperly provided to obtain something else of value.
Malfeasance	Intentional conduct or behavior contrary to the interests of others. Employee theft or substance would be considered employee malfeasance.

Management system standard	A framework of processes and procedures used to ensure that an organization perform activities needed to achieve its objectives.
MeToo Movement	Also called the #MeToo Movement is a global social movement against sexual harassment and sexual abuse where people publicize their allegations of sex crimes committed by powerful and/or prominent men.
Miranda Rights and Warning	Legal rights imparted on those taken into custody when suspect of having committed a crime.
Motive	The reason for having committed a crime or offense.
Operative	An undercover investigator.
Organizational investigations	Investigations performed at the direction of the organization, for the organization. Usually involves the investigation of crimes and offences committed against the organization and/or as a method of establishing the facts and organizational due diligence relating to potential regulatory action. Note: Differs from workplace investigations in that the subject of the investigation may not be an employee or former employee of the organization.
Physical surveillance	Any form of surveillance which uses people. May be augmented with technology but

requires constant human monitoring.

Plaintiff   The party which brings a legal action.

Preemployment   A form of investigation used to verify the
screening   identity, personal history and credentials of an
                       employment applicant.

Preponderance   The amount of evidence needed to prevail in
of the evidence   most civil matters, which is based on a
                       finding that it is more likely than not that an
                       alleged event occurred.

Privacy, the   The expectation of freedom from the
right to privacy   unwanted intrusion of others into one's
                       home, papers, or affairs.

Private   Investigations performed in the private sector
investigations   typically for private citizens involving non-
                       workplace issues.

Private sector   The realm under the management,
                       supervision and authority of non-government
                       entities. May include public and privately
                       owned companies, non-profit organizations
                       and other private institutions. Those not
                       employed by the government are in the public
                       sector. Those suspected of a workplace
                       offence may be the subject of a *private sector*
                       investigation conducted by their employer or
                       agents, and if determined responsible,
                       punished by their employer.

Privilege   A legal protection which permits the lawful withholding of information or evidence from an opponent during the course of litigation. May be used in both criminal and civil cases.

Probative

Relevance, in the common law of evidence, is the tendency of a given item of evidence to prove or disprove one of the legal elements of the case, or to have probative value to make one of the elements of the case likelier or not. Probative is a term used in law to signify "tending to prove."

Pro Bono

A term generally used to describe professional work undertaken voluntarily and without payment as a public service. It is common in the legal profession and is increasingly seen in marketing, technology, and strategy consulting firms.

Process of Investigation

A highly structured and sometimes scientific approach to investigation. Sufficiently structured to provide uniformity and consistency yet, fluid and flexible enough to accommodate any most any situation or fact pattern.

Project manager

The functional manager leading or directing the investigative process and the investigative team under his supervision. The project manager is typically the point of contact through whom those outside the investigative team communicate with it.

Public policy

Unwritten expectations relative to one's

behavior and conduct.

Public sector	The realm under the management, supervision and authority of the government. Those in public law enforcement are employed in the public sector. Those charged with committing a crime or accused of violating the law may be subject to the rule of law and tried in the *public sector.*
Punitive damages	Damages awarded which are intended to punish the defendant and serve as a deterrent to prevent others from engaging in similar behavior.
Restitution	The act of making another party whole. Most often, restitution involves the payment of money.
Return on investment or ROI	The return enjoyed on any particular investment. The return may be monetary or otherwise.
Risk Tolerance	The amount of risk, whether financial or reputational, one willing to tolerate.
Spoliation	Intentional or negligent destruction of evidence.
Standard of Proof	The quality and quantity of proof necessary to make a lawful finding of responsibility.
Statute of Limitations	Law that sets the maximum time the parties involved have to initiate legal proceedings

from the date of an alleged offense, whether civil or criminal.

Subject The individual who is the subject of the investigation or matter in question. Not to be confused with *suspect* as used in the public sector. The subject may or may not be a suspect.

Subrogation The pursuit of another party one deems ultimately responsible.

Surveillance The observing or monitoring of people, places or things.

Trier-of-fact Any person or body charged with the duty of adjudication.

Undercover investigation A method of investigation which entails the surreptitious placement of an investigator into an unsuspecting workforce for purpose of information gathering. These are typically complicated investigations and should only be attempted after other means of information gathering have been ruled out. Referred to as UC in the trade.

Upjohn Warning A written warning (typically in letter form) given to an employee at the onset of an investigative interview to ensure that the employee knows that the privileged relationship (should one exist) is between the attorney conducting the interview and the organization and not the employee. Upjohn

Co. v. United States, 449 U.S. 383 (1981).

Verification and Analysis   That phase of investigation during which the fact-finder interviews those he thinks are most involved in the matter in question.

Workplace Investigations   Any investigation taking place in or involving the workplace. May be conducted by those either in the private or public sector. Typically involving the investigation of employee misconduct, workplace policy violations or work rule violations. The matter under investigation may or may not be a violation of the law. Not to be confused with *private investigations*.

APPENDIX B

CHAIRMAN GRASSLEY'S REFERRAL OF THE MS. JULIE SWETNICK AND MICHAEL AVENATTI, (MS. SWETNICK'S LAWYER) ALLEGATIONS TO AG AND FBI

VIA ELECTRONIC TRANSMISSION

The Honorable Jeff Sessions

Attorney General
U.S. Department of Justice
950 Pennsylvania Avenue,
NW Washington, DC 20530

The Honorable Christopher
A. Wray Director
Federal Bureau of Investigation 935
Pennsylvania Avenue, NW
Washington, DC20535

Dear Attorney General Sessions and Director Wray:

As you know, the Senate Judiciary Committee recently processed the nomination of Judge Brett M. Kavanaugh to serve as an Associate Justice on the Supreme Court of the United States, leading to his eventual confirmation on October 6, 2018. As part of that process, the Committee has investigated various allegations made against Judge Kavanaugh. The Committee's investigation has involved communicating with numerous individuals claiming to have relevant information. While many of those individuals have provided the Committee information in good faith, it unfortunately appears some have not. As explained below, am writing to refer Mr. Michael Avenatti and Ms. Julie Swetnick for investigation of potential violations of 18 U.S.C. §§ 371, 1001, and 1505, for materially false statements they made to the Committee during the course of the Committee's investigation.

ALLEGATIONS BY MR. AVENATTI AND MS. SWETNICK

On September 23, 2018, Mr. Avenatti posted a message on

social media claiming that he was "represent[ing] a woman with credible information regarding Judge Kavanaugh and Mark Judge."[1] Minutes later, Committee staff contacted Mr. Avenatti acknowledging his claim and asking that he "advise [them] of this information immediately so that Senate investigators may promptly begin an inquiry."[2] Mr. Avenatti responded, failing to disclose the identity of his client but representing to Committee staff:

> We are aware of significant evidence of multiple house parties in the Washington, D.C. area during the early 1980s during which Brett Kavanaugh, Mark Judge, and others would participate in the targeting of women with alcohol/drugs in order to allow a 'train' of men to subsequently gang rape them.[3]

Noting Mr. Avenatti's use of "we," Committee staff asked Mr. Avenatti if he did in fact have a client making these claims or was solely doing so himself.[4] He responded that he did have a client, but again did not identify her.[5] On September 24, 2018, Mr. Avenatti posted an additional message on social media "[w]arning ‿ [t]he GOP and others" to "be very careful in trying to suggest that she [Mr. Avenatti's unnamed client] is not credible."[6] Then, on September 26, 2018, Mr. Avenatti publicly revealed that his client was Ms. Julie Swetnick.[7] Ms. Swetnick is a former client of the law firm of Ms. Debra Katz, the attorney for Dr. Christine Blasey ord.[8]

That same day, September 26, 2018, Mr. Avenatti submitted a sworn statement to the Committee purportedly written and signed by Ms. Swetnick, in which she accused Judge Kavanaugh of repeatedly drugging women and/or spiking their punch with alcohol in order to render them inebriated and disoriented so that groups of boys, including Judge Kavanaugh, could gang rape them.[9] Specifically, she alleged in her sworn statement that she met Brett Kavanaugh "in approximately 1980-1981," and that she "attended well over ten house parties in the Washington, D.C. area during the years 1981-1983," some of which she claimed Brett Kavanaugh also attended. "During the years 1981-82," Ms. Swetnick declared, " became aware of efforts by Mark Judge, Brett Kavanaugh and others to 'spike' the 'punch' at house parties attended with drugs and/or grain alcohol so as to cause girls to lose their inhibitions and their ability to say 'No.'" She said that at these parties, which "were a common occurrence in the area and occurred nearly every weekend during the school year," she witnessed Brett Kavanaugh participate in what she believed to be systematic sexual assaults of incapacitated women. " _ witnessed efforts by Mark Judge, Brett Kavanaugh and others to cause girls to become inebriated so they could then be 'gang raped' in a side room or bedroom by a 'train' of numerous boys. have a firm recollection of seeing boys lined up outside rooms at many of these parties waiting for their 'turn' with a girl inside the room," Ms. Swetnick declared, and "[t]hese boys included Mark Judge and Brett Kavanaugh."

Ms. Swetnick's sworn statement, which the Committee received on September 26, 2018, also mentioned for the first time the "Beach Week" parties in Ocean City, Maryland. Ms. Swetnick said that she was "told by other women this conduct also occurred during the Summer months in Ocean City, Maryland," and she "witnessed such conduct on one occasion in Ocean City, Maryland during 'Beach Week.'" However, Mr. Avenatti did not reference "Beach Week" in his September 23, 2018 email to the Committee. Mr. Avenatti's original email only alleged conduct at house parties in the Washington, D.C. area. Notably, Ms. Swetnick submitted her statement broadening the area of the alleged incidents from Washington, D.C. to Ocean City, Maryland, only after the Committee publicly released Judge Kavanaugh's 1982 calendar - which included a notation for Beach Week during the week of June 6-12.[10]

DIVERSION OF COMMITTEE RESOURCES TO INVESTIGATE MR. AVENATTI'S AND MS. SWETNICK'S ALLEGATIONS

The sworn statement Mr. Avenatti submitted on behalf of Ms. Swetnick materially affected the Committee's investigation of allegations against Judge Kavanaugh. Within hours of the submission, all the Democrats on the Senate Judiciary Committee sent a letter to me stating:

> In light of shocking new allegations detailed by Julie Swetnick in a sworn affidavit, we write to request that the Committee vote on Brett Kavanaugh be immediately canceled and that you support the reopening of the B investigation to examine all of the allegations against Kavanaugh or withdrawal of his nomination

The Democrats' letter specifically referenced the fact that Ms.

Swetnick's sworn statement was submitted to the Committee "[u]nder penalty of perjury, which would cause Ms. Swetnick to be subject to criminal prosecution" if her allegations are knowingly, willfully, and materially false.[12]

After receiving the allegations from Mr. Avenatti and Ms. Swetnick, Committee staff immediately began investigating the claims, diverting significant resources to the effort. This included questioning Judge Kavanaugh in a transcribed interview on September 25, 2018, about the allegations Mr. Avenatti made to the Committee via his September 23, 2018 email.[13] t also included questioning Judge Kavanaugh in another transcribed interview on September 26, 2018, about the specifics of Ms. Swetnick's allegations after the Committee received her statement. [14] Under penalty of felony, Judge Kavanaugh categorically denied the allegations and stated he did not know Ms. Swetnick. Committee staff also interviewed ten associates of Ms. Swetnick, working late nights and weekends to gather information to determine the veracity of Ms. Swetnick's claims and evaluate her credibility. Committee staff sought to interview Ms. Swetnick, but Mr. Avenatti refused.

MS. SWETNICK'S AND MR. AVENATTI'S
SUBSEQUENT CONTRADICTIONS OF THEIR ALLEGATIONS

In short, Mr. Avenatti and Ms. Swetnick made grave allegations against Judge Kavanaugh, and the Committee diverted significant resources to investigate the claims. However, in light of Ms. Swetnick's and Mr. Avenatti's own statements to the media, information obtained from Committee interviews of her associates, and publicly reported information about her and Mr. Avenatti, it has become apparent that the statements Mr. Avenatti and Ms. Swetnick submitted to the Committee likely contained materially false claims.

On October 1, 2018, NBC News aired an interview of Ms. Swetnick by Ms. Kate Snow, in which Ms. Swetnick contradicted key claims she had made to the Committee via Mr. Avenatti.[15] When asked about the claim in her sworn statement that she was aware of Brett Kavanaugh spiking punch at parties with drugs and/or grain alcohol, Ms. Swetnick demurred, stating instead that "I saw [Kavanaugh] giving red Solo cups to quite a few girls" but that "I don't know what he did" as far as spiking punch. n this revised account to NBC, she merely claimed she "saw him by" punch containers. This materially contradicted her statement in her sworn statement that she was "aware of efforts by _ Brett Kavanaugh _ to 'spike' the 'punch' at house parties _ to cause girls to become inebriated and disoriented so they could then be 'gang raped.'"[16] Ms. Swetnick's sworn statement to the Committee claimed she had "personal knowledge of the information" stated in it. Yet, when CNN later questioned Mr. Avenatti about the clear contradictions between Ms. Swetnick's statements in her sworn declaration and those to NBC about Judge Kavanaugh spiking punch, he conceded: "One of her friends informed her of what she just put in the declaration or what was attested to in the declaration."

When the NBC interview with Ms. Swetnick addressed claims in her sworn statement that she had "**a firm recollection** of seeing boys," including Brett Kavanaugh, "**lined up** outside rooms at many of these parties" to gang rape incapacitated women, Ms. Swetnick again contradicted her statement to the Committee. She denied both that there were lines of boys outside rooms and that she had any actual knowledge at the time of any gang rapes in those rooms by these boys.

Ms. Snow and Ms. Swetnick had the following exchange in which Ms. Swetnick contradicted her claim of seeing boys lined up outside rooms at these parties she supposedly attended:

Ms. Swetnick: would see boys standing outside of rooms, congregated together and would see them laughing, a lot of laughing.
Ms. Snow: Standing in line outside a room?
Ms. Swetnick: Not a line, but definitely huddled by doors.[18]

So, contradicting her sworn statement claim that she had "a firm recollection" of seeing boys lined up outside bedrooms at parties to systematically rape women, her revised account to NBC merely claimed that she saw groups of boys standing together and laughing in the general vicinity of doors at house parties.

Similarly, although Ms. Swetnick claimed in her sworn statement that, based on "personal knowledge," it was her "firm recollection" that these boys were lined up for the purpose of "waiting for their 'turn' with a girl inside the room," *i.e.*, for their turn to rape a victim incapacitated by punch spiked with drugs or alcohol, she contradicted this as well in her NBC interview, instead admitting that she did not have any knowledge at the time that any such activity was actually happening, but only assumed as much after the fact, stating: "I didn't know what was occurring ... and I didn't understand what it could possibly be." Ms. Snow attempted to clarify, asking: "So you're suggesting that, **in hindsight**, you **think** he [Kavanaugh] was involved in this behavior [gang rapes]?" Ms. Swetnick responded: " would say [pause] yes. It's just too coincidental."[19]

Ms. Swetnick also contradicted the timeline she provided in her sworn statement, in which she stated: "I attended well over ten house parties in the Washington D.C. area during the years 1981-83 where Mark Judge and Brett Kavanaugh were present." n the NBC interview, Ms. Swetnick stated that she was sexually assaulted at one of these house parties when she was 19 and stopped going to them afterwards. According to public records, Ms. Swetnick would have turned 20 toward the end of 1982. So, her claim that she attended these parties through 1983 is contradicted by her claim she stopped attending when she was 19.

In sum, the sworn statement Mr. Avenatti submitted to the Committee on behalf of Ms. Swetnick claimed she had "personal knowledge" that Judge Kavanaugh spiked punch with drugs and alcohol at house parties in 1981-83 in order to cause girls to become incapacitated so that lines of boys would systematically sexually assault them. She later contradicted each of those claims in her interview with NBC.

Those contradictions did not go unnoticed. When NBC introduced her interview segment, Ms. Snow explicitly stated: "There are things that she told us on camera that differ from her written statement last week."[21] When later asked by an MSNBC anchor whether Ms. Swetnick has credibility issues, Ms. Snow stated: "I would say yes because there are - just to be clear there are things that she said to me that differ from her initial statement, which was a sworn statement last week, submitted to the Judiciary Committee."[22] A CNN host similarly noted the contradictions and quizzed Mr. Avenatti about them.[23] While differences between a media report and a statement to the Committee would not necessarily rise to the level of warranting a referral, when the source of the contradictory media reports is the declarant herself, as is the case here, it does.

LACK OF CREDIBLE EVIDENCE MS. SWETNICK
EVER KNEW JUDGE KAVANAUGH

Not only did Ms. Swetnick materially contradict the allegations of sexual misconduct she and Mr. Avenatti made to the Committee about Judge Kavanaugh, there is simply no credible evidence that Ms. Swetnick ever even met or socialized with Judge Kavanaugh. On the contrary, there is substantial evidence they did not know each other. Ms. Swetnick was older and attended a different high school in a different town - one whose students were reportedly not known to regularly socialize with students from Judge Kavanaugh's high school. The only apparent commonality between Ms. Swetnick and Judge Kavanaugh is that they both lived in Montgomery County, Maryland in the early 1980s. That is not particularly meaningful for determining whether they knew each other; according to information from the U.S. Census Bureau, Montgomery County had a population of over 600,000 in 1982.

In addition to denying her allegations, Judge Kavanaugh told the Committee under penalty of felony that he did not know Ms. Swetnick.[24] Mark Judge similarly denied the allegations and stated to the Committee, also under penalty of felony, "I do not know Julie Swetnick."[25] Michael egan, a friend of Judge Kavanaugh's in high school who "attended most of the same social events" as Judge Kavanaugh, stated the following to the Committee under penalty of felony:

> I have never heard of Ms. Swetnick. My understanding is
> that she graduated from Gaithersburg High School three
> years before we graduated from Georgetown Prep. During
> my high school years, did not know any girls from
> Gaithersburg High School. We did not socialize with girls
> from Gaithersburg High School.[26]

Indeed, a letter to the Committee under penalty of felony signed by 64 "men and women who knew Brett Kavanaugh well in high school" called Ms. Swetnick's allegations "[n]onsense" and noted: "In the extensive amount of time we collectively spent with Brett, we do not recall having ever met someone named Julie Swetnick."[27]

NOTE: The letter continues for more than 6 pages. If you would like to see the entire document go to www.InDefenseofTheInnocent.org.

APPENDIX C
DEAR COLLEGE LETTER

UNITED STATES DEPARTMENT OF EDUCATION
FFICE FOR CIVIL RIGHTS
THE ASSISTANT SECRETARY

April 4, 2011

Dear Colleague:

Education has long been recognized as the great equalizer in America. The U.S. Department of Education and its Office for Civil Rights (OCR) believe that providing all students with an educational environment free from discrimination is extremely important. The sexual harassment of students, including sexual violence, interferes with students' right to receive an education free from discrimination and, in the case of sexual violence, is a crime.

Title IX of the Education Amendments of 1972 (Title IX), 20 U.S.C. §§ 1681 *et seq.*, and its implementing regulations, 34 C.F.R. Part 106, prohibit discrimination on the basis of sex in education programs or activities operated by recipients of Federal financial assistance. Sexual harassment of students, which includes acts of sexual violence, is a form of sex discrimination prohibited by Title IX. In order to assist recipients, which include school districts, colleges, and universities (hereinafter "schools" or "recipients") in meeting these obligations, this letter[1] explains that the requirements of Title IX pertaining to sexual harassment also cover sexual violence, and lays out the specific Title IX requirements applicable to sexual violence.[2] Sexual violence, as that term is used in this letter, refers to physical sexual acts perpetrated against a person's will or where a person is incapable of giving consent due to the victim's use of drugs or alcohol. An individual also may be unable to give consent due to an intellectual or other disability. A number of different acts fall into the category of sexual violence, including rape, sexual assault, sexual battery, and sexual coercion. All such acts of sexual violence are forms of sexual harassment covered under Title IX.

The statistics on sexual violence are both deeply troubling and a call to action for the nation. A report prepared for the National Institute of Justice found that about 1 in 5 women are victims of completed or attempted sexual assault while in college.[3] The report also found that approximately 6.1 percent of males were victims of completed or attempted sexual assault during college.[4] According to data collected under the Jeanne Clery Disclosure of Campus Security and Campus Crime Statistics Act (Clery Act), 20 U.S.C. § 1092(f), in 2009, college campuses reported nearly 3,300 forcible sex offenses as defined by the Clery Act.[5] This problem is not limited to college. During the 2007-2008 school year, there were 800 reported incidents of rape and attempted rape and 3,800 reported incidents of other sexual batteries at public high schools.[6] Additionally, the likelihood that a woman with intellectual disabilities will be sexually assaulted is estimated to be significantly higher than the general population.[7] The Department is deeply concerned about this problem and is committed to ensuring that all students feel safe in their school, so that they have the opportunity to benefit fully from the school's programs and activities.

This letter begins with a discussion of Title IX's requirements related to student-on-student sexual harassment, including sexual violence, and explains schools' responsibility to take immediate and effective steps to end sexual harassment and sexual violence. These requirements are discussed in detail in OCR's *Revised Sexual Harassment Guidance* issued in 2001 (*2001 Guidance*).[8] This letter supplements the *2001 Guidance* by providing additional guidance and practical examples regarding the Title IX requirements as they relate to sexual violence. This letter concludes by discussing the proactive efforts schools can take to prevent sexual harassment and violence, and by providing examples of remedies that schools and OCR may use to end such conduct, prevent its recurrence, and address its effects. Although some examples contained in this letter are applicable only in the postsecondary context, sexual harassment and violence also are concerns for school districts. The Title IX obligations discussed in this letter apply equally to school districts unless otherwise noted.

Title IX Requirements Related to Sexual Harassment and Sexual Violence

Schools' Obligations to Respond to Sexual Harassment and Sexual Violence

Sexual harassment is unwelcome conduct of a sexual nature. It includes unwelcome sexual advances, requests for sexual favors, and other verbal, nonverbal, or physical conduct of a sexual nature. Sexual violence is a form of sexual harassment prohibited by Title IX.

As explained in OCR's *2001 Guidance*, when a student sexually harasses another student, the harassing conduct creates a hostile environment if the conduct is sufficiently serious that it interferes with or limits a student's ability to participate in or benefit from the school's program. The more severe the conduct, the less need there is to show a repetitive series of incidents to prove a hostile environment, particularly if the harassment is physical. Indeed, a single or isolated incident of sexual harassment may create a hostile environment if the incident is sufficiently severe. For instance, a single instance of rape is sufficiently severe to create a hostile environment.[10]

Title IX protects students from sexual harassment in a school's education programs and activities. This means that Title IX protects students in connection with all the academic, educational, extracurricular, athletic, and other programs of the school, whether those programs take place in a school's facilities, on a school bus, at a class or training program sponsored by the school at another location, or elsewhere. For example, Title IX protects a student who is sexually assaulted by a fellow student during a school-sponsored field trip.

If a school knows or reasonably should know about student-on-student harassment that creates a hostile environment, Title IX requires the school to take immediate action to eliminate the harassment, prevent its recurrence, and address its effects.[12] Schools also are required to publish a notice of nondiscrimination and to adopt and publish grievance procedures. Because of these requirements, which are discussed in greater detail in the following section, schools need to ensure that their employees are trained so that they know to report harassment to appropriate school officials, and so that employees with the authority to address harassment know how to respond properly. Training for employees should include practical information about how to identify and report sexual harassment and violence. OCR recommends that this training be provided to any employees likely to witness or receive reports of sexual harassment and violence, including teachers, school law enforcement unit employees, school administrators, school counselors, general counsels, health personnel, and resident advisors.

Schools may have an obligation to respond to student-on-student sexual harassment that initially occurred off school grounds, outside a school's education program or activity. If a student files a complaint with the school, regardless of where the conduct occurred, the school must process the complaint in accordance with its established procedures. Because students often experience the continuing effects of off-campus sexual harassment in the educational setting, schools should consider the effects of the off-campus conduct when evaluating whether there is a hostile environment on campus. For example, if a student alleges that he or she was sexually assaulted by another student off school grounds, and that upon returning to school he or she was taunted and harassed by other students who are the alleged perpetrator's friends, the school should take the earlier sexual assault into account in determining whether there is a sexually hostile environment. The school also should take steps to protect a student who was assaulted off campus from further sexual harassment or retaliation from the perpetrator and his or her associates.

Regardless of whether a harassed student, his or her parent, or a third party files a complaint under the school's grievance procedures or otherwise requests action on the student's behalf, a school that knows, or reasonably should know, about possible harassment must promptly investigate to determine what occurred and then take appropriate steps to resolve the situation. As discussed later in this letter, the school's Title IX investigation is different from any law enforcement investigation, and a law enforcement investigation does not relieve the school of its independent Title IX obligation to investigate the conduct. The specific steps in a school's investigation will vary depending upon the nature of the allegations, the age of the student or students involved (particularly in elementary and secondary schools), the size and administrative structure of the school, and other factors. Yet as discussed in more detail below, the school's inquiry must in all cases be prompt, thorough, and impartial. In cases involving potential criminal conduct, school personnel must determine, consistent with State and local law, whether appropriate law enforcement or other authorities should be notified.

Schools also should inform and obtain consent from the complainant (or the complainant's parents if the complainant is under 18 and does not attend a postsecondary institution) before beginning an investigation. If the complainant requests confidentiality or asks that the complaint not be pursued, the school should take all reasonable steps to investigate and respond to the complaint consistent with the request for confidentiality or request not to pursue an investigation. If a complainant insists that his or her name or other identifiable information not be disclosed to the alleged perpetrator, the school should inform the complainant that its ability to respond may be limited.[14] The school also should tell the complainant that Title IX prohibits retaliation, and that school officials will not only take steps to prevent retaliation but also take strong responsive action if it occurs.

As discussed in the *2001 Guidance*, if the complainant continues to ask that his or her name or other identifiable information not be revealed, the school should evaluate that request in the context of its responsibility to provide a safe and nondiscriminatory environment for all students. Thus, the school may weigh the request for confidentiality against the following factors: the seriousness of the alleged harassment; the complainant's age; whether there have been other harassment complaints about the same individual; and the alleged harasser's rights to receive information about the allegations if the information is maintained by the school as an "education record" under the Family Educational Rights and Privacy Act (FERPA), 20 U.S.C. § 1232g; 34 C.F.R. Part 99.[15] The school should inform the complainant if it cannot ensure confidentiality. Even if the school cannot take disciplinary action against the alleged harasser because the complainant insists on confidentiality, it should pursue other steps to limit the effects of the alleged harassment and prevent its recurrence. Examples of such steps are discussed later in this letter. Compliance with Title IX, such as publishing a notice of nondiscrimination, designating an employee to coordinate Title IX compliance, and adopting and publishing grievance procedures, can serve as preventive measures against harassment. Combined with education and training programs, these measures can help ensure that all students and employees recognize the nature of sexual harassment and violence, and understand that the school will not tolerate such conduct. Indeed, these measures may bring potentially problematic conduct to the school's attention before it becomes serious enough to create a hostile environment. Training for administrators, teachers, staff, and students also can help ensure that they understand what types of conduct constitute sexual harassment or violence, can identify warning signals that may need attention, and know how to respond. More detailed information and examples of education and other preventive measures are provided later in this letter.

Procedural Requirements Pertaining to Sexual Harassment and Sexual Violence

Recipients of Federal financial assistance must comply with the procedural requirements outlined in the Title IX implementing regulations. Specifically, a recipient must:

(A) Disseminate a notice of nondiscrimination;
(B) Designate at least one employee to coordinate its
    efforts to comply with and carry out its responsibilities
    under Title IX; and

(C) Adopt and publish grievance procedures providing for prompt and equitable resolution of student and employee sex discrimination complaints.[18]

These requirements apply to all forms of sexual harassment, including sexual violence, and are important for preventing and effectively responding to sex discrimination. They are discussed in greater detail below. OCR advises recipients to examine their current policies and procedures on sexual harassment and sexual violence to determine whether those policies comply with the requirements articulated in this letter and the *2001 Guidance.* Recipients should then implement changes as needed...

NOTE: The letter continues for about 12 more pages. If you would like to see the entire document go on line or visit www.InDefenseofTheInnocent.org.

APPENDIX D

SUMMARY OF MAJOR PROVISIONS OF DOE TITLE IX FINAL RULE 5-6-2020

Summary of Major Provisions of the Department of Education's Title IX Final Rule

Issue	The Title IX Final Rule: Addressing Sexual Harassment in Schools
1. Notice to the School, College, University ("Schools"): Actual Knowledge	The Final Rule requires a K-12 school to respond whenever *any* employee has notice of sexual harassment, including allegations of sexual harassment. Many State laws also require all K-12 employees to be mandatory reporters of child abuse. For postsecondary institutions, the Final Rule allows the institution to choose whether to have mandatory reporting for all employees, or to designate some employees to be confidential resources for college students to discuss sexual harassment without automatically triggering a report to the Title IX office.
	For all schools, notice to a Title IX Coordinator, or to an official with authority to institute corrective measures on the recipient's behalf, charges a school with actual knowledge and triggers the school's response obligations.
2. Definition of Sexual Harassment for Title IX Purposes	The Final Rule defines sexual harassment broadly to include any of three types of misconduct on the basis of sex, all of which jeopardize the equal access to education that Title IX is designed to protect: Any instance of *quid pro quo* harassment by a school's employee; any unwelcome conduct that a reasonable person would find so severe, pervasive, and objectively offensive that it denies a person equal educational access; any instance of sexual assault (as defined in the Clery Act), dating violence, domestic violence, or stalking as defined in the Violence Against Women Act (VAWA).
	- The Final Rule prohibits sex-based misconduct in a manner consistent with the First Amendment. *Quid pro quo* harassment and Clery Act/VAWA offenses are not evaluated for severity, pervasiveness, offensiveness, or denial of equal educational access, because such misconduct is sufficiently serious to deprive a person of equal access.
	- The Final Rule uses the Supreme Court's *Davis* definition (severe *and* pervasive *and* objectively offensive conduct, effectively denying a person equal educational access) as one of the three categories of sexual harassment, so that where unwelcome sex-based conduct consists of speech or expressive conduct, schools balance Title IX enforcement with respect for free speech and academic freedom.
	- The Final Rule uses the Supreme Court's Title IX-specific definition rather than the Supreme Court's Title VII workplace standard (severe *or* pervasive conduct creating a hostile work environment) First Amendment concerns differ in educational environments and workplace environments, and the Title IX definition provides First Amendment protections appropriate for educational institutions where students are learning, and employees are teaching. Students, teachers, faculty, and others should enjoy free speech and academic freedom protections, even when speech or expression is offensive.

Page 1 of 9

287

Summary of Major Provisions of the Department of Education's Title IX Final Rule

3. Sexual Harassment Occurring in a School's "Education Program or Activity," and "in the United States"	The Title IX statute applies to persons in the United States with respect to education programs or activities that receive Federal financial assistance. Under the Final Rule, schools must respond when sexual harassment occurs in the school's education program or activity, against a person in the United States. - The Title IX statute and existing regulations contain broad definitions of a school's "program or activity" and the Department will continue to look to these definitions for the scope of a school's education program or activity. Education program or activity includes locations, events, or circumstances over which the school exercised substantial control over both the respondent and the context in which the sexual harassment occurred, and also includes any building owned or controlled by a student organization that is officially recognized by a postsecondary institution (such as a fraternity or sorority house). - Title IX applies to all of a school's education programs or activities, whether such programs or activities occur on-campus or off-campus. A school may address sexual harassment affecting its students or employees that falls outside Title IX's jurisdiction in any manner the school chooses, including providing supportive measures or pursuing discipline.
4. Accessible Reporting to Title IX Coordinator	The Final Rule expands a school's obligations to ensure its educational community knows how to report to the Title IX Coordinator. - The employee designated by a recipient to coordinate its efforts to comply with Title IX responsibilities must be referred to as the "Title IX Coordinator." - Instead of notifying only students and employees of the Title IX Coordinator's contact information, the school must also notify applicants for admission and employment, parents or legal guardians of elementary and secondary school students, and all unions, of the name or title, office address, e-mail address, and telephone number of the Title IX Coordinator. - Schools must prominently display on their websites the required contact information for the Title IX Coordinator. - Any person may report sex discrimination, including sexual harassment (whether or not the person reporting is the person alleged to be the victim of conduct that could constitute sex discrimination or sexual harassment), in person, by mail, by telephone, or by e-mail, using the contact information listed for the Title IX Coordinator, or by any other means that results in the Title IX Coordinator receiving the person's verbal or written report. - Such a report may be made at any time, including during non-business hours, by using the telephone number or e-mail address, or by mail to the office address, listed for the Title IX Coordinator.
5. School's Mandatory Response Obligations: The Deliberate Indifference Standard	Schools must respond promptly to Title IX sexual harassment in a manner that is not deliberately indifferent, which means a response that is not clearly unreasonable in light of the known circumstances. Schools have the following mandatory response obligations: - Schools must offer supportive measures to the person alleged to be the victim (referred to as the "complainant").

Summary of Major Provisions of the Department of Education's Title IX Final Rule

	- The Title IX Coordinator must promptly contact the complainant confidentially to discuss the availability of supportive measures, consider the complainant's wishes with respect to supportive measures, inform the complainant of the availability of supportive measures with or without the filing of a formal complaint, and explain to the complainant the process for filing a formal complaint. - Schools must follow a grievance process that complies with the Final Rule before the imposition of any disciplinary sanctions or other actions that are not supportive measures, against a respondent. - Schools must not restrict rights protected under the U.S. Constitution, including the First Amendment, Fifth Amendment, and Fourteenth Amendment, when complying with Title IX. - The Final Rule requires a school to investigate sexual harassment allegations in any formal complaint, which can be filed by a complainant, or signed by a Title IX Coordinator. - The Final Rule affirms that a complainant's wishes with respect to whether the school investigates should be respected unless the Title IX Coordinator determines that signing a formal complaint to initiate an investigation over the wishes of the complainant is not clearly unreasonable in light of the known circumstances. - If the allegations in a formal complaint do not meet the definition of sexual harassment in the Final Rule, or did not occur in the school's education program or activity against a person in the United States, the Final Rule clarifies that the school must dismiss such allegations *for purposes of Title IX* but may still address the allegations in any manner the school deems appropriate under the school's own code of conduct.
6. School's Mandatory Response Obligations: Defining "Complainant," "Respondent," "Formal Complaint," "Supportive Measures"	When responding to sexual harassment (e.g., by offering supportive measures to a complainant and refraining from disciplining a respondent without following a Title IX grievance process, which includes investigating formal complaints of sexual harassment), the Final Rule provides clear definitions of complainant, respondent, formal complaint, and supportive measures so that recipients, students, and employees clearly understand how a school must respond to sexual harassment incidents in a way that supports the alleged victim and treats both parties fairly. The Final Rule defines "complainant" as an individual *who is alleged to be the victim* of conduct that could constitute sexual harassment. - This clarifies that any third party as well as the complainant may report sexual harassment. - While parents and guardians do not become complainants (or respondents), the Final Rule expressly recognizes the legal rights of parents and guardians to act on behalf of parties (including by filing formal complaints) in Title IX matters. The Final Rule defines "respondent" as an individual who has been reported to be the perpetrator of conduct that could constitute sexual harassment.

Page 3 of 9

289

Summary of Major Provisions of the Department of Education's Title IX Final Rule

The Final Rule defines "formal complaint" as a document filed by a complainant or signed by the Title IX Coordinator alleging sexual harassment against a respondent and requesting that the school investigate the allegation of sexual harassment and states:

- At the time of filing a formal complaint, a complainant must be participating in or attempting to participate in the education program or activity of the school with which the formal complaint is filed.

- A formal complaint may be filed with the Title IX Coordinator in person, by mail, or by electronic mail, by using the contact information required to be listed for the Title IX Coordinator under the Final Rule, and by any additional method designated by the school.

- The phrase "document filed by a complainant" means a document or electronic submission (such as by e-mail or through an online portal provided for this purpose by the school) that contains the complainant's physical or digital signature, or otherwise indicates that the complainant is the person filing the formal complaint.

- Where the Title IX Coordinator signs a formal complaint, the Title IX Coordinator is not a complainant or a party during a grievance process, and must comply with requirements for Title IX personnel to be free from conflicts and bias.

The Final Rule defines "supportive measures" as individualized services reasonably available that are non-punitive, non-disciplinary, and not unreasonably burdensome to the other party while designed to ensure equal educational access, protect safety, or deter sexual harassment.

- The Final Rule evaluates a school's selection of supportive measures and remedies based on what is not clearly unreasonable in light of the known circumstances, and does not second guess a school's disciplinary decisions, but requires the school to offer supportive measures, and provide remedies to a complainant whenever a respondent is found responsible.

| 7. Grievance Process, General Requirements | The Final Rule prescribes a consistent, transparent grievance process for resolving formal complaints of sexual harassment. Aside from hearings (see Issue #9 below), the grievance process prescribed by the Final Rule applies to all schools equally including K–12 schools and postsecondary institutions. The Final Rule states that a school's grievance process must:

- Treat complainants equitably by providing remedies any time a respondent is found responsible, and treat respondents equitably by not imposing disciplinary sanctions without following the grievance process prescribed in the Final Rule.

- Remedies, which are required to be provided to a complainant when a respondent is found responsible, must be designed to maintain the complainant's equal access to education and may include the same individualized services described in the Final Rule as supportive measures; however, remedies need not be non-disciplinary or non-punitive and need not avoid burdening the respondent.

- Require objective evaluation of all relevant evidence, inculpatory and exculpatory, and avoid credibility determinations based on a person's status as a complainant, respondent, or witness. |

Summary of Major Provisions of the Department of Education's Title IX Final Rule

- Require Title IX personnel (Title IX Coordinators, investigators, decision-makers, people who facilitate any informal resolution process) to be free from conflicts of interest or bias for or against complainants or respondents.
- Training of Title IX personnel must include training on the definition of sexual harassment in the Final Rule, the scope of the school's education program or activity, how to conduct an investigation and grievance process including hearings, appeals, and informal resolution processes, as applicable, and how to serve impartially, including by avoiding prejudgment of the facts at issue, conflicts of interest, and bias.
- A school must ensure that decision-makers receive training on any technology to be used at a live hearing.
- A school's decision-makers and investigators must receive training on issues of relevance, including how to apply the rape shield protections provided only for complainants.
- Include a presumption that the respondent is not responsible for the alleged conduct until a determination regarding responsibility is made at the conclusion of the grievance process.
- Recipients must post materials used to train Title IX personnel on their websites, if any, or make materials available for members of the public to inspect.
- Include reasonably prompt time frames for conclusion of the grievance process, including appeals and informal resolutions, with allowance for short-term, good cause delays or extensions of the time frames.
- Describe the range, or list, the possible remedies a school may provide a complainant and disciplinary sanctions a school might impose on a respondent, following determinations of responsibility.
- State whether the school has chosen to use the preponderance of the evidence standard, or the clear and convincing evidence standard, for all formal complaints of sexual harassment (including where employees and faculty are respondents).
- Describe the school's appeal procedures, and the range of supportive measures available to complainants and respondents.
- A school's grievance process must not use, rely on, or seek disclosure of information protected under a legally recognized privilege, unless the person holding such privilege has waived the privilege.
- Any provisions, rules, or practices other than those required by the Final Rule that a school adopts as part of its grievance process for handling formal complaints of sexual harassment, must apply equally to both parties.

Summary of Major Provisions of the Department of Education's Title IX Final Rule

8. *Investigations*	The Final Rule states that the school must investigate the allegations in any formal complaint and send written notice to both parties (complainants and respondents) of the allegations upon receipt of a formal complaint. During the grievance process and when investigating: - The burden of gathering evidence and burden of proof must remain on schools, not on the parties. - Schools must provide equal opportunity for the parties to present fact and expert witnesses and other inculpatory and exculpatory evidence. - Schools must not restrict the ability of the parties to discuss the allegations or gather evidence (e.g., no "gag orders"). - Parties must have the same opportunity to select an advisor of the party's choice who may be, but need not be, an attorney. - Schools must send written notice of any investigative interviews, meetings, or hearings. - Schools must send the parties, and their advisors, evidence directly related to the allegations, in electronic format or hard copy, with at least 10 days for the parties to inspect, review, and respond to the evidence. - Schools must send the parties, and their advisors, an investigative report that fairly summarizes relevant evidence, in electronic format or hard copy, with at least 10 days for the parties to respond - Schools must dismiss allegations of conduct that do not meet the Final Rule's definition of sexual harassment or did not occur in a school's education program or activity against a person in the U.S. Such dismissal is only for Title IX purposes and does not preclude the school from addressing the conduct in any manner the school deems appropriate. - Schools may, in their discretion, dismiss a formal complaint or allegations therein if the complainant informs the Title IX Coordinator in writing that the complainant desires to withdraw the formal complaint or allegations therein, if the respondent is no longer enrolled or employed by the school, or if specific circumstances prevent the school from gathering sufficient evidence to reach a determination. - Schools must give the parties written notice of a dismissal (mandatory or discretionary) and the reasons for the dismissal. - Schools may, in their discretion, consolidate formal complaints where the allegations arise out of the same facts. - The Final Rule protects the privacy of a party's medical, psychological, and similar treatment records by stating that schools cannot access or use such records unless the school obtains the party's voluntary, written consent to do so.
9. *Hearings:*	The Final Rule adds provisions to the "live hearing with cross-examination" requirement for postsecondary institutions and clarifies that hearings are optional for K-12 schools (and any other recipient that is not a postsecondary institution).

Page 6 of 9

292

Summary of Major Provisions of the Department of Education's Title IX Final Rule

(a) Live Hearings & Cross-Examination (for Postsecondary Institutions)	(a) For postsecondary institutions, the school's grievance process must provide for a live hearing: - At the live hearing, the decision-maker(s) must permit each party's advisor to ask the other party and any witnesses all relevant questions and follow-up questions, including those challenging credibility. - Such cross-examination at the live hearing must be conducted directly, orally, and in real time by the party's advisor of choice and never by a party personally. - At the request of either party, the recipient must provide for the entire live hearing (including cross-examination) to occur with the parties located in separate rooms with technology enabling the parties to see and hear each other. - Only relevant cross-examination and other questions may be asked of a party or witness. Before a complainant, respondent, or witness answers a cross-examination or other question, the decision-maker must first determine whether the question is relevant and explain to the party's advisor asking cross-examination questions any decision to exclude a question as not relevant. - If a party does not have an advisor present at the live hearing, the school must provide, without fee or charge to that party, an advisor of the school's choice who may be, but is not required to be, an attorney to conduct cross-examination on behalf of that party. - If a party or witness does not submit to cross-examination at the live hearing, the decision-maker(s) must not rely on any statement of that party or witness in reaching a determination regarding responsibility; provided, however, that the decision-maker(s) cannot draw an inference about the determination regarding responsibility based solely on a party's or witness's absence from the live hearing or refusal to answer cross-examination or other questions. - Live hearings may be conducted with all parties physically present in the same geographic location or, at the school's discretion, any or all parties, witnesses, and other participants may appear at the live hearing virtually. - Schools must create an audio or audiovisual recording, or transcript, of any live hearing.
(b) Hearings are Optional, Written Questions Required (for K-12 Schools)	(b) For recipients that are K-12 schools, and other recipients that are not postsecondary institutions, the recipient's grievance process may, *but need not*, provide for a hearing: - With or without a hearing, after the school has sent the investigative report to the parties and before reaching a determination regarding responsibility, the decision-maker(s) must afford each party the opportunity to submit written, relevant questions that a party wants asked of any party or witness, provide each party with the answers, and allow for additional, limited follow-up questions from each party.
(c) Rape Shield Protections for Complainants	(c) The Final Rule provides rape shield protections for complainants (as to all recipients whether postsecondary institutions, K-12 schools, or others), deeming irrelevant questions and evidence about a complainant's prior sexual behavior unless offered to prove that someone other than the respondent committed the alleged misconduct or offered to prove consent.

Page 7 of 9

293

Summary of Major Provisions of the Department of Education's Title IX Final Rule

10. Standard of Evidence & Written Determination	The Final Rule requires the school's grievance process to state whether the standard of evidence to determine responsibility is the preponderance of the evidence standard or the clear and convincing evidence standard. The Final Rule makes each school's grievance process consistent by requiring each school to apply the same standard of evidence for all formal complaints of sexual harassment whether the respondent is a student or an employee (including faculty member). - The decision-maker (who cannot be the same person as the Title IX Coordinator or the investigator) must issue a written determination regarding responsibility with findings of fact, conclusions about whether the alleged conduct occurred, rationale for the result as to each allegation, any disciplinary sanctions imposed on the respondent, and whether remedies will be provided to the complainant. - The written determination must be sent simultaneously to the parties along with information about how to file an appeal.
11. Appeals	The Final Rule states that a school must offer both parties an appeal from a determination regarding responsibility, and from a school's dismissal of a formal complaint or any allegations therein, on the following bases: procedural irregularity that affected the outcome of the matter, newly discovered evidence that could affect the outcome of the matter, and/or Title IX personnel had a conflict of interest or bias, that affected the outcome of the matter. - A school may offer an appeal equally to both parties on additional bases.
12. Informal Resolution	The Final Rule allows a school, in its discretion, to choose to offer and facilitate informal resolution options, such as mediation or restorative justice, so long as both parties give voluntary, informed, written consent to attempt informal resolution. Any person who facilitates an informal resolution must be well trained. The Final Rule adds: - A school may not require as a condition of enrollment or continuing enrollment, or employment or continuing employment, or enjoyment of any other right, waiver of the right to a formal investigation and adjudication of formal complaints of sexual harassment. Similarly, a school may not require the parties to participate in an informal resolution process and may not offer an informal resolution process unless a formal complaint is filed. - At any time prior to agreeing to a resolution, any party has the right to withdraw from the informal resolution process and resume the grievance process with respect to the formal complaint. - Schools must not offer or facilitate an informal resolution process to resolve allegations that an employee sexually harassed a student.

Summary of Major Provisions of the Department of Education's Title IX Final Rule

13. Retaliation Prohibited	The Final Rule expressly prohibits retaliation. - Charging an individual with code of conduct violations that do not involve sexual harassment, but arise out of the same facts or circumstances as a report or formal complaint of sexual harassment, for the purpose of interfering with any right or privilege secured by Title IX constitutes retaliation. - The school must keep confidential the identity of complainants, respondents, and witnesses, except as may be permitted by FERPA, as required by law, or as necessary to carry out a Title IX proceeding. - Complaints alleging retaliation may be filed according to a school's prompt and equitable grievance procedures. - The exercise of rights protected under the First Amendment does not constitute retaliation. - Charging an individual with a code of conduct violation for making a materially false statement in bad faith in the course of a Title IX grievance proceeding does not constitute retaliation; however, a determination regarding responsibility, alone, is not sufficient to conclude that any party made a bad faith materially false statement.

Page 9 of 9

295

APPENDIX E
THE PROCESS OF INVESTIGATION FLOW CHART

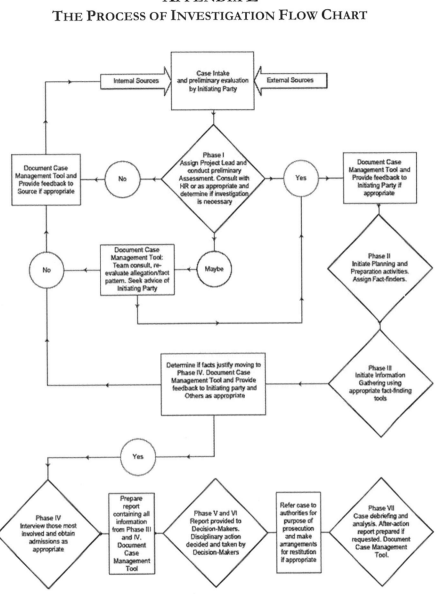

E.F. FERRARO, COPYRIGHT © 2020

NOTE: For a downloadable version of this chart and a copy of the complete policy shown on the following page, please go on line or visit www.InDefenseofTheInnocent.org.

SAMPLE INVESTIGATIONS POLICY

I. PURPOSE

The purpose of this document is to provide those with the responsibility of conducting internal investigations involving suspected or alleged misconduct general guidance relative to the methods and processes used to conduct those investigations.

II. SCOPE

The Policy described herein applies to internal investigations and inquiries conducted by Human Resources as well as those it selects to assist it, whether those resources are internal or external to the organization. It is expected that those conducting investigations be familiar with this Policy and how to use it. However, XXXXX ("the XXXXX" or "XXXXX") recognizes that specific facts and circumstances from time to time may necessitate deviation and modification of this Policy. Accordingly, deviation is permissible when it is for the good of the organization or safety is an issue. The decision to deviate from this Policy should be made on a case-by-case basis by the Human Resources Director in partnership with XXXXX Attorney or their designate.

Remediation and discipline, when appropriate, should be in accordance with the policies and practices established by Human Resources.

III. AUTHORITY AND RESPONSIBILITY

Only the Human Resources Director, XXXXX Attorney or their designee has the authority to initiate an internal investigation or inquiry pursuant to this Policy. The party authorizing the investigation (Authorizing Party) should generally assign a Project Lead at the beginning of each undertaking. Certain circumstances may warrant an investigation to be conducted by an external resource or supported by a Subject Matter Expert (SME). The Authorizing Party is authorized to engage an external resource or SME when necessary after proper approval has been obtained...

APPENDIX F
Investigative Forms and Checklists

Pre-Investigation Checklist

This tool is to be used only as a guide. No two workplace investigations are identical; therefore, a single checklist is not suitable for every type of investigation.

☐ Is the matter employment related and has the organization a duty to investigate?

☐ If allegations have been made, are they credible?

☐ Are there any immediate safety implications which must be considered or addressed?

☐ To whom else should the matter be reported?

☐ Is there a need to report the matter to anyone outside the organization?

☐ Have reasonable objectives been identified?

☐ Have milestones and timelines been established?

☐ Is a budget necessary and has one been decided?

Things to accomplish:

☐ Identify investigative team members and assign responsibilities.

☐ Create a case file.

☐ Perform pre-investigation investigation.

☐ Identify those to interviewed and document cast of characters and potential witnesses.

☐ Gather and secure any physical evidence.

☐ Secure personnel files and store in safe place

☐ Address PR and rumor mill.

☐ Update management and keep those with a need to know properly informed.

☐ *Think Safety.*

Interview Guidelines

☐ Always use black ballpoint pens.

☐ Spell out the full names of all parties involved; do not just use first names.

☐ Print your Employee Information Sheets in black, ballpoint pen. Make all corrections in red, ballpoint.

☐ Always print your name under your signature.

☐ All statements should state the city, county and state in which they are taken.

☐ Always indicate the last time an event occurred and whether or not it occurred on or off organizational property.

☐ Check off each item on the written checklist as you accomplish it. Cross out (x) those items that do not apply. Also, complete the heading entirely.

☐ Always let the interviewee write his own statement. If they cannot, do it for them, but be sure to state in it that you have done so and why.

☐ Write all addendums on statement paper.

☐ If the use of illegal drugs or alcohol took place off organizational property, but the employee returned to work, indicate in the statement whether or not the employee believed he/she was impaired at the time they returned to work.

☐ Sign all written statements and have them witnessed.

☐ Treat every interviewee with respect and dignity.

Written Statement Checklist

Subject:	Written Start:
Interviewer:	Break Start/Finish:
Witness:	Break Start/Finish:
Witness:	Written Finish:
Witness:	Date:

Check each item as covered with interviewee. Indicate "n/a" for those items which do not apply. If interviewee is unable or unwilling to write a statement, ask if he will allow you to write it for him/her. Ask the interviewee to the statement when completed.

☐ Complete opening paragraph according to guidelines.

☐ Document misconduct of subject or other desired information.

☐ Detail when, where, and last time event occurred.

☐ Document known or observed misconduct of others.

☐ Document motive for subject's actions.

☐ Document motive for subject's cooperation.

☐ Document that subject realizes that he has violated organizational policy and/or the law.

☐ Document that subject understands that because of the above he may be disciplined or discharged (or prosecuted if applicable).

☐ Document why the subject has decided to be honest, knowing the possibility of discipline (or prosecution).

☐ Provide subject the opportunity to add anything in his own words.

☐ Close statement as a declaration or affidavit according to guidelines.

☐ Assure all present sign statement.

Following The Introduction of
the Interviewee by Title IX Officer

Indicate that the person making the introduction will not be present during the entire interview and that the subject is free to use the restroom, make a telephone call, take a break or even discontinue the interview at any time. However, before the interview is terminated, a member of the leadership team will return and together with them, the interview will be completed.

During The Interview

Record all start and finish times, including breaks. Take notes and use only black ball point pen. If the subject decides to terminate the interview, notify the designate supervisor and the Title IX Officer immediately. Always treat the interviewee with respect and dignity. Take frequent breaks and make sure the interviewee is comfortable.

ForensicPathways, Inc.
EVIDENCE CHAIN OF CUSTODY TRACKING FORM

Case Number: _____ Issue/Matter: _____

Submitting By: _____

Provider: _____

Date/Time Obtained: _____

Location of Obtained: _____

Description of Evidence		
Item #	Quantity	Description of Item (Model, Serial #, Condition, Marks, Scratches)

Chain of Custody				
Item #	Date/Time	Released by (Signature)	Received by (Signature)	Comments /Location

APPENDIX G
Sample CV

EUGENE F. FERRARO

CPP, CFE, PCI, SPHR, SHRM-SCP

PROFILE

Mr. Ferraro has specialized in the investigation of allegations of behavioral and criminal misconduct for over 30 years. He is the founder and the Chief Executive of ForensicPathways, Inc. He frequently lectures and speaks on the topic of complex investigations involving allegations of harassment and discrimination. He is a graduate of the U.S. Naval Justice School and a former Marine Corps Naval Aviator and combat flight instructor. He is board certified in both Human Resources Management (SPHR and SHRM-SCP designations) and Security Management (CPP designation). He is also a Certified Fraud Examiner (CFE) and a Professional Certified Investigator (PCI).

He is a licensed professional investigator and is the author of numerous books on the topic of complex internal investigations in the private and public sector. Over the course of his career he has competently testified as either a fact or expert witness in over 300 matters. He is a licensed Professional Investigator in California, Colorado, and Illinois and is the founder of Convercent, Inc., a global whistle-blower and compliance company.

CONTACT

BUSINESS PHONE
303.816.1638

Email
Gene.Ferraro@ForensicPathways.com

CORE COMPETENTCIES

The proper investigation and management of whistleblower complaints;

Workplace harassment, discrimination and retaliation prevention and intervention;

Complex internal investigations and fraud examination;

Violence Prevention and Intervention in both the public and private sector;

Security management and crime prevention;

Human Resources management and administration;

Pre-employment screening and background investigations; and

GRC with emphasis on policy development and implementation, regulatory compliance and conformance, culture management, and organizational ethics.

FORMAL EDUCATION

Naval Justice School: U.S. Navy, 1979
Naval Flight School: U.S. Navy, 1978
BS: Florida Institute of Technology, 1975

AUTHORSHIP

In Defense of the Innocent, AuthorVista, 2020

The Professional Certified Investigator, Certification Preparation Study Guide, ASIS International, revised 2019

Virtues & the Virtuous: Inspiring Lessons and Insights about Virtue, Virtuosity, and Essence of the Human Spirit, AuthorVista, 2015

Investigative Interviewing, CRC Press, 2014

Investigations in the Workplace, Second Edition, CRC Press, 2012

5.2020

APPENDIX H
Sample Student Code of Conduct

Grounds for disciplinary action may include one of the following: a) active violation, b) attempt to violate, or c) solicitation of or aiding another in the commission of a violation. Disciplinary action may be taken in any case in which an individual or group is found in violation of any of the following:

1. University Policies—Violation of published university regulations or policies established for any area or academic unit by those having jurisdiction over it, including, but not limited to, parking, Security, Residence Life and Housing, Financial Aid, Health Services, Evans Library and Information Technology.

2. Physical Abuse—causing physical harm to any person or causing reasonable apprehension of such harm.

3. Endangering or Threatening Conduct—Any conduct that imperils or jeopardizes the health and safety of any person or the university community or communicates a serious expression of intent to harm any person or the university community.

4. Harassment—Any action, verbal or nonverbal, in conflict with the university's policy on harassment as stated in the *Student Handbook*. This may include a single action or a series of actions.

5. Hazing—Any action, verbal or nonverbal, in conflict with the university's policy on hazing as stated in the *Student Handbook*. This may include a single action or a series of actions.

6. Hacking—Gaining or attempting to gain unauthorized access to a computer system, whether through damage or

destruction of data or programs, or through disruption of operational practices.

7. Weapons—Unauthorized use, possession or storage of any weapon or explosive material, including, but not limited to, fireworks, firearms, air guns, paint pellet guns, knives, ammunition, martial arts weapons or bombs on university premises or at university-sponsored activities.

8. Failure to Evacuate—Failure to immediately evacuate a university building on the sounding of the fire alarm. Occupants must evacuate a building to points sufficient to ensure their safety. Occupants and/or residents may not re-enter the building at any time or for any reason while the alarm is sounding, unless instructed to do so by the university staff, security and/or local officials.

9. Disorderly Conduct—Disorderly, disruptive or obscene conduct or breach of peace that intentionally or recklessly interferes with normal university-sponsored activities or the rights of other community members on or off university property. Activities include, but are not limited to, studying, teaching, research, university administration, university-sponsored or supervised activities or fire, police or emergency services.

10. Freedom of Expression—Interfering with the freedom of expression of others.

11. Compliance—Failure to comply with the directives of university officials or agents acting in good faith performance of their duties.

12. Fraudulent Behavior—Forgery, falsification, unauthorized alteration or misuse of university documents, records or identification, including but not limited to, electronic software and records.

13. False Information and Impersonation—Furnishing false information to the university, impersonating another person, using another person's identity, or manufacturing or possession of false identification.

14. Academic Dishonesty—All forms of academic dishonesty, including cheating, fabrication, facilitating academic dishonesty or plagiarism.

15. Controlled Substances—Use, consumption, possession, sale, manufacture, trafficking or transfer of any illegal drug or controlled substance, as defined by state or federal law. Use and/or possession of drug paraphernalia. Actions in conflict with university policy and Residence Life policies on illegal drugs as outlined in the *Student Handbook* and other university publications.

16. Theft—unauthorized possession of property of another and/or the university; misappropriation, unauthorized use, access, or reproduction of property, data, records, equipment or services belonging to the university or belonging to another person or entity.

17. Damage—Intentionally or recklessly damaging or destroying university property or the property of others.

18. Public Indecency—Engaging in, but not limited to, public indecency, intoxication and indecent exposure.

19. Facilities Usage—Unauthorized entry or use of university premises, facilities or property.

20. Alcohol—Conduct in conflict with alcohol usage policy as stated in the *Student Handbook.*

21. Responsibility for Guests—Students are responsible for informing their guests, both student and non-student, about university policies and are held accountable for the behavior of their guests.

22. Stalking—Engaging in a course of conduct directed to a specific person or persons that causes substantial emotional distress in such person(s) and serves no legitimate purpose. Course of conduct means a pattern of conduct composed of a series of acts over a period of time, however short, evidencing a continuity of purpose.

23. Violent Behavior—Engaging in the use of physical force or violence to intimidate or to inflict harm to others or the property of the university, such as but not limited to, fighting or physical violence.

24. Sexual Misconduct—Any sexual activity without consent given. Sexual misconduct includes sexual and gender-based harassment, sexual assault, dating violence, domestic violence and stalking.

25. Online Course Conduct and Etiquette—Students participating in online and hybrid programs or courses are expected to conduct themselves professionally when interacting with fellow students, faculty, and staff. Respectful dialog exchanges facilitate proper discourse critical to fostering and maintaining positive learning environment. Students are to strive to maintain an open mind. Respect for one another is critical toward proper discussion of contrary or controversial viewpoints and ideas in discussion boards, group communication forums, and other venues of the online class environment. Posts and communications are expected to further academic discussion relevant to the topic and academic objective. Posts or comments deemed disruptive or inappropriate to the learning environment may be deleted. Communications related to the online classroom deemed disrespectful, inappropriate, unnecessarily disruptive, threatening, or abusive are inappropriate and subject to discipline.

26. Email and Electronic Communications—Mutual respect and civility are expected in all email and electronic communications. All students, on campus and online, are expected to adhere to professional netiquette when communicating with other students, faculty, and staff. Emails and other electronic communication should be reviewed in advance of transmission to ensure they are mindful and respectful of the person receiving the communication. Email and electronic communications deemed unprofessional, unduly argumentative, confrontational, hostile, threatening, offensive, or harassing are inappropriate and subject to discipline.

27. Violations of local, state and federal laws.

Courtesy Florida Institute of Technology, August 2019.

APPENDIX I
What Every Employer Should Know About the Fair Credit Reporting Act (FCRA)

As most employers know, they are permitted to use consumer reports when screening employment applicants and when evaluating employees for promotion, reassignment, or retention purposes—as long as they comply with the Fair Credit Reporting Act (FCRA). FCRA (Public Law No. 91-508) Sections 604, 606, and 615 which spell out their responsibilities and the methods for using consumer reports for employment purposes.

The FCRA, which became law in 1970, was intended to ensure that the information supplied by consumer reporting agencies (then called credit reporting agencies or sometimes, bureaus) was accurate and consumers were afforded recourse when they thought it was not. Amendments to the FCRA—which became effective September 30, 1997—significantly changed the relationship between the user (the employer) and the consumer reporting agency (CRA). It also clarified a number of ambiguities contained in the statute while increasing the legal obligations of users who procured consumer reports. The FCRA was again significantly amended in 2003. That revision, commonly called the FACT Act, clarified prior ambiguities and lessened some of the burdens placed on users in prior amendments. The following revisits some of the more substantial aspects of the FCRA and sheds light on some of the obligations of both users and CRAs. If your organization gets background information on prospective employees, it's likely you're covered by the Fair Credit Reporting Act. Before you request a background screening report, the law requires that you make certain disclosures and get a prospective employee's authorization. Is it time for a FCRA compliance check?

Background screening reports are categorized as "consumer

reports" under the FCRA when they serve as a factor in determining a person's eligibility for employment, housing, credit, insurance, or other purposes and they include information "bearing on a consumer's credit worthiness, credit standing, credit capacity, character, general reputation, personal characteristics, or mode of living."

Clearly, before you request a consumer report regarding a prospective employee, disclose to the applicant that you intend to obtain a report and get their written authorization allowing you to do so.

If the resultant consumer report reveals something that may cause the user to decide not to hire the applicant, the user must notify the individual of the results of the report and provide a copy of the report to that individual. Next, the employer must give the applicant sufficient time to review the report so they can challenge any elements that they claim are inaccurate or incorrect.

If the organization ultimately decides not to hire someone based in whole or in part on the contents of the report, it must provide a notice to that person that states they weren't hired in part because of something revealed in the report.

Organizations often ask how to make the required initial disclosure before it obtains the background report and get the prospective employee's authorization. It's easier than most might imagine. Under the FCRA, the employer must provide the prospective employee with a clear and conspicuous written disclosure that it plans to obtain a consumer report about them and must obtain written permission to compile the report. It is permissible to put the required disclosure and request for authorization in one document. However, be sure to use clear wording that the prospective employee will understand.

Here are few tips:

- Don't include language that claims to release the organization from liability for conducting, obtaining, or using the report.

- Delete any wording that purports to require the applicant to acknowledge that hiring decisions are based on legitimate non-discriminatory reasons.

- Get rid of overly broad authorizations that permit the release of information that the FCRA doesn't allow – for example, bankruptcies.

- Don't include anything else that makes it harder for the applicant to understand the main purpose of the document, and

- Eliminate any additional waivers, authorizations, or disclosures that might be better suited to include in a separate document.

Complying with the FCRA's disclosure requirements is easy. It can be accomplished in a few sentences. Just include a simple, easy-to-understand notification that indicates that the organization intends to obtain a consumer report. The simpler and clearer the better, and remember, it's the law.

APPENDIX J
HOW AN EMPLOYEE TERMINATION SHOULD BE HANDLED

In the world of HR and employment law, the termination of employment is considered the equivalent of capital punishment. As such, it is typically the choice of last resort. For this reason and others, the termination of employees in any one or more protected classes should be very carefully decided and orchestrated.

Additionally, sophisticated employers always consider alternatives to termination. Only when alternatives are not available or have been tried and failed, do such employers chose to terminate. Options include:

1. Changes of classification, duties, schedule, responsibilities, worksite, or other reasonable accommodation(s);

2. One-on-one coaching and counseling; and

3. Skills or technical retraining beneficial to the organization.

When none of these options are available and the decision to terminate is economic, a common option is offer continued employment at a reduced pay rate or salary. Unethical employers sometimes use this option and over time reduce the employee's compensation to level it is no longer economically possible for him/her to stay and thus quit of their own accord. A "bleed out" is a form of constructive discharge and is typically litigated as such. According to HR generally accepted best practices, all terminations should be carefully considered and around the decision to terminate should be a strategy that preserves the dignity of the individual and closely follows the organizations policies, precedents and past practices. Equally, the rights of the employee should carefully be considered and protected. Once the decision to terminate an employee is made and vetted by the appropriate organizational

.

authorities it should be communicated to the employee both verbally and in writing in a timely fashion. Best practices dictate the termination of employees at the executive level should be particularly carefully handled as they pose litigation and reputational risks to the organization. It is common in such cases, counsel is used to provide guidance to ensure both the decision and action are handled appropriately and in accordance to the law. Rarely, is counsel used to communicate the decision to the employee in question.

In instances where the employee chosen for termination raises the issue of discrimination and/or retaliation, and investigation of the allegation is required. Title VII and various EEOC Federal law requires employers who knew or should have known of possible harassment, discrimination or retaliation to investigate (see Bator v. State of Hawaii (9th Cir. 1994) 39 F. 3d 1021; Nichols v. Azteca Restaurant Enterprises, Inc. [9th Cir. 2001] 256 F. 3d 864; Fuller v. City of Oakland [9th Cir. 1995] 47 F. 3d 1522. A delay to investigate may be used as evidence that the employer condoned or even ratified the unlawful conduct. Also supporting "an employer's duty to investigate" are an assortment EEOC Informal Discussion Letters which address the general duty to investigate. Moreover, an employer's failure to investigate:

1. May be used as a basis to show the organization failed to prevent discrimination from occurring or condoned/ratified the unlawful conduct;

2. May be used by the aggrieved employee as an independent cause of action; and

3. May create an inference of malice, which could be basis to award punitive damages.[1]

Additionally it well established that an employer's investigation be "timely and proper." HR best practices suggest that the investigation begin with an interview of the complainant. Doing so benefits the employer is several ways:

1. It demonstrates that the employer considers the allegation(s) serious and that it recognizes its duty to prevent/address discrimination, harassment and retaliation when it suspects (or should suspect) it has occurred;

2. It assists the employer identify the full nature and scope of the allegation; and

3. Enables the employer the opportunity to contain or establish boundaries around the complainant's allegations preventing them from expanding or morphing later.

According the EEOC's website, "An employment policy or practice that applies to everyone, regardless of age, can be illegal if it has a negative impact on applicants or employees age 40 or older and is not based on a reasonable factor other than age (RFOA)."[2] On the same page is this, "The law [ADEA] forbids discrimination when it comes to any aspect of employment, including hiring, firing, pay, job assignments, promotions, layoff, training, fringe benefits, and any other term or condition of employment."
Employment attorneys often advise employers involved in terminations of employees who pose a risk of litigation to not provide a reason for the termination. Instead, they typically suggest

---

[1] Source: http://www.klgates.com/files/Publication/a7a74ba9-634c-444a-ba1a-48cb73ec01d6/Presentation/ PublicationAttachment/8e09ab90-8b03-4534-8858-4ad6b221befd/Conducting_Effective_Workplace_Investigations.pdf
[2] Source: http://www.eeoc.gov/laws/types/age.cfm.

the employer to hold firm to its "at-will" prerogative and communicate such the employee. This is a mistake. For every decision to terminate, there is obviously a reason. Though not required by law, the failure to communicate a reason suggests that the employer's motive is either not easily defendable or unlawful, thus encouraging the litigation it is attempting to avoid. Similarly, using counsel to communicate the decision to terminate suggests the employer is hiding something and is not confident that the decision can be properly communicated by a member of the organization without revealing damaging information. Triers-of-fact typically see through these schemes and judge employers that use them accordingly.

To ease the emotional consequences of termination for the employee and life-disruptions it creates, there are several common HR tools, thoughtful employers use. The most common include:

1. A generous severance package

2. Outplacement services and job search assistance

3. Actively referring the individual to other employers it knows or thinks may be hiring

4. Coaching and counseling

5. Use of organizational office space and or equipment as a place to work while job seeking

6. Reference letters or letters of recommendation

7. A thank you letter to the employee for his/her service

INDEX

A

abuses, 39, 63, 71, 95, 260
accusations, 34, 58, 133, 137, 153, 155, 178, 186, 208, 216, 226
accusatory, 89–90, 111
accuser, 2, 4, 59–60, 124, 127, 132–36, 138, 140–41, 163–64, 169–70, 172, 176–82, 208, 210, 251–53
ACLU (American Civil Liberties Union), 41
actions
　administrative, 136
　disciplinary, 25, 87, 113, 119, 124, 243, 284, 307
　organization's, 206
Acuity, 233
ADEA, 247, 319
adjudicating allegations, 37, 130
admissions, 34, 41, 90, 111–13, 115–16, 118, 121, 145, 150, 255–56, 259, 264
ADR (alternative dispute resolution), 219–20
after-action report, 234
age, 39, 57, 59, 129, 183, 185, 226–27, 239, 244, 247, 319
age discrimination, 39, 53, 231
agreement, collective bargaining, 106, 167
alcohol, 272, 276, 279, 301, 309

alleged event, 48, 210, 266
AMA (American Motorcyclist Association), 123
Amazon, 120, 122, 199, 214
amendments, 6, 28, 34–36, 53, 59, 126, 211, 313
American Civil Liberties Union (ACLU), 41
American Motorcyclist Association (AMA), 123
Amherst College student, 43
ANSI/ASIS Investigations Standard, 263
ANSI standards, 81
API, 205
appeals, 49–50, 178, 214, 242, 256
Apple, 7
ASIS (ASIS International), 82, 122–23, 131, 192
ASIS International. *See* ASIS
assailant, 24, 58, 60, 253
assault, 18–19, 43, 46, 59, 87, 158, 172, 182, 216, 256–57, 276
assault and battery, 172, 182
Assistant Secretary, 41–42, 279
attack, 20, 24, 29, 87, 154, 176, 213, 218
attorney, 142–43, 150–51, 164–65, 167, 169–72, 174, 176–77, 180, 196, 198, 208–10, 230–31, 257, 269, 272
Attorney Client Privilege, 257
Attorney General, 271

interrogatories, 188
interviewee, 146, 151, 255,
    301–2
interviewer, 114, 144, 146–47,
    171, 229, 255, 263, 302
interviewing, 86, 89, 110–11,
    145–46, 150
interviews, 86, 89–90, 111,
    113–14, 144, 148–50,
    162, 165, 175–76, 210–
    11, 255, 274, 276
  administrative, 111, 115,
    118–19, 255
investigation, 16, 64–65, 67–
    69, 82–88, 90–99, 107–
    11, 113–19, 121–22, 124,
    127–29, 131–38, 150–53,
    163–65, 198–99, 204–5,
    210, 233–35, 258–59,
    263–67, 269–71
  good faith, 113, 124, 262
  impartial, 152, 262
  institutional, 91–92
  organization's, 186, 189
  pre-investigation, 97, 299
  private, 266, 270
  private sector, 68, 88, 98,
    188, 229, 256, 266
  proper, 64, 69–123, 128,
    212
investigation findings, 263
Investigation Flow Chart, 235,
    297
investigation policy, 79, 140
  written, 133–34
investigation practices, 81
investigation process, 263
investigation program, 82, 264
Investigations Standard, 81–

83, 85, 87, 98, 119–20,
    122, 205–6, 235
investigation team, 263
investigation team leader,
    263–64
investigation templates, 233
investigative experience, 2, 88
investigative interviewing, 90,
    114, 120, 148, 151, 168,
    199
investigative interviews, 90–
    91, 111, 113–14, 118,
    178, 264, 269
investigative misconduct, 95
investigative policies, 85, 119
investigative process, 79, 92,
    119, 187, 255, 267
  established, 119
investigative report, 151–52,
    199–200, 210
Investigative unit (IU), 264
Investigative unit manager
    (IUM), 264
investigators, 49, 52, 55, 74,
    78, 83, 88–89, 109, 113,
    116, 196, 198, 264
  experienced, 1, 150, 229
  undercover, 110, 265
investigatory interviews, 90,
    114, 119–20, 128–29,
    144, 167, 198, 255
IRS, 122, 203
IU (Investigative unit), 264

J

job abandonment, 25
judges, 20, 53, 79, 116, 191,
    193, 209, 211, 217, 252,
    257

patents, 70, 122
Paterno, Joe, 68, 77
PDCA (Plan-Do-Check-Act),
    82–83, 234
Penn State, 68, 77–78
Pennsylvania State University,
    192
PG&E CORP, 23
phases of investigation, 85,
    114, 117, 234, 270
physical restraint, 157, 183
physical sexual acts, 279
physical surveillance, 98–100,
    106, 265
plaintiff, 95, 157, 164, 170,
    190–91, 194, 218, 222,
    230, 258–59, 266
Plan-Do-Check-Act. *See*
    PDCA
police, 32, 89, 137, 143, 150,
    166, 206, 256, 308
police interrogations, 32, 166
policies, 25–26, 45, 47, 103,
    119–20, 128–30, 132–33,
    135, 144, 148, 206, 234–
    37, 243–44, 257, 307
precedents, 53, 97, 245, 317
predators, v, 3, 51, 154
Pregnancy Discrimination
    Act, 39
Pre-Investigation Checklist,
    299
prejudice, 116, 152
premises, 101, 136, 180, 308–
    9
preponderance, 49, 266
preservation, 187–88, 259,
    261, 264
President Bill Clinton, 181

President Richard Nixon, 41
President Trump, 13
prevention and education, 86,
    114, 117
prisons, 181, 224
privacy
    invasion of, 106, 172, 180
    reasonable expectation of,
    101, 180
private sector, 39, 82, 90–92,
    111, 121, 129, 145, 197,
    266
private sector investigators,
    88–89
privilege, 35, 129–30, 267
Pro Bono, 267
process, 15–16, 33, 50–51, 55,
    77–81, 83–87, 89, 94–95,
    115–18, 120, 122–23,
    128–29, 150–51, 177–78,
    190–91, 202, 219–21,
    234–35, 242
  decision-making, 164, 236
  lawful, 242
  organization's, 197
process improvement, 77, 82
process rights, 178–79, 241–
    42
professional investigators, 24,
    85, 137, 150–51, 196,
    199, 209
programs, school's, 42, 280–
    81
prohibition, 29, 38–39
project manager, 92, 94, 96,
    114, 261, 267
Proper Internal Investigation,
    24, 67, 122
property, private, 28–30, 126

S

safety, 26, 85, 244, 300, 307–8
Sample Student Code of
 Conduct, 307
Sandberg, 3–4, 22
 Sheryl, 3, 22, 253
Sandberg and Geisha
 Williams, 10
Sandford, 35
Sandusky, Jerry, 68, 77
SCARCITY of RIGHTS, 25–
 35
SCARCITY of RIGHTS
 AND PROTECTIONS,
 37–53
schemes, 191, 247, 320
school administrators, 46,
 154, 210, 223, 282
School policies and practices,
 241
schools, 36–37, 41–42, 44–51,
 54–55, 136, 138, 144,
 150, 170–71, 177–80,
 205–6, 212, 217–18, 240–
 41, 279–84
science, forensic, 204, 225
Secretary DeVos, 46, 54
sector, public, 83, 88, 266,
 268–70
security management, 82, 85,
 192
Seligmann, Reade, 253
seizure, 28, 126
self-incriminate, 153
self-incrimination, 28, 30–32,
 126
Senate, 16–17, 21, 41, 55, 127
Senator Birch Bayh, 41
Senator Feinstein, 18, 58

Senator Hirono, 251, 253
Senator Warren, 10
services, 70, 74, 80, 90, 123,
 196, 198, 204–5, 239,
 241, 248
sex, 37–39, 41, 46, 185, 279
sex crimes, 224, 265
 alleged campus, 46
sex discrimination, 38, 279,
 285
sex offenders, 208, 224
sexual abuse allegations, 7
sexual assault, iii–iv, 5, 19–20,
 22, 24, 42–46, 54–55, 58–
 60, 152–53, 155–56, 175–
 76, 185–87, 209, 226–27,
 279–80
sexual harassment, 4–5, 8–9,
 37, 41–42, 46, 48–49, 56,
 228, 236, 279–82, 284–85
sexual harassment cases, 56
sexual harassment lawsuits, 56
sexual misconduct, 8, 21, 36,
 45, 47, 55, 60, 65, 177–
 78, 207, 310
sexual misconduct allegations,
 5
sexual misconduct
 complaints, 48
sexual violence, 41–42, 45, 47,
 138, 156, 166–67, 200,
 279–81, 284–85
 acts of, 279
Shakespeare, 22
 William, 12
shareholders, 23, 71
SHRM (Society of Human
 Resources Management),
 131, 204

78, 223, 227, 229, 307–10
university policies, 307, 309
Upjohn Warning, 269

V

values statements, 130
vehicle, 105–6, 149, 161, 163
victims, 5, 8, 42–43, 48, 57–
    58, 60–61, 154, 156, 158,
    208, 227–28, 251–53,
    256–57, 280
  alleged, 32, 40, 43, 58, 122
violence, 69, 108, 158, 213,
    280, 282, 284, 310
  sexual harassment and
    sexual, 42, 138, 280–81,
    284–85

W

walkouts, 23, 26
Wall Street Journal, 23–24, 66
Warren, Elizabeth, 10
Washington, 46, 103, 173–74,
    214, 271–73, 276
Washington Post, 11
Wayne, Lisa M., 175, 176
weapons, 58, 174, 241, 243,
    308
whistleblowers, 70, 72, 74,
    122
whistleblowing, 69
Williams, 4, 12–13, 22–23
Williams College, 12–13
witnesses, 19–20, 28–29, 31,
    34, 50–51, 75, 126–29,
    133–35, 143–45, 149,
    151–52, 158, 186–87,
    193–95, 302
women, iii–v, 1–4, 7, 9–11,

21, 38, 42–44, 47, 62–63,
    65, 176, 206–7, 251–52,
    272–73, 277
workplace investigations, 105,
    158, 259, 265, 270, 299

335

Additional Resources

Standards

ANSI/ASIS Inv. 1-2015 Investigations Standard.

ASIS/SHRM Workplace Violence Prevention and Intervention ANSI Standard (WVPI.2).

Conformity Assessment and Auditing Management Systems for Quality of Private Security Company Operations (PSC.2) 2019 Edition.

Conformity Assessment and Auditing Management Systems for Quality of Private Security Company Operations (PSC.2) 2019 Edition.

Websites

InDefenseofTheInnocent.org	News, blog, forms, checklists and other informational recourses.
ForensicPathways.com	Professional investigative services, litigation support, consulting, training and other resources.
ASISonline.org	Formerly the American Society of Industrial Security, for all things security related, including standards and guidelines related to organizational security and safety.
EEOC.gov	How to file a charge of employment discrimination and much more.
ED.gov	U.S. Department of Education
Justice.gov	U.S. Department of Justice

ABOUT THE AUTHOR

Eugene F. Ferraro, SPHR, SHRM-SCP

Gene has specialized in the investigation of allegations of behavioral and criminal misconduct for over 32 years. He is the founder and former Chairman of the whistle-blower technology company, Convercent, Inc. He is also the founder and currently the Chief Executive Officer of ForensicPathways, Inc. and frequently lectures and trains on the topic of complex investigations involving allegations of harassment, discrimination, sexual assault, and other serious misconduct in the workplace and schools. He is a graduate of the U.S. Naval Justice School and a former U. S. Marine Corps Naval Aviator and combat flight instructor. He is board certified in both Human Resources Management (SPHR and SHRM-SCP designations) and Security Management (CPP designation). He is also a Certified Fraud Examiner (CFE) and a Professional Certified Investigator (PCI).

Gene is a member of ASIS International and served on the ASIS Standards and Guidelines Commission for 10 years. He co-chaired the working and technical committees which developed the 2015 national *ANSI/ASIS Inv. 2015 Investigations Standard* and the 2011, *ASIS/SHRM Workplace Violence Prevention and Intervention ANSI Standard*. He is a licensed professional investigator and is the author of over a dozen books on various aspects of complex internal investigations and investigative interviewing in the private sector. He has competently testified as either a fact or expert witness in over 200 matters in U.S. courts and currently lives in the mountains of Colorado with his wife Shelley, and their four magnificent horses.

Made in the USA
Columbia, SC
30 July 2020